CONTAIN yourself

CONTAIN yourself

Kerstin P. Ouellet

101 fresh ideas for fantastic container gardens

Ball Publishing
Batavia, Illinois

Ball Publishing
P.O. Box 9
335 N. River St.
Batavia, IL 60510, U.S.A.
www.ballpublishing.com

Cover and interior designed by Sharon Fabsik.
Edited by Rick Blanchette.

Library of Congress Cataloging-in-Publication Data

Ouellet, Kerstin P.
 Contain yourself : 101 fresh ideas for fantastic container gardens / Kerstin P. Ouellet.
   p. cm.
 ISBN 1-883052-33-5 (alk. paper)
 1. Container gardening. I. Title.

SB418 .O93 2003
635.9'86–dc21

                              2002151466

Printed and bound by Imago in Singapore
09 08 07 06 05 04 03   1 2 3 4 5 6 7 8 9

To my sons, Dylan and Devin.
To be able to watch you grow up is one of the greatest privileges in life.
Without you, gardening would be only half the fun.

In memory of Paul Ecke Jr. (1925–2002) and
Hector Harrison (1920–2002),
with admiration and respect for their tremendous contributions to
horticulture and gardening.

Contents

Acknowledgements

I'd like to thank the many people who have helped make this book possible through their generosity in providing help and advice. My sincerest thanks to all of you!

My editor, Rick Blanchette, for his guidance, ideas, and suggestions;
My husband, Rich, for his understanding and patience during countless hours that I spent writing this book;
My family in Germany, who's always close although we're 6,000 miles apart;
My teachers and professors at *Fachhochschule Weihenstephan,* especially Prof. Dr. R. Roeber.

Thank you to the following people for their work:
Dawn Bewely, Bob Bretell, Claire Curran, Malinda Romine, and Gene Sasse.

A special thanks to the following companies:
Braun Horticulture for donating baskets, stone planters, and topiary frames.
EuroAmerican Propagators for providing plant material, labor, and growing space.
Fred Meyer Stores for donating pottery and planters.
Molbak's Garden Center for photography on page 281.
Roger's Gardens for permission to take the pictures on pages 6, 7 (middle and bottom), 9, 34 (top), 279 (bottom), 282, 283.

Introduction

Growing up in Germany, I witnessed the birth of the container garden boom. Ever since I can remember, my mom set out each spring to decorate our entire housefront with window boxes. My mom wasn't the only one—pretty much the entire village planted window boxes, vying for a prize in the local garden club's annual window box contest. In the 1970s and early 1980s, geraniums were the clear favorites. Then, in the late '80s and early '90s, the more "adventurous" gardeners tried their luck with such exotics as *Bidens, Scaevola,* and 'Surfinia' *Petunia*—and they quickly became the talk of the town.

When I started horticulture school in 1989, container garden production had become an important part of the curriculum. Our school would plant an abundance of spectacular window boxes brimming with color. Every year, the countless combinations of plants drew gardeners from near and far. When I moved to the United States and started my horticulture career in 1994, I witnessed the sprouting passion for container gardening on this side of the Atlantic.

Since then, the container garden trend has exploded. You'll be hard pressed to find a garden center in May that doesn't carry at least a few mixed planters and baskets. But as with so many things, it's better if it's homemade. And there is no reason to be intimidated by the gorgeous container gardens you see at garden centers and in public places, because you can create your own that are just as beautiful. If you like plants, you'll love container gardening. And with a few tips and guidelines, you'll turn into a pro in no time.

This book will help you make your own container garden dreams come true. The step-by-step instructions will make designing, planting, and caring for them a breeze. In the first part, you'll learn everything from design principles to planting and care information. You'll learn the pros and cons of the different container choices available, how to use color effectively, how to utilize texture and proportion, how to plant and care for your container gardens, and much more.

The second part introduces you to the many different plants that were used in this book. You'll find out about their growth characteristics and special care needs so that you'll feel more confident using them and eventually integrating them into your very own designs. From *Acorus* to *Yucca*, you'll learn about eighty plant species and their many varieties.

When you get to the third part, it's time to get your hands dirty. Here you can utilize an abundance of detailed planting diagrams that not only show you how to plant the pictured container gardens, but they'll also teach you about some of the effects of particular plants in combination with others. By learning why I used a specific plant or color combination, you'll become more confident in venturing out to create your own designs.

Over the years that I've spent working with and writing about gardening, the need for a detailed, step-by-step guide on container gardening became obvious, especially when it comes to using the many wonderful new plants that have come to the market over the last few years. I hope you'll find *Contain Yourself* to be an indispensable resource in making your container garden dreams come true. I believe you'll treasure it for many years to come, either as step-by-step guide or merely as inspiration for your own creativity.

Part 1

The Basics and Beyond

1

Container Gardening—
A Passion for All Gardens

Wouldn't we all love to have an acre of gardening space plus all the time we need to turn it into our own little paradise? The truth is, however, that our lots are getting smaller and smaller, leaving little room for elaborate gardens. And even if we are fortunate enough to have a large gardening space, we often don't have the time to turn it into one of those beautiful, abundant gardens we admire in gardening magazines. How then to make the most of limited space and limited time? Create a miniature paradise with container gardens.

Container gardens are the most versatile way of using plants. There is no limit to how big or small they can be or to the shapes they come in. You can move them to wherever you like, and if they are in the way of your big summer party crowd, you can simply move them around to accommodate your guests. And if you don't have any room on the deck or patio for containers, no problem—use hanging baskets!

A Very Brief History

Container gardens first became popular in Europe in the 1980s. European countries are much more densely populated than North America, and many Europeans rent apartments rather than own their own house. When a European does own a home, it's often an attached home, similar to townhomes in the States. Despite—or maybe because of—this lack of space, Europeans are highly appreciative of plants, and they garden in the small spaces available to them.

As Europeans have always been innovative when it comes to gardening trends, it was only a question of time before the container garden craze hit North America. This finally happened in the early 1990s and has since spread like a wildfire. Plant breeders quickly responded to this trend and have focused their efforts on developing plants that work well in container gardens. Today, we have an abundance of new and unusual plant varieties available that make container gardening more fun than ever. This book will show you that container gardening with the latest varieties is not only rewarding, it's also easier than you might think.

2

Designing Container Gardens

The design often makes or breaks a container garden. True, care might be equally as important, but without careful plant selection and the right combination of colors, the design simply won't look good, at least not in the long run. For me, designing container gardens is the most fun part of gardening. Strolling through your garden center and choosing the right plants that complement each other and bring out the best in each other, plus selecting among the endless container choices available to find what's just right for your taste and décor is a joy you might get addicted to. You'll soon find out that designing container gardens is a passion and that you can't have just one.

Container Choices

The question whether you should first choose the plants and then the container or vice versa is like the question about the chicken and the egg. But while some might argue, it doesn't really matter in my opinion. Assuming that you might already have a container that you want to plant, or that the selection of containers that meet your budget and taste is narrower than the choice of plants available, let's start with the container.

Well-stocked garden centers carry a variety of container choices in many different sizes, shapes, materials, and colors.

Random House Webster's Unabridged Dictionary defines "container" as "anything that contains or can contain something," and that's pretty much true for container gardening as well. The choice of containers that you can use to plant into is nearly endless. The only limit is your imagination. For now, let's look at some of the more commonly used container types.

Terra cotta and clay containers

Terra cotta containers are some of the most popular choices for container gardens. Their look and function are equally excellent. The term *terra cotta* is derived from the Latin *terra cocta*, which means "baked earth." Terra cotta pots are made of fired clay and have the classic, Mediterranean style that is so popular for container gardens today. They range from plain, elegant pots to elaborately ornate planters, so you are likely to find one that suits your taste. Their simple elegance works well for many different plant combinations. Plant performance is very good in terra cotta containers because the porous surface allows for air circulation, which is important for plants. That also means that the risk of overwatering your container gardens is smaller. Over time, terra cotta pots take on an interesting, aged look, which adds character.

Glazed planters can be skillfully incorporated into the design. This dark brown glazed planter looks great with the warm-colored flowers.

While terra cotta containers are one kind of clay pot, there are also other clay pots available that are not considered terra cotta. Those clay pots range in color from gray to beige to brown, depending on the kind of clay used. Clay pots are available in their natural or unglazed form as well as glazed. While the glaze reduces the air circulation, it can add a rainbow of colors to broaden your design possibilities.

Terra cotta and clay containers are most commonly available as round, square, and rectangular planters, but they can also be found as wall baskets, or oval-shaped planters, or hanging baskets. Terra cotta and other clay pots have the disadvantage of being quite heavy and are prone to chipping and breaking, so they need to be handled carefully. But their attractive look more than makes up for their disadvantages. They also aren't frost resistant, so you need to protect them from frost in winter, or they might break.

Terra cotta containers are popular choices for container gardens, whether they are plain and elegant or ornate.

Strawberry pots are—as the name suggests—great for growing strawberries in containers, but their rustic appeal also looks great if planted with herbs or flowering plants.

Plastic

Plastic pots used to be quite plain, but this is no longer the case. Since the 1990s, beautiful, ornate plastic containers that look just like terra cotta or stone containers have become widely available. These types of containers are made of materials such as molded polyethylene, polyurethane, recycled plastic, fiberglass, or others. Their main advantage is that they are very lightweight and break- and chip-resistant compared to clay pots. Plastic is also an inexpensive material for hanging baskets, although I prefer the look of natural materials in hanging baskets.

Molded plastic planters like this look like clay but are lightweight and chip resistant.

Air circulation and water evaporation are lower in plastic pots compared to clay pots. This can be both good and bad. During hot weather, your pots won't dry out as fast, but during cool and rainy weather the risk of overwatering is higher. Some plastic containers are treated to protect them from UV damage, while others aren't. Those that aren't sunproof can get brittle over time and/or fade.

Plastic containers are available in almost any imaginable size and shape, ranging from plain pots to hanging baskets, window boxes, wall baskets, and ornate patio planters. You will have no trouble matching up a container with any colors, themes, or décor.

Wood

Wooden containers are great for a natural, rustic look. You can find wooden planters that were specifically manufactured to serve as container gardens, but you can also turn an existing wooden tub, box, crate, trough, or whiskey barrel into a container garden. Wooden planters have good air circulation, which is important for good plant performance. Their rustic look often intensifies over the years, as the irrigation water ages the wood and gives it more character.

Redwood and cedar can often be found as window boxes and square hanging baskets, while planters are often "recycled" barrels and tubs. If you want to make your own wooden planters or if you want to plant an existing pot or barrel, make sure that the wood hasn't been treated with chemicals that might harm the plants.

This rustic basket was lined with burlap to protect the potting mix from being washed out during watering.

Wooden planters give a rustic look and look good with many different color combinations.

Wicker baskets and planters also belong in this category. They're great if you want a rustic, country garden look. Herb gardens, for example, look especially beautiful in wicker baskets. The only problem with wicker is that it can become quite messy when you water, as

Cedar baskets are great, natural looking choices for hanging baskets.

some of the potting mix washes through the baskets. You could combat that by lining it with plastic, but then you have the problem of overwatering. If you decide to line your wicker baskets with plastic, it's best to cut a few small drainage holes so the excess water can drain while very little or no soil is washed out. Another—and, in my opinion, even better—solution is one that a professional plant grower once shared with me: Line the wicker basket with burlap. The water can drain while the soil is retained.

Upscale metal planters like the one pictured add an elegant touch to container gardens.

Metal

Metal containers come in a wide range of designs and price tags. From an inexpensive, plain, galvanized bucket or trough to elaborate cast iron urns, the selection is endless. Although metal is not as commonly used for container gardens as clay and plastic, it offers many design possibilities. Cast iron is very heavy and can be fairly expensive, but also looks outstanding and often classy. On the other end of the price range are galvanized metal and aluminum, which are usually fairly plain, keeping all of the focus on the plants. The silver look of galvanized metal looks best with cool-colored plants, such as pink, blue, and purple. You can also find copper planters, which age nicely.

Moss and coco fiber

Moss is my favorite material for hanging baskets because of its natural look and outstanding plant performance. Although most moss is used in hanging baskets, you can also find wall baskets, window boxes, and even planters made of moss. The structure of these containers is usually a wire or metal cage, which is so thickly lined with moss that you often can't even see the metal.

Moss baskets not only look great, but they also give you the option to plant along the sidewalls of the basket, which results in a fuller look and gives you a faster color impact than if you plant only at the top.

The downside of moss baskets is that they dry out much faster than most other materials. This is especially significant in hot climates and after the plants have grown larger. Don't be surprised if you need to water your baskets daily. Some moss baskets come with built-in water reservoirs, shallow tins that are hidden in the moss at the bottom. They retain a certain amount of water to slow the drying out process. If your moss basket doesn't have a water reservoir, you can also put a piece of plastic in the bottom after you poke drainage holes in it. The water will drain slower, allowing the plants and potting mix to absorb more water.

Some moss baskets come with built-in water reservoirs that retain water longer and reduce drying of the potting mix.

Today, moss baskets are readily available so that you don't need to go through the work of assembling your own from a wire frame and loose moss. But if you choose to make your own, be sure to moisten the moss well and pack it very tightly. That way you can pack more moss in, which helps retain as much water as possible.

Coco fiber is a material that can be used as alternative to moss. It usually has a beige to light brown color and stays together more tightly than moss. It is also slightly lower priced. I personally prefer the look of moss, but coco fiber is an excellent alternative. Plant performance is outstanding in both moss and coco fiber, as both provide very good air circulation and drainage.

Moss baskets are natural looking and beautiful even if plants don't cover their sides.

Other Containers

This section could be endless. After all, you could use your worn out rubber boots or great-grandma's chamber pot as planters. We'll just look at some of the slightly more commonly used materials.

Ceramic

Ceramic pots are similar in performance to glazed clay. Ceramic can sometimes be found in painted Asian pottery or antique planters.

Stone

Stone planters look beautiful, but they're usually heavy and can be pricey. However, one type of stone planter will appear frequently in the section of this book that features the planting diagrams. Braun

Stone planters are beautiful, but they can be quite heavy, like the one pictured on the left. On the right is a more lightweight model from Braun Horticulture.

Horticulture makes this fairly new type, and the planters are not nearly as heavy or pricey as you might expect. As they are more porous than many stone planters, plant performance in them is excellent. And because they are porous, they age beautifully over time, giving them more and more character over the seasons.

Molded fiber

Baskets and planters made of molded fiber surfaced in the late 1990s. They are made of recycled paper and are a good, fairly natural looking alternative to moss and coco fiber baskets. However, if you want to plant baskets along the sidewalls, you should look for baskets with pre-drilled holes in the walls.

A Final Thought about Containers

There are three things that are very important in a container—drainage, drainage, and drainage. If your planter doesn't have drainage holes, you are almost certain to overwater it. Besides, after heavy rains all the water has nowhere to go. Without proper drainage, the potting mix stays too wet, which leads to poor air circulation and root rot.

When you shop for pots and planters, evaluate them for their drainage abilities. When you buy clay or ceramic containers, make sure that they already have drainage holes. Depending on the container size, a few medium-sized holes are better than just one tiny one, especially for large pots. If you buy plastic or metal containers without drainage holes, you can drill holes in them when you get them home. Containers made of natural fibers such as moss drain naturally.

If you are worried about the surface you plan to put your container gardens on, you might want to use saucers or "pot feet" to protect the surface. This might be especially important for wood, marble, or expensive

If plastic or metal containers don't have pre-drilled holes in them, drill a few holes manually before planting.

tile. As water, nutrients, and soil wash out during watering, they pool under the container and can cause stains over time.

Working with Color

I've always viewed working with color as the most exciting part of container gardening. Grouping together just the right colors to create a certain theme, complement a décor, or achieve high color impact is a rewarding experience. Color usually catches the viewer's eye first, whether you choose a subtle pastel theme or bold colors. Color combinations can often make or break a good container garden design.

Color—when used effectively—distinguishes a high-impact container garden from an ordinary one.

The good news is that working with color is not as hard as you might think.

If you are new to designing, you might want to utilize the help of a color wheel. This is a simple tool that you can buy at an artist's or crafts store for a few dollars. It displays colors around a wheel, which makes it easy for you to identify the right combinations. Pick colors on opposite ends of the color wheel and you get complementary colors; pick colors next to or close to each other (also called analogous colors) and you get harmonizing combinations; or pick different shades and tints of one color and you achieve a monochromatic design.

Warm colors

Warm colors are considered those in yellow, orange, and red tones. They evoke a warm, spirited feeling in the viewer. Different nuances of yellow, orange, and red, such as amber or terra cotta, are also in this category. Warm colors are often used in Southwest-themed designs. They are a good choice if you want to make an impact. Their bold colors capture the eye of the viewer, but they can also be overpowering to some tastes, especially if used in masses. While a monochromatic design in red can be quite provocative, a combination in soft shades of yellow seems friendly and even mellow.

Warm colors look best with terra cotta containers, reddish and brownish glazed containers, and wooden planters. If you wish to mix foliage other than green with your warm-colored flowers, choose yellow and golden tones.

Cool colors

Blue, purple, and pink are considered cool colors, as well as their shades and hues, such as lavender, lilac, or powder blue. Cool colors are very popular, as they evoke calm, serene feelings. Just imagine a tranquil lake, and you will understand. Since cool colors are so unobtrusive and go well with many different designs, they are quite widely used. When you shop for plants, you will also notice that you can find a lot of plants in these tints.

Cool-colored flowers look good in neutral-colored containers, such as a light stone color, beige or gray clay, or in glazed containers in blue, green, or teal. White or metal containers are also a good choice. And you can never go wrong with terra cotta. For foliage accents beyond green, choose silver, gray, or purple- and pink-tinged foliage.

Complementary colors

Complementary colors are those on opposite ends of the color wheel. They bring out the best in each other and enhance one another. In other words, one color really makes the other jump. Popular combinations for container gardens in comple-

Warm-colored flowers and foliage evoke a warm, spirited feeling in this brown glazed container.

The serene, cool colors of this container garden are a friendly welcome at a front entrance.

The yellow and purple flowers are complementary and make each other look even more vibrant.

mentary colors are blue and orange or purple and yellow. Just imagine a blue verbena with an orange coreopsis, or yellow marigold with purple petunia—both duos are extremely vibrant. You can create the most striking contrasts by combining just two pure colors, or if you're after a slightly more subtle look, combine several colors that are close to each other on each end of the color wheel. For example, combining all four plants listed earlier together is a little more subdued, especially if you let the blue and purple tones dominate and use earthier tones of yellow and orange.

Analogous or harmonious colors

Harmonious colors are those that are next to each other on the color wheel, for example blue, blue-purple, and purple. Because they are similar, their combination results in a harmonious design, which is very pleasing to the eye. The more neighboring colors you add, the less harmonious the design becomes, but it gains impact. Harmonious—also called analogous—designs are very popular and look especially stunning in high-end containers for an elegant, upscale look.

This analogous design features yellow-green foliage of *Lysimachia* 'Goldilocks', yellow, button-shaped flowers of *Ajania*, and yellow-orange in the center of the strawflowers. White brightens the design.

Monochromatic designs

Monochromatic means that the design uses only one color in different intensities. Monochromatic designs are very pleasing to the eye and very trendy in Europe right now. You can plant your own monochromatic container gardens by planting different shades of one color, such as different shades and tints of purple. If you want to give your design more impact, use a contrasting container, but if you want to carry the subtle theme throughout, use a container in a similar color or choose a neutral one, such as a stone color.

Color themes

Besides using one of the color principles mentioned above—which are proven guidelines that professional designers use—you can also create your own color themes that don't necessarily follow these principles. For example, you could create your own container garden using the colors of your favorite sports team. Or

This monochromatic design uses different intensities of yellow for a sophisticated look. The dark-brown glazed container gives it contrast.

show your patriotic pride with flowers by creating container gardens in red, white, and blue. Mixed containers in patriotic colors are a beautiful way to greet visitors at your front door, but equally as attractive as patio decorations. Not only are they popular for Memorial Day and Independence Day, but also any time of the year. You can create very simple hanging baskets by combining verbenas in red, white, and blue, or you can plant more intricate designs by combining completely different plants. One of my favorite combinations is the hanging basket to the right.

This hanging basket in patriotic colors combines *Dianthus* 'Tiroler Gebirgshaengenelke', a cascading carnation from Europe with a hard-to-pronounce name but beautiful, vibrant red, fragrant flowers; *Scaevola* 'New Wonder', also known as blue fan flower; and *Verbena* 'Babylon White', a trailing verbena with pure white flower clusters.

Texture

Texture is a bread-and-butter component of container gardening. Texture gives the design movement and interest. Besides, it's fun to not only combine different colors, but also varying textures. A container garden rich in texture can be achieved by using flowering plants with different foliage and flower sizes and shapes, but also by adding non-flowering foliage plants that are primarily used for the purpose of adding texture. By working with different textures, your design becomes more natural looking. Just take a stroll outside, and you'll discover all the different textures nature has to offer. By incorporating texture into your design, you bring nature's intention into your container garden.

You can also use texture very skillfully to create a certain theme. For example, what about a container garden with only daisy-shaped flowers in different sizes and colors? Or a very fine-textured or coarse-textured combination? It's really up to you what you want to create, but generally the eye is more drawn to a design that features various textures—it keeps the viewer's interest longer.

The texture of the spiky, star-shaped flowers is repeated in the deeply dissected leaf in front.

One of the best ways to add texture is by incorporating foliage plants into your design. When you shop for foliage plants, you are likely to find a good selection, as they have become very popular for container gardening over the years. Texture plants come in all shapes and sizes. If you are looking for tall, upright texture plants and have grown tired of the oh-so-frequently-used dracaena spike, your chances to find the perfect substitute are much better than they were just a few years ago. This is because ornamental grasses are becoming much more readily available to gardeners and are experiencing a general popularity boom.

Ornamental grasses are some of my very favorite plants to use in container gardens. For simplicity's sake, I also group grasslike plants, such as sedges or New Zealand flax (*Phormium*), in this category, as they serve similar purposes as ornamental grasses, and nurseries that carry one usually also carry the other. Ornamental grasses and grasslike plants come in nearly all sizes, colors, and growth habits. From dainty, three- to four-inch-tall grasses that are great for petite container gardens to stately four-foot-plus grasses to rule a majestic planter, the choices are endless. Ornamental grasses also come in a wide range of colors, from yellow to green, bronze, burgundy, purple, and almost black. While most ornamental grasses have attractive foliage, they often surprise with an extra bonus when they come into bloom. The foxtail-shaped flowers of purple fountain grass (*Pennisetum setaceum* 'Rubrum'), for example, not only catch your eye,

but their soft texture also encourages touch. What's also great about using tall ornamental grasses in the center of a container is that they add height without over-powering the combination due to their airy habit.

Besides ornamental grass-es and grasslike plants, there are many other plants that are exceptional texture plants for container gardens. They also come in many different col-ors, shapes, and growth habits. To name just a few, you will find strictly trailing

This container design uses several ornamental grasses for texture, such as *Carex flagellifera* 'Toffee Twist' and *Hakonechloa macra* 'Aureola'. The black-leaved *Trifolium* 'Dark Dancer' adds even more texture.

components in the golden-leaved *Lysimachia nummularia*, the silver-green variegated *Glechoma*, variegated vinca vine, or the endless colors of English ivy varieties. Some mounding or semi-trailing plants are

Foliage plants, such as *Helichrysum* 'White Licorice', are wonderful texture plants that add interest to container gardens.

Lamium, which are available in several different colors; *Helichrysum petiolare,* also called licorice plant, with its various colors; or variegated mint (*Mentha*). Upright plants include variegated sages (*Salvia*) and coleus, which comes in nearly any color of the rainbow. As you browse through the section with the planting diagrams, you will frequently find texture plants and examples of texture-rich flowering plants. Use them as inspirations for your own experiments with texture. You'll soon find out how much fun you'll have!

Proportion

You might think that container, color, and texture, are enough to concentrate on when container gardening. They are very important, but there are still other considerations. Now let me introduce you to proportion!

This is an example where the plants are too small in relation to the container. The planter is not a showpiece, so the plant portion should be much bigger in relation to the container.

Proportion often determines whether a container garden seems balanced or not. If the planter is too big and the plants are barely noticeable, the result is unbalanced. As a rule of thumb you should aim for the plant portion to be at least twice as big as the visible part of the container. Of course, as plants grow, the ratios change, but plan your proportions considering the fully grown size of the plants. But as with every rule, there are exceptions. As a matter of fact, the exceptions are so significant that I'm not sure if it should even be called a rule. You don't have to worry about the rule if you have a beautiful showpiece planter that you want to show off. If the focus should remain on the pot, it's perfectly acceptable to use plants more sparingly. And as the available pottery choices become better and better, you'll find yourself increasingly in situations where you don't want to hide your planters with plants. Chances are you spent a fairly high amount of money on your show-pieces, so why would you want to cover them up? On the other hand, if the planters are anything but attractive, you'll want to cover as much of them as possible. If you're using average-looking containers, keep the rule of thumb in mind.

Plant Habit

Plant habit refers to how a plant grows—upright, mounding, or trailing. For most

If you have a beautiful planter that you want to show off, you can use plants simply to accentuate it and not hide any portion. In this case, the royal blue pot is complemented by striped New Zealand flax (*Phormium*) and variegated English ivy.

successful designs, you'll want to have all three categories incorporated, with the upright plant in the center, mounding plants around it, and trailing ones along the edges. Combining all three growth habits helps achieve a harmonious design. This is especially important for upright planters, where you need to add height in the center to balance the size of the planter. The exception is if you are planting hanging baskets that will hang so high that the center won't be visible. Then you can use exclusively trailing plants if you wish.

Make yourself familiar with a plant's habit before you put your design together. Remember that the plant is likely to be young when you buy it. So while one might be six inches tall when you buy it, it could reach a mature height of two feet, while another plant that's six inches tall when you buy it might start trailing and not gain any more height. If you are not familiar with the plant, look at the label or ask a garden retail professional for help.

This design combines upright growing plants (purple fountain grass) with mounding varieties (*Pelargonium, Osteospermum*) and trailing types (*Muehlenbeckia*).

You should also know how vigorous your plants are and only combine those with similar growth vigor. Otherwise, plants with a more vigorous habit will dominate and outperform those that grow more slowly. The licorice plant (*Helichrysum petiolare*), for example, is very vigorous and can outgrow a plant like alyssum or *Brachyscome* easily, but other vigorous plants, such as trailing verbena, can keep up with its fast growth. If you combine very vigorous plants with slow-growing ones, your design will change over time and the slow growers might disappear altogether. However, if you find out after you've planted your container garden that some plants are trying to take over, you can always cut them back.

Plant Growing Needs

Considering plants' needs for light, water, and fertilizer when you design a container garden doesn't contribute to its initial aesthetics, but to its longevity and success. Plants have different preferences and perform best if they are given their ideal growing needs. If you put a plant that prefers shade in the sun, it's likely to burn or at least not grow as well as it could otherwise. Plants that are given adverse conditions might die or be outgrown by those that are growing in ideal conditions. This will change the look of your container garden and might even leave bare spots. This is easy to imagine if you picture succulents mixed with plants that need moist conditions or hostas—classic shade plants—with sun-loving verbenas. To ensure the highest success rate, combine plants that have similar requirements to sun, water, fertilizer, and type of potting mix.

If this sun-loving container garden were placed in the shade, the adverse growing conditions could be a breeding ground for diseases and poor plant performance.

3

Planting Container Gardens

Now that you've learned how to design gorgeous container gardens, it's time to get your hands dirty. I guess one could say that container gardening is a little bit like baking: If you use high-quality ingredients, you'll achieve better results. And since container plants depend on the limited amount of potting mix in the container and can't take up water and nutrients from surrounding areas, container gardens require a little more attention than plantings in the ground. So if you put a little bit of care (and money) into choosing your potting mix, fertilizer, and plants, you're very likely to succeed.

Potting Mix

Although often referred to as "potting soil" or simply "soil," the best potting mix doesn't contain any soil at all. Regular topsoil or garden soil does not have the requirements container plants need. Besides, real soil may contain weeds or diseases. So look for a good potting mix at your garden retailer. Good potting mixes often contain peat moss or bark, plus inorganic matter to increase drainage and stability. There are different quality levels available, so it's best to ask for assistance if the label doesn't reveal enough information. Don't hesitate to ask your garden retailer which mix they use themselves, then you'll know it's good.

There are several factors to look for in a potting mix:

Drainage capacity

Your potting mix must have the ability to drain water well. A mix that remains waterlogged cuts off the air supply to the roots and can cause root rot. A good potting mix often has nonorganic matter such as perlite or vermiculite added to it to ensure good drainage.

Water-holding capacity

This sounds contradictory to what you just read, but it's true—you need both good drainage as well as good water-holding capacity. The trick is to find a mix that has a balance of both because once your plants get big and the weather gets hot, container gardens need a lot of water. Remember that they only have a limited amount of potting mix available to supply water. That's why you want a mix that holds water fairly well, so that you don't have to water all the time. Some potting mixes have wetting agents mixed in that retain water, or you can buy wetting agents and mix them in before planting. Wetting agents usually come in granular form and turn into a gelatinous substance when they absorb several times their volume in water.

How much water-holding capacity you need depends on the climate you live in. If you are in a summer-dry climate such as the Southwest, you'll want a higher water-holding capacity. If you live in a climate with moderate summer temperatures and/or frequent rain, drainage is more important than water retention.

pH

The pH of a potting mix determines how acidic or alkaline it is, which in turn influences the performance of the plants and the availability of nutrients. Most of the plants used in this book prefer a pH range of 5.5 to 6.5. Look at the label and make sure that your potting mix is approximately in this range. But although it's important to start with the right pH, that doesn't guarantee that the pH will remain right for the rest of the season. Other factors, such as the alkalinity of your water and the type of fertilizer you use, can change the pH over time. We'll talk more about that when we get to the care section of this book.

Nutrient content

Some of the best potting mixes have fertilizer already mixed in. This helps give your plants a good start, but it doesn't replace regular fertilization throughout the season. If your mix doesn't have fertilizer mixed in already, add some slow-release fertilizer to the mix before you plant. This will take care of the plants' initial needs, but you should follow up with regular fertilization.

Planting tip

It's more pleasant to work if you moisten your potting mix slightly before you plant. It significantly reduces the amount of dust particles that you might otherwise get in your eyes and inhale. It also makes it easier to thoroughly moisten the mix after the container garden is planted.

Planting Basics for Pots and Window Boxes

How you should arrange the plants in a pot depends on how it will be viewed. If you'll be looking at it from all sides, you'll want it to look great from all angles. In that case, place an upright plant in the center, mounding plants around it, and trailing plants along the edges.

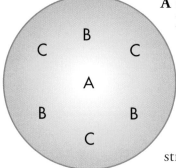

A = Upright plant
B = Mounding plants
C = Trailing plants

This is an example of a basic planting schematic for a round pot with a symmetrical structure. Whether you use only one variety for each of the mounding and trailing types or multiple varieties is up to you. You can also use more or less than three plants of each type, depending on the size of your container, the size of the plants, and your taste.

This container garden follows the basic planting schematic with an upright plant in the center (*Phormium*), mounding plants around it (*verbena* and *Osteospermum*), and trailing plants around the edges (*Glechoma* and *Brachyscome*).

If you are planning on placing a container garden in a corner or against a wall where it will only be viewed from one, two, or three sides, you can place the upright plant in the back and not plant it symmetrically. You will still be able to use a lot of different plants and will not "waste" any that would be hidden in the back.

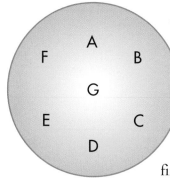

A = Upright plant
B, G, F = Shorter upright and mounding plants
C, D, E = Trailing plants

A planter that follows this layout definitely has a "face." You'd be looking at it from the front or side, where the upright plants build the backdrop. The top picture on page 29 shows what the finished container garden looked like.

Before you start planting, decide if you will be able to move your container after it's planted. Some planters get so heavy that it's best to plant them in their final spot. Smaller and lighter pots can be planted on an elevated surface such as a potting bench or table so you don't have to bend down and strain your back.

For the actual planting, fill your planter partially with slightly moist potting mix. Some gardeners prefer to fill it only to the level of the largest plant, but I find it easier to fill it up to about three to four inches from the rim and then place the plants by digging a hole with my hands. That way the plants have more stability from the beginning, which makes the whole planting process easier. If you are not sure of your arrangement, place the plants in their intended spot to visualize the design, make adjustments if necessary, then remove them to start planting.

The mouth of this asymmetrical pot was toward the front and not in the center. That gives it a definite "face," meaning it clearly has one side that you'll be viewing it from. Following the above planting schematic gives it a face and balances the asymmetrical planter.

Start planting in the center and work your way out; or, if you plant asymmetrically, start in the back with the tallest plants and work your way to the front. Remove each plant—one at a time—from its existing pot gently. If you have trouble removing it, turn the pot upside down, slide your fingers into the base of the plant, support the plant with one hand, and gently tap the rim of the pot onto the edge of a firm surface such as a potting bench or step. If you still can't remove it, use scissors to cut the pot open. If you find the roots to be

When designing your own container gardens, it is easier to visualize the end result if you prearrange the pots in the container, then take them out and start planting.

coiled around the bottom of the pot, gently pull them apart. Place the plant at a level so that the new potting mix is at the same level where the old root ball is. If you bury the plant stems, the stems might rot.

Planting Steps at a Glance:
- Fill the planter with potting mix, leaving about three inches from the rim
- Gently remove plants from their old pot
- Start planting upright plants in the center or back, then work your way outward or toward the front
- After each plant, press the potting mix down firmly
- Press down along the edges to eliminate air pockets
- Water thoroughly

ly. If you want to squeeze a plant into a tight spot, you may gently pull some of the potting mix from the old root ball off or squeeze the root ball so that it fits. When you are finished planting, push your hands into the mix along the edges firmly to compress it well and to eliminate air pockets. Add additional potting mix if needed. If the roots have good contact with the surrounding potting mix, they will resume growing sooner and will experience less stress. Make sure to leave at least one to two inches between the top potting mix level and the rim of the pot to provide enough room for watering. When you are finished planting, water the container thoroughly with gentle pressure until water drains through the holes in the bottom. If your potting mix was dry and the water runs through immediately, water several times until the entire container is soaked thoroughly.

If you are planting window boxes, you might want to choose a tiered look, especially if you actually place them against a window. In this case, place a row of upright plants in the back, a row of mounding plants in the middle, and a row of trailing plants in the front. If your window box doesn't allow for three rows, you can alternate upright and mounding plants in the back, or alternate mounding and trailing plants in the front.

If you place your window box in front of a window, it's best to use tall plants that are airy so they don't block the view and the light coming into your house. *Argyranthemum*, for example, has a

This window box uses upright and mounding plants in the back (Persian shield and rex begonias) and mainly trailing plants in the front (*Lysimachia* and *Muehlenbeckia*) with another mounding plant interspersed in the front center (*Heuchera*).

dense growth habit and is not as good for window boxes, while plants with an open habit, such as *Scabiosa* or ornamental grasses, work well.

Planting Hanging Baskets

When planting hanging baskets and you use those made of natural materials such as moss or coco fiber, the question is, Should you plant them along the sidewalls or not? The truth is that there is no right or wrong answer, but rather both techniques have their merits and challenges. There is so much beautiful plant material available that is very trailing, so you don't need to plant the sidewalls to get a basket that's completely covered with flowers without any part of the basket being visible. But if you choose to work with different plant material or simply don't want to wait until the plants reach a certain length, planting along the sidewalls is a good option.

Before we get into details, let's first look at some basics that apply whether you plant the sidewalls or not. If your basket will be hung at, slightly above, or below eye level, you will want to follow a planting schematic similar to that for planters. That means you'll want to have one or more upright plants in the center, mounding plants around it, and trailing plants along the edges. But make sure that your upright plants are not too tall. Depending on the size of the basket, you'll want to look for upright plants that are a maximum of fourteen to sixteen inches tall, but shorter plants are even better. As a rule of thumb, I like to make sure the upright plants don't go beyond the hanger. Mounding or semi-trailing plants are good choices to put around the upright plants, and trailing plants are very important, since they are often the signature of hanging baskets.

A = *Nemesia* 'Compact Innocence'
B = *Petunia* 'Supertunia Mini Blue Veined'
C = *Verbena* 'Tukana White'

This planting diagram uses a moderately upright plant in the center (*Nemesia*), a compact-growing petunia that can be considered semimounding around it, and trailing verbena along the edges. While the *Nemesia* is upright enough for a hanging basket with its twelve- to fourteen-inch finished height, it would be considered mounding if it were used in a large, upright planter. The result is shown in the top picture.

This basket features exclusively trailing varieties with *Diascia* 'Red Ace', *Petunia* 'Supertunia Priscilla', and *Verbena* 'Babylon White'. If your baskets hang above eye level, you will want to focus on trailing varieties like these.

If your baskets will be well above eye level, you can eliminate upright plants because they will not be seen at such a height. Baskets that hang very high can be planted with trailing plants exclusively since even the mounding plants would be out of view.

If you decide not to plant along the sidewalls, select varieties that are very trailing (but still use upright and mounding plants as explained earlier). A lot of trailing verbena fit in this category, as well as trailing petunias such as the 'Supertunia' series. Supertunias, for example, can reach up to three feet in length, which makes them the ultimate basket plants. Other great trailing choices are bacopa (*Sutera*), *Scaevola*, and *Calibrachoa*, to name just a few. Baskets that are planted only from the top will show greater parts of the container for a while. But if you use an attractive basket, such as one made of moss, it won't matter; in fact, it adds quite a bit of character to show parts of such a container.

The main advantages of planting only from the top are:

• Cost savings. You need fewer plants, which keeps your cost down.

• Time savings. It is a lot faster to plant only from the top than to plant along the sidewalls.

• Easier maintenance. If you plant only from the top, you use fewer plants, which translates to more potting mix volume per plant. Fewer plants are competing for water and nutrients, which means that each plant has more water and nutrients available, and you won't have to worry about replenishing those resources constantly.

Baskets that are planted only on the top show parts of the basket in the beginning (left), but if you use trailing plants, they will eventually cover all visible parts of the container (right).

On the other hand, planting along the sidewalls has its advantages. If you want to use varieties that are not very trailing, such as pansies, alyssum, or some *Brachyscome* varieties, you'll want to plant along the sidewalls. It lets you create a round color ball filled with flowers. You can incorporate the basket itself into your design. You could, for example, embellish the basket by using wire to attach decorative pieces of wood to it, which gives it a very rustic look. It also allows you to use more plants, which gives you more design possibilities.

To plant along the sidewalls, select smaller plants than the popular four-inch pots so that you can fit them through the wire frame. Look for packs with multiple small plants, or if the plants you want to use are only available in four-inch pots, select smaller ones. Sometimes you can find pots with multiple small plants in them. In that case, you can take them apart carefully.

I first saw wood tied to moss baskets at Roger's Gardens in Corona Del Mar, California. This technique gives moss baskets a rustic look. These baskets were planted on the top as well as along the sidewalls.

There are two main techniques in planting along the sidewalls. The first option is to buy assembled baskets and cut holes into the sidewalls, where you then insert the plants. If you plant in this manner, it's important to moisten the moss first. This not only makes the whole process easier, it also reduces the amount of dust created. Fill the container with potting mix level by level as you insert plants along the sidewall. Finally, finish by planting plants on top. As spreading plants

Soak the basket in a tub of water for one to two minutes to moisten the moss well.

Using a sharp knife, cut a hole into the moss where you plan to insert the first plant (left). The hole has to go all the way through the moss so that the plant's roots will be completely surrounded by potting mix. Fill the basket with potting mix to the level where the first row of plants will be inserted. Insert the plant into the hole (center) all the way until it gets in touch with the potting mix in the basket (right). If necessary, squeeze the root ball to fit the plant through the wire cage.

start to grow and develop multiple branches along the sidewall, they can be trained to cover a larger area by pinning the branches to the moss. This works especially well with trailing verbena and English ivy, as they quickly develop roots along the branches. The result is a uniform color ball with plants closely hugging the container.

Finish one row, then insert more potting mix to the next level. Work your way around the basket and up. When finished, plant on the top.

The second option is to assemble a moss basket from scratch, using a wire cage and loose moss. The plants can then be planted as the moss basket is being assembled. With this method, the moss must be moistened well before starting. Begin from the bottom of the wire basket, packing the moss tightly. As you reach the level where you'll insert plants, begin adding plants after filling the bottom with potting mix. Continue with layers of firmly packed moss, potting mix, and plants until the basket is complete. In the end, finish by planting on the top.

Moss baskets that are planted according to these two techniques usually require watering not only from the top, but also along the sidewalls. This is especially important until the plants on the sides develop a sufficient root system that can provide moisture from the core, after which you can just water from the top. Keep a close watch on the plants along the sides to make sure that they are getting enough water.

Water your baskets with gentle pressure not only from top, but also thoroughly along the sidewalls. Apply low water pressure to avoid damaging the plants.

If you assemble moss baskets from scratch, insert the plants as you assemble the basket.

4

Caring for Container Gardens

There's no doubt that putting the right plants together is a big part of the success of container gardens, but the proper care is just as important. With the right care, your plants will flower profusely, and their foliage will look healthy and lush for several months. Adhering to the following guidelines and care tips will bring you a lot closer to container gardening success.

Watering

Watering is often believed to be a no-brainer, but the truth is that you can make a lot of mistakes while usually meaning well. Adequate moisture levels promote plant growth and plant performance. Too much water cuts off the oxygen supply to the roots and can cause root rot, while too little water leads to plant stress. Plants that are stressed don't grow as well as they could and are more susceptible to diseases and insect problems. Some plants actually don't recover very well from drying out. Some respond by dropping their flowers, others drop their foliage, while yet others break open in the middle and create an unsightly growth habit.

Lotus vine responds to severe drying out by dropping its needle-thin, silver foliage.

Watering problems can arise from the beginning if the plants you use together in a container don't start out with the same moisture level. If some are very dry, they won't be able to absorb enough water during the first thorough watering after planting. This means an uneven moisture level from the start. Although it can be corrected with very thorough watering early on, it is better to generously water the plants up to one day before planting so that they all have the same moisture content when they are planted.

Immediately after planting, water your containers well, until water leaks through the drainage holes in the bottom. Slowly fill the space between the top of the potting mix and the rim of the container with water. Repeat several times as needed until the potting mix is evenly wet and water leaks through the drainage holes. Remember to start with slightly moist potting mix, otherwise the water will run straight through without being absorbed. Use a nozzle that produces a shower-like water flow, and always use low pressure so that you don't wash out the potting mix and damage the plants.

When watering by hand, always use a gentle spray and low pressure to avoid damaging the plants and washing out potting mix.

The water requirements of your container gardens can change dramatically throughout the season, depending on the size of the plants and the weather. If you start your container gardens early in spring, the weather might still be cool and gloomy. If in addition you have relatively small plants and a large container with a big potting mix volume, you will need to water very little in the beginning. As a matter of fact, you even need to make sure not to overwater your containers. But even if your plants need little water, it's always better to water thoroughly and less frequently than to water often but only a small amount. Always water until the water leaks through the drainage holes (as described earlier), but wait with the next watering until the top two inches of potting mix are dry to the touch.

As your plants grow and the weather warms up, the water needs of your container gardens increase. Check your pots frequently and adjust your watering schedule accordingly. Once the plants are fully grown and the weather is hot, container gardens can dry out very quickly. Don't be surprised if you need to water them daily in hot climates. Hanging baskets that are exposed to drying winds might even need water twice a day in extreme conditions. A built-in reservoir will help keep the basket from drying out as quickly.

Factors that reduce the water requirements are:
- Plastic containers and containers with poor drainage
- Potting mix with high water-retaining capacities and/or poor drainage
- Water-retaining soil amendments mixed into the potting mix
- High potting mix volume in relation to the plant size
- Low light levels/cloudy skies
- Cool temperatures
- The use of slow-growing, drought-tolerant, or succulent plants
- Frequent rain.

Factors that increase the water requirements are:
- Natural-fiber containers such as moss or coco fiber baskets
- Potting mix with low water-retaining capacities and/or very good drainage
- Low potting mix volume in relation to the plant size
- High light levels/sunny skies

- High temperatures
- Exposure to drying winds
- The use of fast-growing and/or moisture-loving plants.

There are water-retaining soil amendments available that can hold several times their volume in water. They usually come in a granular form that you mix into the potting mix and then expand into a gel-like substance when in contact with water. The gel releases the moisture gradually to the surrounding potting mix.

While this sounds like a good concept, many container garden designers question its merits. One of the problems is that you usually need quite a lot to make it effective. The other problem is that you would have to mix it

Baskets made of natural fiber dry out faster, especially if they are exposed to dry winds after the plants get big. If those factors are a problem, look for moss baskets with a built-in water reservoir. If they dry out severely, put them in a tub of water for a half hour or more until the potting mix is completely saturated.

into the potting mix before planting, but—as we just discussed—you might be facing the danger of overwatering in the beginning while the plants are small and the weather cool. That means you would have increased water-holding capacity at a time when your plants don't need a lot of water. You also can't adjust its water-holding capacity throughout the season as the weather changes. So if you have a rainy period, chances are your containers will be too wet for too long. In other words, it is often better to adjust the water needs of your plants manually than to rely on a water-retaining agent. On the other hand, if you live in a hot climate with little or no summer rain, water-retaining soil amendments might very well be right for you.

Another important question that you need to ask yourself is whether to put your container gardens on drip irrigation or to water by hand. If you have several container gardens, drip irrigation is a great help. One of its advantages is that it dispenses water slowly and with basically no pressure. This means that the potting mix can absorb the water thoroughly. It also lets you direct the water flow to the base of the plants. That means that you won't be damaging the plants with high pressure, and you minimize getting the foliage wet. Wet foliage promotes the spread of diseases, so keeping the foliage dry is an important step toward plant health. Drip irrigation is especially helpful if you can put it on an automatic schedule. Then you don't have to worry about daily watering or about watering while being on vacation.

Large, tall, glazed containers hold a large volume of potting mix and allow for little evaporation. Take care not to overwater them, especially if the plants are small.

If you decide to water by hand, always use low pressure. Direct the water flow as low to the base of the plants as possible. If you water on top of the plants, you might damage the plants, and a bare spot can develop if you always water on the same spot. No matter which method of watering you chose, don't water late in the day. It is better if you water earlier so that the plants don't go into the night wet, which promotes diseases.

Fertilizing

Plants don't just grow on their own—they need water and food, just like humans. Proper fertilizer levels help make your plants look healthy and grow and bloom vigorously. Keep in mind that your container plants have only a limited amount of potting mix available to draw nutrients from. That's why it is even more important to fertilize container-grown plants than those planted in the ground.

To give plants a boost from the start, it's a good idea to mix some slow-release fertilizer into the potting mix before planting. This is especially helpful if you tend to forget about regular fertilization. Slow-release fertilizer releases nutrients over a certain period of time. This time frame is listed on the label, but it's also influenced by the temperature and the amount of water applied to the container gardens. Some potting mixes already have slow-release fertilizer mixed in. In that case you don't need to add additional slow-release fertilizer to the mix before planting.

Personally, I do not like to rely on slow-release fertilizer as the sole source of nutrition for container gardens. It might fail to release enough nutrients at one time, the nutrients might get used up earlier than expected, or you might forget to replenish the fertilizer after it is used up. Consider slow-release fertilizer as "insurance" for your plants, as it provides nutrients if you forget to fertilize. Water-soluble fertilizer gives you more control over the amount of nutrients available to your plants. Use it exclusively or in addition to slow-release fertilizer. Choose a high-quality, well-balanced fertilizer, ideally one that contains micronutrients. The main nutrients you can find in a fertilizer are nitrogen (N), phosphorus (P), and potassium (K). You can determine the ratio in which they are used by the so-called NPK ratio that's given on the label as three numbers, for example 20:10:20 (or 20–10–20).

You might have heard that nitrogen is important for leafy growth, while phosphorus is important for blooming. This is basically true and is the reason why gardeners often recommend a fertilizer high in phosphorus for annuals. Typical annuals grow first, then they flower, then they die, all in one season. At the stage when you buy them, they have usually completed their leafy, or vegetative, growth, and you only have to worry about keeping them blooming.

Proper fertilization is important for healthy growth and vibrant blooms.

But a lot of the plants used in this book are not your typical annuals. Many of the plants that are so popular for container gardening today are not really annuals, but tender perennials. That means that they are perennials in their native habitat but are not frost hardy. Although most parts of North America use them like annuals (because they wouldn't survive the winter), they would actually continue to live and grow if frost wouldn't kill them. Consequently, they have a different life cycle than "typical" annuals. While typical annuals often stop growing when they start flowering, these new types continue to grow as they flower. In some parts of the country and in their native habitat, they even grow and often flower throughout the winter. This translates into a greater and different need for nutrients throughout the growing season, as you need to provide the right nutrients for vegetative growth as well as for bloom production. Their need for nitrogen remains high throughout the summer. That's why I like to use a fertilizer that's fairly high in nitrogen, such as a 20:10:20 or 20:5:15.

Many new types of annuals are actually tender perennials. Their fertilizer needs are different from those of typical annuals.

Container-grown plants should be fertilized about every other week. Follow the package direction for concentration recommendations. It is better to fertilize when the potting mix is slightly moist than completely dry. If you apply fertilizer to dry soil, the thirsty plants immediately take up fertilizer solution, which can be too highly concentrated and can cause plant damage. If the plants are not thirsty when you apply fertilizer, they will absorb the fertilizer solution more slowly and without harm.

Adequate fertilization is necessary for lush, healthy plant growth and abundant blooms.

If you live in an area where the water has a high salt content or in hot climates that require frequent watering, gradual salt buildup in the potting mix can be a problem. High salt levels can cause burn marks on the foliage and poor plant performance. If this is a problem, leach periodically with clear water.

The availability of fertilizer is influenced by the pH of the potting mix. If the pH is too high, it locks up the fertilizer, which means that the plants can't absorb the nutrients even though the nutrients are present. This often shows in yellowish foliage with dark veins, an indicator of iron deficiency. While giving more fertilizer or applying a fertilizer high in iron can help green up the foliage, it actually only masks the problem. Unless you lower the potting mix pH, the same problem will continue to occur. The potting mix pH can be influenced by the kind of nitrogen that you use in your fertilizer. Generally, ammonia-based nitrogen lowers the soil's pH, while nitrate nitrogen raises it. Ask your garden center to recommend a nitrogen source suitable for your needs.

Pruning and Trimming

Some people shy away from pruning their plants, but most plants respond very well to pruning. A lot of the plants used in this book don't require pruning, but they may tolerate it very well. Some even benefit from it, in which case I noted it with each planting diagram.

The main reasons to prune plants are to deadhead spent flowers or to trim them back if they get too big or leggy. Deadheading means cutting off spent flowers. This has two purposes. One is simply aesthetic, as flowers may turn brown and unsightly after their bloom. The second reason is that plants that set seeds waste energy that could otherwise be spent on developing new flowers. In that case, plants truly benefit from deadheading. Pinch off spent flowers either with scissors, garden shears, or your fingers. Remove them close to the stem, so that no unsightly stem ends remain.

If plants get too big or out of hand, you may cut them back liberally. If your container gardens are just a little bit out of overall shape, trim the entire container by a few inches. Plants usually respond well with healthy, new growth and abundant flowers. If the plants in the container get too big or leggy, you may trim them back by a third or even by half. The new growth will be much thicker and more lush. Sometimes it's hard to predict how vigorously a plant will grow in relation to its companions, or you may simply want to use a particular plant for its aesthetic effect even

Container gardens can be pruned so that they maintain a clean, uniform shape.

though it is more vigorous than the others are. In that case, keep a close eye on the fast-growing variety and cut it back if it tries to overtake the others.

Pest and Diseases

By combining many different plants in container gardens, you are offering a smorgasbord for pests and diseases. While one plant might be attractive to aphids, others might be favorites of spider mites or mealybugs. Not only are you growing plants that may attract different pests in a small space, but the foliage in container gardens can also get very thick, often providing ideal growing conditions and hiding spaces for insects and other pests and a moist growing ground for diseases.

To keep your containers healthy, you need to check for insects and diseases frequently and thoroughly. Look closely at the flowers and new growth, then divide the foliage with your hands and check older growth. Besides looking for visible insects, look for discolored foliage or deformed flowers and leaves, as they may be indicators of an insect problem. Insects not only cause direct, visible damage, they can also carry diseases that may harm the plants and affect their performance. Such insects, known as vectors, may infect each new plant they feed on as they move through your container.

Hanging baskets can be especially hard to scout for insects. It's best to take the baskets down and start searching in the center, as insect problems can often start there, where the growth is especially dense. If you don't take the baskets down, only checking from below, you are likely to overlook the onset of a problem. By the time you discover a problem, it might have gotten out of hand. Remove affected plant parts, if possible, and treat the insect problem following recommendations from your garden retailer.

Disease problems often arise if the growing conditions are unfavorable or if the plants are otherwise stressed. Too much moisture, insufficient light levels, poor air movement, and damp conditions can all be breeding grounds for diseases. Make yourself familiar with the growing requirements of the plants you use (such as light levels/sun exposure and water requirements) and try to adhere to them as much as possible.

As a general precaution, it is always best to start with healthy, high-quality plant material. This doesn't mean that you won't have any future problems, but healthy plants are less susceptible to insects and diseases. So look for high-quality plants from a good garden retailer and give your container gardens a healthy start.

When it comes to diseases, prevention is always better than treatment. But if you have problems with fungal or bacterial diseases, look for the appropriate remedy at your local garden retailer. Root-borne diseases are best treated with a drench, while diseases on stems and foliage can be sprayed.

Part 2

Plant Profiles

T he plants in this section all appear in the baskets, pots, and window boxes found in Part 3. Here you'll find out all about each plant—how large it grows, flowering time, light and water needs, ideal potting mix, and frost hardiness. Each plant will also have information about how it should be used in containers, such as for trailing over the edges, mounding in the middle, or adding height to the container. If foliage or flowers are notable, you'll see that. The varieties used in the book will be listed as well.

The USDA Zones referred to here are based on the 1990 edition of the USDA Hardiness Zone Map (see p. 286). USDA was working on a new edition at the time this book went to print.

Acorus gramineus
Sweet flag

- Exposure: Partial shade to full sun
- Height: 12–16"
- Frost hardiness: USDA Zone 5
- Flowering time: Insignificant

Sweet flag is a popular grass for container gardens due to its medium height and noninvasive character. Use it as a middle-height plant in planters or as a center plant in hanging baskets. The variegated forms 'Ogon' and 'Variegatus' are especially attractive with their striped, arching leaves. *Acorus* prefers partial shade, but tolerates full sun. Provide sufficient moisture, which is especially important in sunny locations.

Ageratum Hybrid

- Exposure: Full sun
- Height: 6–12", some varieties up to 24"
- Frost hardiness: Not hardy; use as an annual in most climates; hardy in USDA Zones 10–11
- Flowering time: Spring through fall, or all year in Southern, frost-free climates

A mounding plant that is well suited as a middle-height plant in containers. Smaller varieties can be used along the edges; the tall varieties can be used as cut flowers. Flowers are most common in shades of blue and purple, but also come in white and bicolored. Ageratum prefers a fertile, well-drained potting mix that is kept slightly moist at all times. In very hot and humid climates, ageratum is best used in fall, winter, and spring. Varieties used in this book are 'Artist Alto Blue', 'Artist Blue', and 'Artist Purple'.

Ajania Hybrid 'Bea'

- Exposure: Full sun
- Height: 12–14"
- Frost hardiness: USDA Zone 6
- Flowering time: Fall

There are significant differences in the *Ajania* hybrid varieties, and since I used only this one, I will focus on 'Bea'. It's related to *Ajania pacifica*, which used to be known as *Chrysanthemum pacificum*. It flowers in fall, with small, button-shaped, golden yellow flowers that appear in umbels. The foliage is green with silver undersides. Because of its limited flowering time, it's best used for autumn-themed designs—or you can use it year-round for its foliage. Good drainage is important.

Ajuga reptans
Bugle weed

- Exposure: Full sun to partial shade
- Height: 2–4"; flowers 6–8", spreading
- Frost hardiness: USDA Zone 3
- Flowering time: Spring

This hardy perennial is mostly used for its colorful foliage. It has a low-growing, spreading habit that's ideal for the edges of containers. The blue flower panicles are vibrant and attractive, but they appear mainly in spring. Extensive breeding work has resulted in a wide range of foliage colors available, from olive green to purple, pink, and multicolored. *Ajuga* prefers well-drained potting mix. If planted in full sun, adequate moisture is especially important. At the end of the season, *Ajuga* can be taken out of the container and used as a groundcover in the garden, but it's quite aggressive. Varieties used in this book all belong to *Ajuga reptans*: 'Burgundy Glow', 'Catlin's Giant', 'Chocolate Chip', and 'Mahogany'.

Angelonia angustifolia Hybrid
Summer snapdragon

- Exposure: Full sun
- Height: 2–3'
- Frost hardiness: Not hardy; use as an annual in most climates; hardy in USDA Zones 10–11
- Flowering time: Spring through fall, or all year in Southern, frost-free climates

Angelonia is one of my favorites as a center plant in an upright container. It provides height and color at the same time. *Angelonia* is a heat lover and can stand up even to heat and humidity in Southern climates, but is also an excellent annual in cooler regions. A well-drained, fertile potting mix is best, which should be kept slightly moist. Flowers come mostly in blue, purple, and bicolored, but also white and pink. In this book, you can find the varieties 'Angelface Blue Bicolor' and 'Angelface Violet'.

Anisodontea Hybrid
African mallow

- Exposure: Full sun
- Height: 3–4'
- Frost hardiness: Mostly used as annual, but may die to the ground and come back in USDA Zones 8–9; perennial in Zones 10–11
- Flowering time: Spring through fall, or all year in Southern, frost-free climates

This is another favorite of mine for the center of planters because it provides height without being overpowering, due to its open and airy habit. It has an "English cottage garden" look. African mallow prefers well-drained potting mix and adequate moisture, but watch for aphids and spider mites. It usually blooms in pink, and the dead flowers are inconspicuous. The only variety I used in this book is 'Elegant Lady', which has fairly large flowers.

Arctotis Hybrid

- Exposure: Full sun
- Height: 10–18"
- Frost hardiness: Not hardy; use as an annual in most climates; hardy in USDA Zones 10–11
- Flowering time: Spring through fall, or all year in Southern, frost-free climates

Arctotis has flowers that remind me of gerberas, which it displays on long stems over compact, silver foliage. It's a good middle-height plant in large planters, or center plant in smaller containers. Flowers are usually shades of yellow, orange, and red. One disadvantage is that its flowers close at night and sometimes stay closed under low-light conditions. *Arctotis* prefers slightly moist, well-drained potting mix, but doesn't like to have wet feet. Watch for aphids. Deadheading is important to keep it blooming continually. The only variety used in this book is 'Sunspot'.

Argyranthemum frutescens
Marguerite daisy

- Exposure: Full sun
- Height: 12–20"
- Frost hardiness: Not hardy; use as an annual in most climates; hardy in USDA Zone 10–11; tolerates 26 to 28°F if well established
- Flowering time: Spring through fall, or all year in Southern, frost-free climates

Marguerite daisy is a great choice as a center plant if you want a high color impact—it's densely covered with flowers most of the year. Some of the more compact varieties can also be used as mounding elements in large planters. Deadheading is recommended to keep the flowers coming. If too many flowers are dead at once, a good trim usually brings out a new flush of blooms. Marguerite daisies use quite a lot of water and fertilizer once they are big, so make sure to keep both in adequate supply. Varieties used here are 'Butterfly', 'Courtyard Daisy Blanche', 'Harvest Snow', and 'Summer Angel'.

Artemisia 'Oriental Limelight'

- Exposure: Full sun to partial shade
- Height: 12–36"
- Frost hardiness: USDA Zone 3
- Flowering time: Summer, but prized for foliage

Of the many different *Artemisia* types out there, 'Oriental Limelight' is a hybrid with variegated leaves in green and yellow. It stays low and mounding at first, but as the season progresses, it builds long, upright branches that are eventually topped with inconspicuous flowers. Although it's a hardy perennial that's excellent for the perennial border, it's also a popular container garden plant used for its attractive foliage. It's easy to grow and has few pests or disease problems.

Bacopa, see *Sutera*

Barleria obtusa

- Exposure: Full sun to partial shade
- Height: 12–18"
- Frost hardiness: Not hardy; use as an annual in most climates; perennial only in frost-free climates
- Flowering time: Late summer, but grown primarily for foliage

This heat-lover is best used as a middle-height component plant because of its colorful foliage. The pink accents are especially prominent on young growth, while older growth is mainly green and white. The two-tone pink flowers appear in late summer and are an added benefit, since they play second fiddle to the foliage. Because it's a heat-lover, it's best to wait until the temperatures have warmed before you plant *Barleria*. Temperatures below 45°F stall growth. *Barleria* is not very frequently grown, and the only variety used in this book is 'Amethyst Lights'.

Begonia obliqua

- Exposure: Full sun to shade
- Height: 10–12"
- Frost hardiness: Not hardy; use as an annual in most climates; hardy in USDA Zones 10–11
- Flowering time: Spring through fall, or all year in Southern, frost-free climates

With dark, mahogany-colored foliage and blush pink flowers, this is a good plant with multiple attributes. It can be used as a center plant in small pots or as mounding element in larger planters. It tolerates sun and shade, but its colors are most intense in full sun. In the shade, its foliage is primarily green and the flowers almost white. The variety used here is 'Maribel Pink Shades'. This type of begonia is similar to *Begonia* 'Richmondensis', which might be easier to find and can be substituted, especially the pink form.

Begonia Rex-Cultorum
Rex begonia

- Exposure: Partial to full shade
- Height: 6–12"
- Frost hardiness: Not hardy; use as an annual or houseplant
- Flowering time: Insignificant

　　Rex begonias are excellent foliage plants for shady locations. Their multicolored foliage adds intriguing accents to mixed containers. Their colors range mostly from green to silver, pink, and purple—sometimes even with all four in one variety. They are often used as houseplants but can be placed in shady spots outdoors once the temperatures remain above 45°F. While they like warm temperatures, they are not suitable for extremely hot weather. The varieties used in this book are from the 'Great American Cities' series. Since most varieties have a similar color theme, they can often be used interchangeably.

Bergenia cordifolia

- Exposure: Sun to shade
- Height: 10–18"
- Frost hardiness: USDA Zone 4
- Flowering time: Spring

　　Bergenia is a popular perennial with large, round, leathery leaves. The flowers are pink and appear in whorls on long stems in spring and sporadically through early summer. But even when the flowers are gone, the foliage alone is attractive. To prolong flowering for as long as possible, deadhead *Bergenia* regularly. In fall, when the temperatures drop, the leaves turn an attractive bronze color, which makes it also a great selection for autumn-themed designs. Plant it near the edge of planters so that its pretty foliage isn't hidden. The variety in this book is 'Autumn Glory'.

Bidens ferulifolia

- Exposure: Full sun to shade
- Height: 10–12", trailing
- Frost hardiness: Not hardy; use as an annual in most climates; hardy in USDA Zones 10–11
- Flowering time: Spring through fall, or all year in Southern, frost-free climates

Trailing plants with yellow flowers are not too common, so it's no surprise that *Bidens* has become so popular. Other reasons would be its excellent heat tolerance, low maintenance, and honey-sweet fragrance. The first *Bidens* introductions were quite vigorous, but the more recent varieties are better behaved though it's still a fast-growing plant. Varieties used in this book are 'Goldie' and 'Peter's Gold Carpet'.

Black Mondo Grass, see Ophiopogon

Brachyscome Hybrid
Swan River daisy

- Exposure: Full sun
- Height: 6–12"
- Frost hardiness: Not hardy; use as an annual in most climates; hardy in USDA Zones 10–11
- Flowering time: Spring through fall, or all year in Southern, frost-free climates

Brachyscome is one of the most popular container garden plants. The most commonly available varieties have delicate, ferny foliage and a mounding or trailing growth habit. Other varieties have broader leaves. They are best used along the edges of planters, where they can cascade as they get older. The less trailing varieties are good mounding elements. Their small, daisylike flowers are most common in shades of pink and purple, but white and yellow varieties are also available. *Brachyscome* doesn't like to be too wet, but don't let it dry out either or the flowers will shrivel up. Varieties used in this book are 'City Lights', 'New Amethyst', and 'Toucan Tango'.

Bracteantha bracteata
Strawflower

• Exposure: Full sun
• Height: 10–18"
• Frost hardiness: Not hardy; use as an annual in most climates; hardy in USDA Zones 10–11
• Flowering time: Spring through fall, or all year in Southern, frost-free climates

Bracteantha comes mainly in two different growth habits: The mounding or semi-trailing varieties can be used in hanging baskets or along the edges of planters. The upright types vary in height, reaching up to eighteen inches, and are ideal for the center of pots. The more compact types are good as center plants in smaller planters or as middle-height plants in larger ones. Their flowers can be used in fresh or dried arrangements. Regular deadheading is important to keep the plants looking neat and the flowers coming. Strawflowers don't like to be too wet; otherwise their foliage turns yellow. The varieties most frequently used in this book belong to the 'Sundaze' series, which are compact and upright.

Calibrachoa Hybrid

• Exposure: Full sun
• Height: Varies—mounding types 8–12"; trailing types 4–6" and trailing
• Frost hardiness: Slightly hardy; commonly used as an annual, but has been known to overwinter in USDA Zone 7 if well established
• Flowering time: Varies by variety; mostly spring through fall, but all year for some varieties in Southern, frost-free climates

A newcomer over the last decade, *Calibrachoa* has quickly found its way into the hearts of gardeners across the country. When in bloom, *Calibrachoa* is covered with hundreds of small flowers that resemble a miniature petunia, one of its relatives. There is a considerable variation in bloom time and growth habit among the varieties, so make sure that you read the label carefully or ask a nursery professional for advice. Some varieties grow strictly trailing and should only be used along the edges of containers. Others are mounding and are suitable either as middle-height plants or as trailing components. Also, some varieties start flowering earlier in spring than others, flower even in winter in frost-free climates, and don't close their flowers at night. It's important to know these differences, but no matter which ones you choose, you'll love these low-maintenance varieties when they're in full bloom. Just make sure that you give them enough fertilizer. Another thing to watch for are aphids, especially in summer. A very broad range of colors is available, including many shades of pink, blue, purple, red, yellow, orange, white, and even multi-toned varieties. The varieties used in this book belong to the 'Million Bells' and 'Superbells' series.

Carex buchananii
Leatherleaf sedge

- Exposure: Full sun to partial shade
- Height: 14–20"
- Frost hardiness: USDA Zone 6
- Flowering time: None

Leatherleaf sedge is, botanically speaking, not a grass, but it is known and handled as one. I've heard people call it "dead grass" because of its bronze-colored leaves that feel dry to the touch. Leatherleaf sedge grows upright, and its thin leaves are slightly curled on top. It's best used to add height and texture in the center of planters and pots. Because of its thin leaves, it has a very subtle effect. It tolerates sun to partial shade. The more sun it gets, the more moisture it needs.

Carex flagellifera

- Exposure: Full sun to partial shade
- Height: 10–16"
- Frost hardiness: USDA Zone 7
- Flowering time: None

Carex flagellifera is very similar in color and texture to *Carex buchananii,* but has a more mounding, weeping habit. It's good for the center of small planters or in the middle or along the edges of larger planters. It looks especially graceful if it can cascade over the rim of an elegant container. Because of its earthy color, it's a great component for warm-colored or autumn-themed designs. Care requirements are also similar to *Carex buchananii,* but it's slightly less frost tolerant. The variety used in this book is 'Toffee Twist'.

Chasmanthium latifolium
Northern sea oats

- Exposure: Full sun to partial shade
- Height: 2–3'
- Frost hardiness: USDA Zone 5
- Flowering time: Summer

This is a beautiful ornamental grass with an upright growth habit, arching stems, and showy, drooping flowers. Its foliage changes colors from green to copper to rich brown over the course of the season. It's even valuable in winter, when the rich foliage builds a striking contrast against a snow-covered landscape. With its substantial height, it's ideal for the center of large planters in full sun to partial shade. This grass likes moist conditions, especially if it's in full sun. A big plus is that it appears to be pest- and disease-free.

Chrysocephalum apiculatum

- Exposure: Full sun
- Height: 10–12"
- Frost hardiness: Not hardy; use as an annual in most climates; hardy in USDA Zones 10–11
- Flowering time: Spring through fall, or all year in Southern, frost-free climates

This plant went through a name change within the last decade; it used to be called *Helichrysum apiculatum.* Its small, button-shaped, golden-yellow flowers are ideal for mixed containers. They are fairly inconspicuous by themselves, and its growth habit is very open, but in container gardens they mingle with the other plants and stick out their flower heads among the other plants. The foliage is delicate, silver in color, and velvety to the touch. *Chrysocephalum* is one of the most easy-to-care-for container garden plants that also has very few pest and disease problems. The variety used in this book is 'Baby Gold', but very similar varieties are sold under different names.

Cleome
Spider flower

- Exposure: Full sun
- Height: 1–5', varies greatly by variety
- Frost hardiness: Not hardy; use as an annual in most climates; some varieties are perennial in USDA Zones 10–11
- Flowering time: Spring through fall

Commonly called spider flower, this old-fashioned plant is a favorite in garden beds due to its unusual flowers that—at least to some people—look like spiders, which gave the plant its name. The plants that are most commonly seen in gardens belong to *Cleome hassleriana,* which is a seed-grown species with relatively tall flower stems and unpleasant thorns. It also reseeds quite freely. What you can find in this book is a new hybrid called 'Linde Armstrong'. It flowers even when it's less than a foot tall, with rosy pink flowers and no thorns. Brought to the market by Dr. Allan Armitage, 'Linde Armstrong' is ideal for container gardens, where it reaches a mature height of typically two to two-and-a-half feet. It is also very heat and humidity tolerant. Make sure not to keep it too wet, but other than that, this is a great, low-maintenance variety.

Coleus Hybrid (syn. *Solenostemon*)

- Exposure: Shade to sun
- Height: 12–36"
- Frost hardiness: Not hardy; use as an annual; temperatures below 40°F cause damage
- Flowering time: Insignificant

You probably remember coleus as an old-fashioned, seed-grown shade plant from way back when, but things have changed. Coleus started experiencing a renaissance in the 1990s, when more and more vegetatively grown varieties came to the market. The plants that you can find at your garden retailer today are likely to be grown from cuttings and are much more sun tolerant than their seed-grown predecessors. I can't think of another plant that comes in as many foliage colors, which makes it so versatile for container gardens. One and the same variety might actually change its color, depending on how much light it gets. You can also find a wide variety of heights, from compact forms that get only about one foot tall to vigorous types that grow three feet tall or more. For the planters in this book, I used 'Amora', 'Dark Star', 'Dipt in Wine', 'Kingswood Torch', 'Pineapple', 'Sky Fire', 'Super Sun Plum Parfait', and 'Texas Parking Lot'.

Cuphea llavea

- Exposure: Full sun
- Height: 8–12"
- Frost hardiness: Not hardy; use as an annual in most climates; hardy in USDA Zones 10–11
- Flowering time: Spring through fall

If you're looking for a fun plant to use in container gardens, try *Cuphea llavea*. Its flowers look like faces with huge ears, which gave it the variety names under which it can be found: 'Tiny Mice' and 'Bat Face'. While 'Tiny Mice' is, in my opinion, the nicer name, it also describes the flower shape better. As far as growth habit, this is not the greatest stand-alone plant, but it's excellent in container gardens, where its branches can weave in between other plants and its flowers stick out to attract attention.

Cuphea x purpurea

- Exposure: Full sun
- Height: 8–10"
- Frost hardiness: Not hardy; use as an annual in most climates; hardy in USDA Zones 10–11
- Flowering time: Spring through fall

Here's another plant that's fun in container gardens. Its scarlet red flowers have six showy petals that are arranged in a pinwheel shape, with the top two petals being significantly larger than the rest. Similar to *Cuphea llavea* in growth habit, this species is best used in mixed containers rather than as a stand-alone. Like most *Cuphea*, it tolerates heat well. The best-known variety in this species is 'Firefly'.

Dianthus caryophyllus
Carnation

- Exposure: Full sun
- Height: 7–16"
- Frost hardiness: USDA Zone 6
- Flowering time: Spring through fall

Carnations are wonderful plants for garden beds and container gardens alike. Their ruffled, double flowers are often fragrant and one to two inches in diameter. Some grow mainly upright, while others grow upright at first, but as the flower clusters open up, their weight makes the stems cascade gracefully. This effect is especially attractive in container gardens. You can use them in the center of a hanging basket or small planter, where their branches spill like fountains of color, or along the edges of larger pots, where they can cascade over the rim. Another plus is that their fragrant flowers can be used as cut flowers. The foliage is also attractive and often silver in color. Carnations like a fertile, well-drained potting mix that's kept evenly moist. You can find varieties 'Devon Cottage Rosie Cheeks' series in this book.

Diascia
Twinspur

- Exposure: Full Sun
- Height: 7–16"
- Frost hardiness: USDA Zone 7
- Flowering time: Spring through fall, or all year in Southern, frost-free climates

Diascia used to be a plant that was ideal for moderate climates, but intense breeding work since the 1990s (and even earlier in Europe) has resulted in not only more varieties, but also more heat-tolerant types. The late English *Diascia* breeder Hector Harrison bred some of the best varieties available today. *Diascia* is used in all parts of the country, although it may still suffer a bit in very hot and humid climates of the Southeast, but those locales can use them as a winter-flowering plant from autumn through spring. Their growth habit ranges from trailing to upright, but most are semi-trailing and best used along the edges of planters or in hanging baskets. Also called twinspur due to its flower shape, *Diascia* is most commonly available in different shades of pink and red—including coral and apricot—but white varieties can also be found. Keep *Diascia* moist at all times, as drying out can lead to dropped flowers. For this book, I used 'Little Charmer', 'Red Ace', 'Strawberry Sundae', 'Summer Celebration Coral Belle', and 'Summer's Dance'.

Eragrostis
China love grass

- Exposure: Full sun
- Height: 18"
- Frost hardiness: USDA Zone 7
- Flowering time: Summer

An especially showy ornamental grass, *Eragrostis* gets its charm from its clouds of pinkish-red flowers that appear in late spring and last through most of summer before turning golden yellow in fall. This mounding type is a good middle-height plant in pots and planters. The flowers can be used in fresh and dried arrangements.

Erysimum linifolium
Wallflower

- Exposure: Full sun to partial shade
- Height: 12–16"
- Frost hardiness: USDA Zone 6
- Flowering time: Spring and early summer

Erysimum is a hardy perennial that does well in full sun but benefits from light shade in very hot climates. I used the variety 'Variegatum' in this book. It has narrow, creamy yellow and green variegated leaves and purple flowers that appear in early spring and last into summer. It's an excellent component plant for container gardens because of its attractive foliage. The plant is usually chosen for its foliage and the flowers are an added bonus, which should be considered when you design your containers, although *Erysimum* doesn't flower all season. *Erysimum* likes good drainage, but it's very easy to grow otherwise. The variegated foliage and purple flowers look especially good with purple-flowering plants and dark purple foliage.

Felicia amelloides
Blue marguerite

- Exposure: Full sun to partial shade
- Height: 8–12"
- Frost hardiness: Not hardy; use as an annual in most climates; hardy in USDA Zones 10–11
- Flowering time: Spring to fall

You can never have too many daisies, especially when they come is such a lovely shade of blue. Felicia is a classic container garden plant with delicate foliage and long flower stems topped by blue-petaled flowers with yellow centers. Use them as middle-height plants in your container gardens. *Felicia* prefers well-drained potting mix and doesn't like wet feet, which could lead to root rot. In hot climates, afternoon shade is beneficial. The variety used in this book is 'Cape Town Blue'.

Fuchsia

- Exposure: Shade to partial shade
- Height: 8–16"
- Frost hardiness: Not hardy; use as an annual; temperatures below 40°F cause damage
- Flowering time: Spring through fall

When you think of fuchsia, you might think of hanging baskets in shade, but there are also types that grow mostly upright and can even tolerate a bit of sun. Those are the kinds I used in this book. You can find fuchsias that have small, single flowers, and they are great for container gardens as middle-height plants. The trailing types are excellent for mixed hanging baskets in partial or full shade, or along the edges of planters. There are even types with variegated foliage, which give you double impact—foliage and flowers. Some fuchsias set seedpods that turn blackish purple in color. If you don't like the seedpods, make sure to deadhead regularly, which also keeps the flowers coming more profusely. The varieties in this book are 'Ballerina Blau', 'Golden Marinka', 'Lohn der Liebe', and 'Sun Ray'.

Gaura lindheimeri

- Exposure: Full sun to partial shade
- Height: 10–36"
- Frost hardiness: USDA Zone 5
- Flowering time: Summer

Gaura has become a well-known perennial that tolerates many different climate zones, even the hot and humid South. While many of the previous introductions grow three feet tall, more recently, compact forms have emerged that are suitable for container gardens. 'Perky Pink' is such a variety and grows not much more than a foot tall. Its foliage is burgundy red, and the flowers are medium pink on long stems. *Gaura* prefers well-drained potting mix. Deadhead the spent flower stems regularly to encourage continuous blooming.

Glechoma

- Exposure: Full sun to shade
- Height: 3–6", trailing
- Frost hardiness: USDA Zone 6
- Flowering time: None

Although it's a perennial, *Glechoma* is one of the most popular plants for mixed containers due to its variegated foliage in silver-green and white. Its growth is strictly trailing, so place it along the edges of planters and baskets. It's quite vigorous and can easily cascade three feet in one summer. If it gets too big, simply cut it back liberally. The leaves have a distinct scent—I wouldn't call it a necessarily pleasing fragrance, but then again, tastes vary. Because it roots freely, you can use it as a topiary plant to grow along moss baskets or structures filled with moss. The downside of this ability is that it also becomes quite invasive if planted in the ground. *Glechoma* is tolerant to sun as well as shade, but the more sun it is exposed to, the more moisture it requires. The most commonly available variety and the one used in this book is 'Variegata'.

Hakonechloa macra
Hakone grass

- Exposure: Partial shade to full shade
- Height: 12–16"
- Frost hardiness: USDA Zone 5
- Flowering time: None

An excellent ornamental grass for shady locations, *Hakonechloa* excels in container gardens as well as in landscape beds. The variety I used in this book is 'Aureola', with yellow leaves striped with green. Its growth habit is mounded/weeping, which looks especially stunning if planted along the edges of a planter. It can tolerate partial sun if enough moisture is provided, but protection from midday sun is important. A seemingly pest- and disease-free selection, it prefers a well-drained, fertile potting mix that's kept moist at all times.

Hedera
English ivy

- Exposure: Sun to shade
- Height: 3–5", trailing
- Frost hardiness: USDA Zone 5
- Flowering time: None

Without a doubt, English ivy is a classic container garden plant. With their use dating back hundreds of years, they continue to be favorites today. Few other plants are so easy to care for and so adaptable to as many different conditions. Although primarily a shade plant, ivies can tolerate full sun as long as they're given adequate moisture. You can also find them in many different colors, so if you can't find the particular varieties that I used in this book—'Glacier', 'Goldstern', 'Ritterkreuz', and 'Yellow Ripple'—you are likely to find something similar. English ivy is also a great topiary plant because it roots freely and easily creeps along moss baskets or wire structures filled with moss. Aside from watching for spider mites, you'll need to give ivies little maintenance.

Helichrysum petiolare
Licorice plant

- Exposure: Full sun to partial shade
- Height: 6–12"
- Frost hardiness: Not hardy; use as an annual in most climates; hardy in USDA Zones 10–11
- Flowering time: Prized for foliage

One of the most popular component plants is *Helichrysum petiolare,* commonly called licorice plant. This South African native has ultrasoft, velvety leaves and a spreading growth habit that turns trailing in hanging baskets. It's a very vigorous grower, especially the silver-leafed form, and you should keep an eye on it so that it doesn't outgrow other plants in the container. To control it, you can use it sparingly and/or trim it back if it threatens to get out of hand. The varieties commonly used today are 'White Licorice' with silver leaves; 'Lemon Licorice', which is similar—if not identical—to 'Limelight' and has soft lemon-yellow foliage; 'Licorice Splash' with creamy white and silver-gray leaves, similar to 'Variegatum'; and a small-leafed form called 'Petite Licorice', which is the one I used in this book. The variegated and small-leafed forms are less aggressive. Because most parts of the country grow licorice plant as an annual, gardeners don't get to see the small, soft yellow flowers that appear in late winter and early spring, but they're not much to look at anyway—this is clearly a plant grown for foliage. Good drainage is important. Make sure you don't keep the plants too wet, especially while they're young. Otherwise they might rot.

Heliotropium arborescens Hybrid
Heliotrope

- Exposure: Partial shade to full sun
- Height: 10–24"
- Frost hardiness: Not hardy; use as an annual in most climates; hardy in USDA Zones 10–11
- Flowering time: Spring to fall

Heliotrope is a classic plant for container gardens and flowerbeds. The flowers come in different shades of purple and blue and vary by variety. Most are very fragrant, with a sweet vanilla scent. The finished plant height also varies by variety, but most are moderate in height and are good as mounding components in a planter. Heliotrope prefers a well-drained, fertile potting mix in full sun to partial shade. The more sun a plant gets, the darker its flowers. So one and the same variety can actually look quite different depending on the light conditions. The varieties used in this book are 'Atlantis' and 'Nagano'. Heliotrope likes warm temperatures, so don't plant it too early.

Heuchera

- Exposure: Partial shade
- Height: Foliage 8–12"; flowers 16–30"
- Frost hardiness: USDA Zone 4–5
- Flowering time: Spring and summer

Many *Heuchera* species are native to North America, but most of the ones used in this book are hybrids. Although *Heuchera* produces dainty flowers that are usually white or pink and displayed on long flower stems, when I selected *Heuchera* for the container gardens in this book, I looked exclusively at their foliage. Many have different shades of purple; others are green variegated. *Heuchera* does well in climates with moderate summer heat and can lack in performance in the Deep South. However, research gardens, such as the one at the University of Georgia, have identified selections that perform well even in heat and humidity. *Heuchera* is susceptible to aphids and vine weevils. The varieties used in this book are 'Amethyst Myst', 'Green Spice', 'Purple Petticoats', and 'Splish Splash'.

Hosta

• Exposure: Shade to partial shade; some sun-tolerant varieties
• Height: Foliage 8–24"; flowers 12–36"
• Frost hardiness: USDA Zone 4
• Flowering time: Summer

Although hostas have quite attractive flowers—some are even fragrant—there is no doubt that most varieties were selected for their beautiful foliage, which ranges from blue-green to golden yellow, with many green-yellow and green-white variegated forms. Some varieties appear to be quite sun tolerant, but hostas are, without a doubt, excellent plants for shady areas, where we're often lacking good plant selections. Hostas prefer fertile, well-drained potting mix that's kept consistently moist. Drying out can quickly lead to leaf damage. Unfortunately, hostas are a favorite with snails and slugs, which will make your plants look like Swiss cheese if you don't control them early. This problem is more prominent in the landscape rather than in containers, but you still need to watch out. Especially in the landscape, deer, gophers, voles, and weevils can also become a problem. For this book, I used the variety 'Golden Prayers', but with the wide selection of varieties available today, you are likely to find an appropriate substitute if you can't find it.

Ipomoea batatas
Sweet potato

- Exposure: Sun to partial shade
- Height: 10–14", trailing
- Frost hardiness: Not hardy; use as an annual; temperatures below 40°F cause damage
- Flowering time: Insignificant

Prized for its foliage, ornamental sweet potato has quickly become a favorite among container gardeners. The most popular form is chartreuse, which looks especially stunning in combination with rich purples and magenta. Other forms are dark purple—almost black—or tricolor gray-green, white, and pink. Sweet potato loves warm temperatures and performs well even in the Deep South. This also means that you shouldn't plant it too early in spring if you live in a climate with cooler temperatures. It can even get quite aggressive once the temperatures rise, so pair it with other vigorous growers and cut it back if needed. For a stunning but simple combination, plant one chartreuse sweet potato ('Terrace Lime' or 'Margarita') with three magenta trailing *Petunia* (such as 'Supertunia Royal Magenta') in a hanging basket. Sweet potato weevils can be a serious problem, but they're limited to certain areas of the country. In this book, you can find 'Black Heart', which is very similar to 'Ace of Spades'; 'Blackie'; 'Terrace Lime'; and 'Tricolor', which is also sold under the name 'Pink Frost'.

Isolepis, see Scirpus

Kalanchoe 'Elves' Bells'

- Exposure: Sun to partial shade
- Height: 8–12"
- Frost hardiness: Not hardy; use as an annual in most climates or as a houseplant
- Flowering time: Spring

Kalanchoe is a plant that you probably didn't expect in outdoor container gardens, but using unusual plants every once in a while is fun. I selected a variety that has attractive, deep green and red-tinged foliage in addition to its bell-shaped, dusty rose pink flowers, so that you still have the value of the foliage after the flowers are gone. Kalanchoe flowers naturally in spring, after going through a period of short days. This particular variety is different from the popular houseplant because its flower shape and leaf shape are different. It also has a semi-trailing growth, which is especially prominent if it's given the chance to spill over the rim of a planter. Provide adequate moisture, especially if placed in full sun, and watch for aphids.

Lamiastrum galeobdolon

- Exposure: Shade to sun
- Height: 6–10", trailing
- Frost hardiness: USDA Zone 4
- Flowering time: Spring and summer

The name of this genus has changed so much that I'm not sure what to call it, so I'll use the name that's most commonly found on plant tags. At some point in its life, this plant was called *Lamium* and *Galeobdolon*. *Lamiastrum* produces white flowers in spring and summer, but it's primarily noted for its beautiful, variegated foliage. With its trailing habit, its foliage is best show-cased along the edges of a planter, where it can cascade over the rim, or in a hanging basket. *Lamiastrum* prefers a well-drained, slightly moist potting mix. Moisture is especially important with increasing exposure to sun. Although a popular shade plant, *Lamiastrum* can tolerate sun in moderate climates. The only variety used for this book is 'Hermann's Pride'.

Lamium maculatum

- Exposure: Shade to sun
- Height: 6–12"
- Frost hardiness: USDA Zone 4
- Flowering time: Spring and summer

Just like its close relative *Lamiastrum, Lamium* is a tremendous shade plant that's prized for its beautiful, variegated foliage. Breeding work has resulted in many different leaf colors, including 'White Nancy' with silver foliage edged in green and white flowers and 'Golden Anniversary', a yellow and green variegated form that holds its purple flowers quite well through the summer. Other forms include pink flowers and have different variegations. *Lamium* is not quite as trailing as *Lamiastrum*—some varieties are even primarily mounding. But the trailing forms are still best used along the edges of planters, and the mounding ones can either be used along the edges or as mounding components further toward the center of the planter. The requirements for placement and care are the same as for *Lamiastrum*.

Lantana

- Exposure: Full sun
- Height: 10–40"
- Frost hardiness: Mostly used as annual; all hardy in USDA Zones 10–11; some forms hardy to USDA Zone 7
- Flowering time: Spring through fall, or all year in Southern, frost-free climates

Lantana is a great plant for container gardens because of the many forms and colors it comes in. While some varieties are trailing, others are upright and grow into a shrub in mild climates. This gives them a broad range of applications, from middle-height plants to trailing elements along the edges. The color range is also quite broad, but mostly in the warmer tones—yellow, orange, red, and their shades such as rose, magenta, and pink. Lavender is also a popular color. The more vigorous the variety, the more water and fertilizer it needs. The leaves of some varieties are quite fragrant, and certain varieties set inedible seeds. While most seeds are black and inconspicuous, one of the varieties used in this book—*Lantana trifolia* 'Lavender Popcorn'—develops bright lavender-colored seeds the size of popcorn kernels. You can also find 'New Gold' used in this book.

Lobelia erinus Hybrid

• Exposure: Full sun
• Height: 6–12"
• Frost hardiness: Not hardy; use as an annual in most climates; hardy in USDA Zones 10–11
• Flowering time: Spring through fall, or all year in Southern, frost-free climates

Lobelia has long been a bread-and-butter plant in flowerbeds and containers. But besides the well-known seed annual, breeders have developed forms that are grown from cuttings. Some of those appear to be more heat-tolerant and flower longer. However, hot and humid Southern climates are advised to use lobelia as a fall-, winter-, and spring-flowering container garden plant. Some varieties are trailing, but many are mounding. The taller varieties can be used as middle-height plants, but most are best along the edges of planters. Lobelia is famous for its blue flowers, but lavender, pink, and white forms are also available. You'll find 'Laguna Pink' used in the containers in this book.

Lotus berthelotii
Lotus vine

• Exposure: Full sun
• Height: 6–8", trailing
• Frost hardiness: Not hardy; use as an annual in most climates; hardy in USDA Zones 10–11
• Flowering time: Spring

Lotus vine is a wonderful container garden plant because of its fine-textured, silver foliage and cascading habit. What some people don't know is that it also has absolutely stunning flowers—because it needs cool temperatures to induce blooms, many people never see the flowers, which appear in early spring, and flowering might never occur if the plants were grown in a heated greenhouse. Some newer varieties require less chill, and the chance of seeing them in bloom is higher. Nevertheless, the foliage is outstanding on its own. Use it along the edges of planters or in hanging baskets. The silver texture is especially stunning with cool-colored flowers such as blue and purple. Make sure not to let lotus vine dry out, or it might lose its needle-thin leaves. The variety that you can find in this book is 'Amazon Sunset', but if you're only looking for foliage accents, you may substitute another silver-leafed form.

Lysimachia congestiflora

- Exposure: Partial to full shade
- Height: 6–10", trailing
- Frost hardiness: Not hardy; use as an annual; temperatures below 40°F cause damage
- Flowering time: Spring through fall

With its big, golden yellow flower clusters and green foliage, this *Lysimachia* species has become a popular selection for container gardens in partial shade locations. It thrives in warm temperatures and doesn't like the cold. Its trailing habit is best showcased along the edges of planters and in hanging baskets. If the temperatures are warm enough, this is quite an easy-care plant, but watch for aphids. I like using 'Outback Sunset', which has the same, rich yellow flower clusters as the species, but with gold and green variegated leaves. This gives you double impact, once through the flowers and once through the foliage.

Lysimachia nummularia
Creeping Jenny

- Exposure: Shade to sun
- Height: 2–4", trailing
- Frost hardiness: USDA Zone 3
- Flowering time: Grown for foliage

Another species of *Lysimachia,* this one has little in common with *Lysimachia congestiflora. L. nummularia* is a frost-hardy perennial with small, round, shiny golden leaves and an extremely low-growing, trailing habit. It can be used as a groundcover in the shade, but owes its fame to its use in container gardens, where the fine-textured foliage can spill over the rims of planters and out of hanging baskets. Although botanical books speak of its flowers, I have never seen the variety that I use—'Goldilocks'—bloom and always use it for its foliage. Creeping Jenny prefers partially shady locations, but can be quite sun tolerant in some climates, especially if adequate moisture is provided. Sometimes the taller plants in a cleverly designed container garden provide enough shade so that it can withstand a full-sun location. I don't believe there's much difference between variety names currently on the market, but I frequently see 'Goldilocks' and 'Aurea'.

Mentha spicata
Mint

- Exposure: Full sun to partial shade
- Height: 6–16"
- Frost hardiness: USDA Zone 4
- Flowering time: Spring through fall

There are so many different mint species and varieties on the market that describing them would fill a book on its own, but I like to use some of the more ornamental forms in container gardens—not only in herb planters, but also herbs mixed with ornamentals. In this book, I used *Mentha spicata* 'Nigra', a variety of spearmint with dark purple, almost black, leaves and purple undersides and stems. It grows upright, arching at first, but starts to cascade as it gets bigger. It's quite aggressive, so pair it with other vigorous growers, or give it a good trim if it gets out of hand. Many other varieties with ornamental value are also available.

Muehlenbeckia
Creeping wirevine

- Exposure: Full sun
- Height: 4–8", spreading
- Frost hardiness: USDA Zone 4
- Flowering time: Insignificant

Muehlenbeckia is a greatly underused plant for container gardens. It has a wiry growth that weaves between other plants, sticking out its branches with shiny, round, emerald green leaves here and there. With its spreading growth, use it along the edges of planters or in hanging baskets. Creeping wirevine is easy to care for and has few insect and disease problems. It can get quite vigorous, but you can easily cut it back if it starts to get out of hand.

Nassella, see Stipa

Nasturtium, see Tropaeolum

Nemesia fruticans

- Exposure: Full sun
- Height: 10–16"
- Frost hardiness: USDA Zone 8
- Flowering time: Spring through fall, or all year in Southern, frost-free climates

Nemesia has won the hearts of gardeners worldwide. That's no surprise if you consider its abundant blooms, well-behaved growth habit, and often-fragrant flowers. With its medium height, it's best used in the middle of planters, as a second tier after the center plant. It's also an excellent plant for the center of hanging baskets. Flowers are commonly white, pink, and different shades of blue and purple. Some varieties are more fragrant than others. Many re-seed, so you're likely to find some surprise colors in your garden the next year, unless you were diligent in cutting off spent flowers. The varieties used in this book are 'Blue Bird', 'Blue Lagoon', 'Candy Girl', 'Compact Innocence', 'Safari Pink', and 'Safari Plum'.

Ocimum basilicum
Basil

- Exposure: Full sun
- Height: 8–24"
- Frost hardiness: Not hardy; use as an annual
- Flowering time: Summer

We all know annual sweet basil as a culinary herb, but there are also forms of basil that are beautiful as ornamentals. The different varieties vary significantly in height, so I'll focus on the one I used in this book. One of my favorites is 'African Blue', which I used here. It has dark purple-green leaves with purple undersides. In summer, lavender-colored flowers appear that are hummingbird magnets. You can use it as a culinary herb, but if you let it grow, you'll be able to enjoy the flowers. Once it's fully grown, it can reach two feet or more. Use it as a middle-height plant in large containers, or as one of the dominant plants in medium-sized planters. Basil is a heat-lover, so don't plant it too early in spring.

Ophiopogon planiscapus
Black mondo grass

- Exposure: Sun to shade
- Height: 4–8"
- Frost hardiness: USDA Zone 6
- Flowering time: Summer

Black mondo grass is an unusual, grass-like plant with nearly black leaves. Its compact habit is best used in small planters. It grows slowly, so pair it with nonaggressive plants. Don't expect much growth during one summer, so make sure that you use well-developed plants so the other plants in the design don't outgrow it. It's a specialty item that's not always easy to find, especially in some parts of the country. But if you can locate it, take advantage of it in designs that are beyond the ordinary.

Origanum
Oregano

- Exposure: Full sun to partial shade
- Height: 6–12"
- Frost hardiness: USDA Zone 4
- Flowering time: Summer

Here's another popular culinary herb with ornamental value. Some oregano varieties have textured leaves or attractively curved branches. The variety I used is 'Santa Cruz'. Oregano prefers sunny locations, but it can tolerate partial shade. Keep it slightly moist, but make sure not to overwater. Oregano is a popular culinary herb in pasta dishes, salads, and many Italian dishes.

Osteospermum
African daisy

- Exposure: Full sun
- Height: 8–24"
- Frost hardiness: Not hardy; use as an annual in most climates; hardy in USDA Zones 10–11
- Flowering time: Spring through fall, or all year in Southern, frost-free climates

Osteospermum used to be a popular flowering plant for spring and early summer, but plant breeders have created varieties that are more heat tolerant and flower throughout the summer. However, in very hot, Southern climates with high night temperatures, many *Osteospermum* varieties still flower sparsely in summer, but those locales can use them from fall through spring. The different varieties also vary greatly in height. Traditionally, *Osteospermum* grows upright and gets 14–24" tall, but many newer types are more compact and mounding. Use the tall, upright varieties in the center of planters; medium-height types can go in the middle; and the mounding, semi-spreading types are good along the edges or even in hanging baskets. Because of the significant difference between varieties, make sure to inform yourself before you buy. *Osteospermum* prefers a sunny spot in a well-drained, fertile potting mix. Watch for aphids. Varieties in this book are the 'Symphony' series in 'Cream', 'Lemon', 'Orange', and 'Peach', and the 'Dandenong Daisy' series in 'Purple Blush', 'Rose', and 'Variegated Pink'.

Oxalis crassipes
Sorrel, wood sorrel

- Exposure: Full sun to shade
- Height: 6-8"
- Frost hardiness: USDA Zone 5
- Flowering time: Spring through fall

You might think of oxalis as a weed, but there are better-behaved species available that are quite valuable ornamentally. Whereas the regular *Oxalis crassipes* has pink to purple flowers, the one I used in this book is 'Alba', a pure white form. It does well in a wide range of conditions but prefers a fertile, well-drained potting mix and doesn't like to be too wet. Like many oxalis, it closes its flowers at night. Because it's sterile, it doesn't reseed, which makes it noninvasive. It also doesn't develop runners. It's not very widely grown, so you might have trouble locating it, but if you can get your hands on it, you'll find this to be an easy-to-grow plant for container gardens and perennial beds.

Pelargonium
Geranium

- Exposure: Full sun to partial shade
- Height: 10–24", some trailing
- Frost hardiness: Not hardy; use as an annual in most climates; hardy in USDA Zones 10–11
- Flowering time: Spring through fall, or all year in Southern, frost-free climates

What we commonly call a geranium is actually, botanically speaking, a *Pelargonium*, which can be confusing since there is also a genus *Geranium*. The geraniums that are most commonly used in container gardens and landscape beds are upright-growing bedding geraniums and mounding or trailing ivy geraniums. Bedding geraniums often require more care because regular deadheading is important for most varieties. Without it, they may flower less, and the clusters of spent flowers can be a breeding ground for *Botrytis*. However, the type that I used is the 'Fireworks' series of *Pelargonium zonale*. Their star-shaped flowers are less prone to diseases. I used 'Red-White Bicolor' and 'Scarlet' from this series. The best types for hanging baskets and the edges of planters are ivy geraniums. Many of them are trailing and also less prone to diseases. I used the varieties 'Blue' and 'White' from the 'Blizzard' series. Geraniums like an even moisture level and a generous amount of fertilizer. Watch for aphids and spider mites.

Pennisetum messiacum
Fountain grass

- Exposure: Full sun
- Height: 18–36"
- Frost hardiness: USDA Zone 7
- Flowering time: Summer

This type of fountain grass is an excellent choice if you're looking for a subtle plant in the center of a planter. Its foliage is compact and lush green with burgundy highlights that become more intense under cool temperatures. The fun part is its flowers, which are stocky and very soft, like a rabbit's tail. That's what got it its variety name 'Red Bunny Tails', but you're likely to find it under different names as well. It's an easy-to-grow ornamental grass with very few pests or disease problems.

Pennisetum setaceum
Fountain grass

- Exposure: Full sun
- Height: 18–48"
- Frost hardiness: Not hardy; use as an annual in most climates; hardy in USDA Zones 9b–11
- Flowering time: Summer

I believe fountain grass is the single most frequently used ornamental grass in container gardens, especially its purple and dwarf purple form. Since I only used those two in this book, I will focus on them rather than the entire species. Purple fountain grass, commonly sold as 'Rubrum', has beautiful, burgundy-colored leaves and foxtail-shaped flower plumes that range from purple to pink and creamy white. It reaches three to four feet in height and is recommended for the center of large planters. Its dwarf form grows only 18–30" tall and is much more suitable for a larger range of container sizes, while its foliage and flowers are just as beautiful. The dwarf form of purple fountain grass is commonly sold under the names 'Dwarf Rubrum', 'Red Riding Hood', and 'Eaton Canyon'. Fountain grass is used as an annual, and even in areas where it survives the winter, it still goes dormant. It's a warm-season grass, so wait until the temperatures have warmed up before you plant it. Fountain grass flowers can be used in arrangements. Very few pest and disease problems afflict it.

Persicaria microcephala

- Exposure: Full sun to partial shade
- Height: 15–36"
- Frost hardiness: USDA Zone 5
- Flowering time: Summer; inconspicuous

This *Persicaria* is a vigorous perennial that loves the heat and grows quickly, especially once the temperatures have increased. The only variety I am familiar with is 'Red Dragon', a beautiful plant with deep purple leaves accented by silver chevron marks. It produces cream-white flowers in summer, but is really grown for its foliage. The flowers are inconspicuous, so they don't really distract, but you can cut them off if you want to enjoy the foliage exclusively. Because it's such a vigorous grower, you might have to trim it back if it tries to take over any of the other plants in the planter. Give *Persicaria* a well-drained, fertile potting mix that's kept slightly moist and you'll have an easy-to-care-for plant.

Petunia

- Exposure: Full sun
- Height: 6–12", trailing
- Frost hardiness: Not hardy; use as an annual in most climates; hardy in USDA Zones 10–11
- Flowering time: Spring through fall

Who knows if container gardening would have ever become so popular if it weren't for trailing petunias. Likely it would have, but petunias are certainly a bread-and-butter ingredient. The only petunias I used for this book are the trailing types, as they are simply outstanding for container gardens. Let them spill over the sides of your planters, window boxes, and hanging baskets—they'll create a waterfall of color. They are fast growing, and some varieties can easily grow three feet long in one summer. Naturally, plants that get that big need a lot of water, so make sure to water frequently. And because they grow so fast, they also need a lot of fertilizer; you can almost double your fertilizer dose that you would give other bedding plants. In some areas, budworms can cause significant damage, so check your plants frequently, especially if you've had problems before. I used varieties from the 'Supertunia' series for this book.

Phormium
New Zealand flax

- Exposure: Full sun
- Height: 2–5'
- Frost hardiness: Not hardy; use as an annual in most climates; hardy in USDA Zones 10–11
- Flowering time: None

New Zealand flax is another one of my favorite plants for container gardens. Unfortunately, it can be hard to find. It's excellent for the center of a large planter where you want height, color, and texture. There are many different varieties on the market, with foliage colors ranging from green to red and almost black. Many varieties are variegated, either green and yellow or shades of burgundy with different colored stripes. Quantities are often limited, but because it's becoming so popular, your chances of finding it get better each year. *Phormium* grows slowly, so choose a plant that has almost reached the final size that you're looking for. Your *Phormium* should definitely be larger than the other plants in the planter, or else it's likely to get outgrown.

Plectranthus

- Exposure: Full sun to partial shade
- Height: 8–36"
- Frost hardiness: Not hardy; use as an annual in most climates; hardy in USDA Zones 10–11
- Flowering time: Summer; often inconspicuous or none

Plectranthus is an excellent component plant that provides texture to container gardens. There are many different species and varieties on the market, and they vary greatly in color, growth habit, and height, and only some have showy flowers. *Plectranthus coleoides* 'Variegata', also known as trailing Swedish ivy, is one of the best forms for container gardens. Its branches have a fountain-like growth, and its leaves are green with white margins. *Plectranthus amboinicus* is a more upright form with fragrant leaves reminiscent of oregano. *Plectranthus ciliatus* has purplish-green leaves, an upright growth habit, and lavender-colored flowers. *Plectranthus* seems to be gaining in popularity, so you'll likely find new types on the market in the near future. It's easy to grow and has few pests or disease problems.

Poinsettia

Poinsettias are most likely not what you expected in an outdoor container garden book, but since I used one, I should mention it here. This beautiful plant that decorates nearly every household around Christmastime can only be used in Southern, frost-free climates as an outdoor container garden plant during winter, when it's most readily available. Don't expect it to grow much, so choose a plant that's the final size you want in your container, while other plants will grow into your design. Keep your poinsettia evenly moist and you'll enjoy it throughout the holiday season. A side note: Poinsettia is the common name for this plant, and you'll rarely see the botanical name, *Euphorbia pulcherrima*. Try referring to your poinsettias as *Euphorbia* if you want to impress your family and friends with your horticultural know-how.

Salvia officinalis
Sage

- Exposure: Full sun
- Height: 8–18"
- Frost hardiness: USDA Zone 5
- Flowering time: Insignificant or none

What's known as a popular culinary herb is also a great ornamental—or at least some varieties are. Common sage has an upright growth habit and grows to medium height, which makes it a good middle-height plant in container gardens. There are several varieties available with beautiful foliage, ranging from golden yellow to purple and silver. Some are variegated with two or three colors. For some, especially the purple and tricolor varieties, the colors become more intense as the temperatures drop. Intense sunlight also intensifies colors. Although sage is quite drought tolerant in the ground, it needs a lot of water in container gardens. A perk with this plant is that you can use the leaves from these containers for cooking. Varieties used in this book are 'Icterina', 'Purpurascens', 'Tricolor', and 'White-edged'.

Santolina chamaecyparissus
Lavender cotton

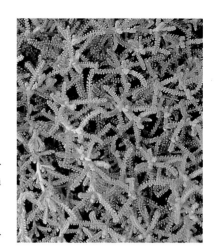

- Exposure: Full sun
- Height: 10–16"
- Frost hardiness: USDA Zone 6
- Flowering time: Spring and summer

    As a Mediterranean native, santolina likes hot and dry summers. While moderate temperatures are tolerated just as well, it doesn't perform well in humid conditions and in poorly drained soils. Although it produces yellow, button-shaped flowers, it's mostly grown for its fine-textured, silver foliage. There are also green forms available, but the silver ones have more decorative value. With its mounding growth, it's a good middle-height plant in container gardens and looks especially great with cool colors such as blue and purple.

Saxifraga stolonifera
'Harvest Moon'

- Exposure: Partial to full shade
- Height: 4–6"; flowers up to 12"
- Frost hardiness: USDA Zone 6
- Flowering time: Summer

    This variety of *Saxifraga* produces lacy white flowers in summer, but its true attraction are its leaves, which vary from greenish-yellow to bronze, depending on temperature and light exposure. The leaves have pinkish-red undersides. The more sun the plant gets, the darker the foliage. It forms tight clumps before it starts to develop runners on long stems as it gets older. Because of this habit, it's best used along the edges of planters in semi-shady locations. Its earthy colors look especially enticing in terra cotta pottery. Good drainage is important.

Scaevola
Fan Flower

- Exposure: Full sun
- Height: 8–12", trailing
- Frost hardiness: Not hardy; use as an annual in most climates; hardy in USDA Zones 10–11
- Flowering time: Spring through fall

Had you asked somebody in the early 1990s what a *Scaevola* was, you would have likely received blank stares. Today, *Scaevola* is as much part of container gardening as are moss baskets. Commonly called fan flower because of its fan-shaped flowers, *Scaevola* is excellent for the edges of planters and for hanging baskets due to its abundantly trailing habit. Heat seems to be as unproblematic as cool temperatures. The flowers are most common in shades of blue, but pink and white varieties are also available, though the white varieties are sometimes slower to grow. *Scaevola* likes a healthy dose of fertilizer, but keep phosphorous as low as possible, otherwise phosphorous toxicity can develop. Keep the potting mix slightly moist at all times. There are also miniature and upright-growing varieties available, but the vigorous trailers are the most popular ones. Varieties used in this book are 'New Wonder'—which might be the single best-selling variety—'Pink Fanfare', and 'Spring Rhapsody'.

Scirpus cernuus
Fiber-optic grass

- Exposure: Full sun to partial shade
- Height: 12"
- Frost hardiness: Not hardy; use as an annual in most climates; hardy in USDA Zones 10–11
- Flowering time: Summer

Scirpus cernuus is commonly called fiber-optic grass because of the small flowers that sit atop the thin, emerald green leaves. Its botanical labeling can be confusing—I've also seen it marked as *Isolepis cernua*. With its short habit and slightly cascading growth, it's best used along the edges of planters. Because of its moderate height, it's also good for hanging baskets, where many ornamental grasses are too tall. Technically speaking, it doesn't belong to the grass family, but it's handled as a grass because of its appearance. Keep the potting mix moist at all times, especially if it's in full sun. Otherwise, fiber-optic grass is a low-maintenance plant with little or no pests or disease problems.

Sedum Hybrid
Stonecrop

- Exposure: Full sun
- Height: 14–20"
- Frost hardiness: USDA Zone 4
- Flowering time: Late summer and fall

Sedum is a huge genus with hundreds of different species, many of which are used in rock gardens. However, the hybrid that I used in this book is an upright growing one with succulent, fleshy leaves. 'Matrona' has light salmon-pink flowers that appear in late summer and last into fall. Its foliage takes on a bronze color in fall as the temperatures drop. 'Matrona' is a more compact variety, but if you can't find it, you can substitute the easier-to-find 'Autumn Joy', which is similar in color and habit but is slightly taller. This plant is ideal for autumn-themed container gardens.

Stipa tenuissima
Mexican feather grass

- Exposure: Full sun
- Height: 12–18"
- Frost hardiness: USDA Zone 7
- Flowering time: Summer

I can never resist touching Mexican feather grass, as its needle-thin leaves sway in the gentlest breeze. It looks and feels like a well-groomed horse's mane, except that its almost iridescent green. Use it in the middle or along the edges of containers, but keep it fairly unobstructed so that it can get the attention it deserves. In summer, it produces subtle flowers that turn from green to a soft wheat color as they mature. It tolerates hot and dry conditions very well, but stays green longer if the temperatures are moderate and moisture is adequate. It's a very low-maintenance grass with few or no pests or disease problems.

Strobilanthes dyerianus
Persian shield

- Exposure: Full sun to partial shade
- Height: 3–4'
- Frost hardiness: Not hardy; use as an annual
- Flowering time: None if used as annual

Commonly called Persian shield—which is a lot easier to pronounce—
Strobilanthes is another one of my favorites that's experiencing a popularity
boom right now. Its stunning foliage is purple with a metallic sheen. With
its stately height, it's ideal for the center of large planters, where you want
height, color, and texture. Persian shield is a real heat lover, but it can be
grown in all climates in North America during the summer. It just stays
shorter in cooler climates, and growth stalls at temperatures below 40 to
45°F. Although USDA Zones 10 and 11 could use it as perennial, the
short days in winter induce flowers and the attractive vegetative growth
gets lost. It's best used as an annual in all climate zones.

Sutera
Bacopa

- Exposure: Sun to shade
- Height: 4–12", mostly trailing
- Frost hardiness: Not hardy; use as an annual in most climates; hardy in USDA Zone 10–11
- Flowering time: Spring through fall, or all year in Southern, frost-free climates

Bacopa is one of the hottest newcomers on the container gardening scene over the last ten years. With its small, delicate flowers that appear in abundance and its trailing habit, it has quickly won the hearts of gardeners worldwide. What we commonly call bacopa is actually *Sutera.* What seems like a plot to confuse gardeners is due to a misnaming when the plant was first introduced. Nonetheless, its an excellent plant along the edges of mixed planters and in hanging baskets, where it can easily trail three feet in just one season. *Sutera* performs best in partial shade, but it tolerates full sun in northern climates, provided that moisture is adequate. Drying out can cause the flowers to drop, although the plant often recovers. In very hot climates, shade is recommended. Hot weather can also lead to smaller flower size. The first varieties that were introduced were white, but pink, purple, and lavender varieties are also available. One form even has variegated leaves and white flowers. The varieties used in this book are 'Bermuda Sky', 'Cabana', 'Giant Snowflake', 'Glacier Blue', 'Gold 'n' Pearls', 'Lilac King', and 'Snowstorm'.

Thymus
Thyme

- Exposure: Full sun
- Height: 3–14"
- Frost hardiness: USDA Zone 5
- Flowering time: Spring and summer

We all know thyme as a culinary herb, but it's also a great ornamental. Of the many species, I often used *Thymus vulgaris,* the common thyme, and *Thymus citriodorus,* lemon thyme. Thyme is available in many different colors, some with silver foliage, others with green and yellow variegated leaves. Height and growth habit also vary, from very low-growing, matt-forming types to bushy, upright ones. It's an easy-to-grow herb that doesn't like to be kept too wet. Use it mainly along the edges of planters and in herb baskets. The variety I used is 'Golden King', but you can choose among the many different varieties and pick your favorite.

Torenia
Wishbone flower

- Exposure: Partial shade to full sun
- Height: 6–10", trailing
- Frost hardiness: Not hardy; use as an annual in most climates; hardy in USDA Zones 10–11
- Flowering time: Spring through fall

Torenia has been a bedding plant for many years, but the advent of more vigorously trailing varieties has made it a popular choice for container gardens. Besides the common seed varieties, cutting-grown types are also available and often more trailing. The more recent introductions are also often more heat tolerant. Use the trailing types along the edges of planters and in hanging baskets. The plant is commonly called wishbone flower because of the way the stamens are connected, forming a wishbone. *Torenia* does well in partially shady locations, but can tolerate full sun, especially in northern climates. Too much sun can turn the foliage into a yellowish bronze color, which usually doesn't cause damage but may be considered unsightly. Keep moisture levels even at all times and watch for aphids. Varieties in this book are 'Summer Wave Amethyst' and 'Summer Wave Blue'.

Trifolium repens

- Exposure: Sun to partial shade
- Height: 3–6"
- Frost hardiness: USDA Zone 4
- Flowering time: Grown for foliage

When you look at the foliage shape, you can see that *Trifolium* is part of the clover family. The variety I used is called 'Dark Dancer', also sold as 'Atropurpureum'. It has dark purple leaves with bright green margins and stems. It's very low growing, almost mat forming, and is best used along the edges of small containers. It's a small plant, so it could get lost in large planters, but it's a nice specialty plant for designs that go beyond the ordinary.

Tropaeolum majus
Nasturtium

- Exposure: Full sun
- Height: 6–12", often spreading
- Frost hardiness: Not hardy; use as an annual in most climates; hardy in USDA Zones 10–11
- Flowering time: Spring through fall

You might be used to finding nasturtium in herb books because it's a beautiful, edible plant. But it has also tremendous ornamental value! Some varieties can get quite aggressive and sprawling, but I like to use a particular variety called 'Red Wonder'. It is much more compact than the species and never gets out of hand. It has scarlet red, double flowers that are surprisingly fragrant. Its foliage is dark green with a hint of silver. It has a mounding growth habit and is best used as a middle-height plant. For use in the kitchen, toss the edible flowers in salads and use the leaves in cream cheese and egg dishes. If you are planning on using it in recipes, don't use any pesticides on it.

Verbena

- Exposure: Full sun to partial shade
- Height: 4–14", often trailing
- Frost hardiness: Mostly used as annual; some varieties hardy to USDA Zone 8
- Flowering time: Spring through fall.

Besides petunia, verbena is one of the most important plants in container gardening. They come in many different forms, with upright and trailing growth habits. I especially like the trailing types because they are terrific for the edges of planters and in hanging baskets. The mounding and upright types are great middle-height plants. Verbenas have really boomed over the last ten years. Today, the selection of varieties is nearly endless, all with different claims to earliness and disease resistance. Many of the trailing types are grown from cuttings. The color spectrum offers almost anything except yellow and orange shades. Verbenas are heat tolerant and are quite disease resistant—especially the newer varieties. If you've had problems with mildew on verbena in the past, look for mildew-resistant varieties. The varieties that I used for this book are from the 'Babylon', 'Superbena', 'Tapien', 'Temari', and 'Tukana' series.

Vinca
Vinca vine

- Exposure: Sun to shade
- Height: 3–6", trailing
- Frost hardiness: USDA Zone 4–7, depending on species
- Flowering time: Spring; grown for foliage

Vinca vine is an old-fashioned container garden plant that is still popular today. There are basically two types, but the gardener who wants to use them just for the container garden season doesn't really need to distinguish the two. *Vinca major* is frost hardy to USDA Zone 7, while *Vinca minor* is hardy to USDA Zone 4. Both are commonly used in container gardens for one season. Their growth habit is very trailing, so they are ideal for the edges of planters, window boxes, and hanging baskets. Varieties with variegated foliage are especially attractive, often in white and green or yellow and green. Vinca vine prefers shady and partially shady locations, but can tolerate sun if adequate moisture is provided and especially if larger plants in the container provide some shade. Besides common, variegated vinca vine, I also used an especially decorative variety called 'Illumination'.

Yucca

• Exposure: Full sun
• Height: Varies by species
• Frost hardiness: Varies by species; some hardy to USDA Zone 4
• Flowering time: Spring and summer

There are many different yuccas, many of which turn into trees in the Southwest. A good species for container gardening is *Yucca filamentosa,* which is a small type that stays low, growing only about three feet tall. The variegated forms are especially attractive. 'Golden Sword' and 'Color Glory' are just a few examples. It's definitely a specialty item that's not easy to find, but if you find it—or a somewhat similar one— use it to attract attention. Yucca needs well-drained potting mix and a warm spot.

Part 3

Planting Recipes and Ideas

Container Garden Recipes

The following are 101 detailed planting diagrams and design ideas to help you make your own container gardens. Each container "recipe" has a picture of the finished pot, a diagram showing plant placement, and a list of the plants and varieties used. Each recipe also has some thoughts on Plant Personalities, Container Characteristics, and Care Clues. This information will be enough to let you plant with confidence the container shown.

Here are a few thoughts on how to get the most out of this section.

Diagrams

If you wish, you may follow the diagrams exactly and use only the plants specified. This is especially helpful if you are new to container gardening. However, once you feel more confident in designing container gardens, the diagrams may merely be inspirations for your own creations. Feel free to substitute with your favorite plants.

Next to each picture is a sun icon, illustrating each container's light requirement. A yellow sun indicates an arrangement that's suited to a full-sun location. A half-shaded sun icon means the container should be placed in a partially shaded location, and a gray sun indicates a shaded location.

Variety Selection

I listed the exact varieties that I used for each container, but plant selections change frequently and garden centers can't carry all of the varieties available, considering the huge number of varieties to choose from. If you can't find a particular variety, try to substitute with one from the same genus (i.e., *Verbena*), and try to match flower color and growth habit. In other words, if you can't find a particular trailing purple verbena, simply look for a substitute with a similar growth habit, so that you don't exchange a trailing component with an upright one. There is so much excellent plant material out there today that you'll have a great time finding your favorites.

Plant Size

Unless otherwise specified, I used plants in four-inch pots to plant the container gardens pictured. If you work with different sized plant material, keep in mind that you might have to use a different sized planter or that your plants will fill the container faster or slower, depending on if you purchased larger or smaller plants. Even if you use four-inch pots, what you find in the stores often varies, not only from store to store, but also depending on the time of the year that you buy. Generally, look for well-developed plants that aren't overgrown or root-bound. In the end, initial plant size doesn't really matter that much. If you use more or larger plants, your container fills out faster; if you use fewer or smaller plants, it'll take longer. Simply consider your container size, your plant sizes, and your budget, and use your own judgment. But one more word of caution: If you jam pack a container with a lot of plants or large plants, it will be harder to keep the container watered and fertilized because you'll have more plants competing for the available moisture and nutrients. Admittedly, containers planted with fewer plants take longer until they are lush and beautiful, but they also last longer in your garden.

Container Characteristics

I described the exact container that I used, although I realize that it's quite unlikely that you'll find a 100 percent match. I provided that information so that you know what kind of container I used and why I selected it. I also included advantages and disadvantages in some instances. The information given should serve as an aid for you to make the right container selection. When it comes to container size, make sure that you measure the inside diameter if you're trying to figure out what size planter you need. Manufacturers often list the outside dimensions, so don't trust the size marked on the pot. Simple math can help you chose the right size: If you are planting four four-inch pots in a row, you'll need at least a sixteen-inch planter, unless you really want to jam them in. Keep in mind that a larger pot provides more potting mix volume, which makes proper maintenance easier.

Care Clues

In this section, I only pointed out any *special* care requirements. Please refer to the general section of this book (starting on page 37) for more detailed information.

Plant Personalities

This is a beautiful container garden that combines exquisite plant selections with an elegant container. It's perfect for a prime spot, like here next to a pool, or anywhere where it gets the attention it deserves. It combines many different colors and textures so you discover something new almost every time you look at it.

The texture plants were all chosen for their dark foliage. This effect leads the eye from one plant to the next. The height comes from purple fountain grass. Its soft, foxtail flower plumes give height without overpowering due to their airy appearance. Depending on how big your container is, you can choose either regular purple fountain grass or its dwarf version, which is sold under the variety names 'Red Riding Hood', 'Eaton Canyon', and 'Dwarf Rubrum'. The choice is yours, as both tall and dwarf varieties have the same color, but while the regular form gets three to four feet tall, the dwarf version reaches only eighteen to thirty inches.

Other foliage accents in the back are *Begonia* 'Maribel' and *Carex* 'Toffee Twist', also called weeping brown New Zealand sedge. The begonia's mahogany-colored foliage is especially intense under high light levels. It has delicate, blush-pink blooms as an added bonus. The sedge rounds out the corners with its needle-thin leaves that drape elegantly over the edges.

In the center and front corners we have even more foliage accents that provide texture and interest. The coleus in the center adds vibrant specks

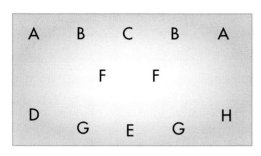

A = *Carex flagellifera* 'Toffee Twist' (2)
B = *Begonia* 'Maribel Pink Shades' (2)
C = *Pennisetum setaceum* 'Rubrum'
D = *Sedum* 'Matrona'
E = *Osteospermum* 'Orange Symphony'
F = *Coleus* 'Kingswood Torch' (2)
G = *Verbena* 'Babylon Blue Carpet' (2)
H = *Ajuga* 'Catlin's Giant'

of red with maroon edges, while the sedum and ajuga visually connect the two corners by having similar leaf colors and shapes. Although sedum is a fall-flowering perennial, it is used here as a foliage accent—its flowers will be a bonus. If you can't find the variety 'Matrona' in stores, look for a similar variety, such as 'Autumn Joy'. Ajuga might surprise you with bright blue flower umbels in spring. For the rest of the year, enjoy its large, lush, mahogany-colored leaves.

The flower and trailing elements in this container garden are *Osteospermum* 'Orange Symphony' and *Verbena* 'Babylon Blue Carpet'. The soft orange daisy flowers of *Osteospermum* have a dark blue center the color of the verbena. 'Orange Symphony' is a mounding and heat-tolerant variety of *Osteospermum*, whereas some other *Osteospermum* varieties might get too tall or stop flowering in the heat of summer.

Container Characteristics

I chose a stunning iron container that's full of character. Its elegant, formal look is softened over time, as it ages beautifully to an antique look. The dimensions of this particular planter are twelve by twenty-two inches. When you find one like it, make sure that it has drainage holes; if it doesn't, drill some before planting.

Care Clues

None of the varieties used require deadheading, but the *Osteospermum* and verbena benefit from it. The flowers of fountain grass can be used in fresh or dried arrangements. At the end of the season, you may take the plants apart carefully and plant the sedge, sedum, and ajuga in the ground. They are frost hardy to USDA Hardiness Zone 6 for the sedge and 3 for sedum and ajuga. Climates with little or no frost can also plant the *Osteospermum*, verbena, begonia, and fountain grass in the garden.

Plant Personalities

This basket is excellent for a partially shady location or for filtered sunlight.

The fuchsia in the center is an upright type with small, single flowers. It's part of a series from Europe that tolerates more sun and heat than many fuchsias. As fuchsias grow a bit slower than the other varieties, you might want to look for a well-developed plant when you plant this basket—you could even use one pot size larger than the rest of the plants. If you can't find this 'Ballerina Blau' (this might also be sold as 'Blue Ballerina'), look for a similar color with an upright growth habit. The color of its hot pink sepals is echoed in the veins of the ivy geraniums (*Pelargonium*). The 'Blizzard' series of ivy geraniums has a trailing habit and also good heat tolerance. If you wish to substitute, make sure that you get a semi-trailing or trailing type. The two colors that were used are 'Blue Blizzard', whose flowers are actually more lavender than blue and have attractive dark veins, and 'White Blizzard', a variety with clean white flowers accented by dark pink veins.

Finally, the color theme in pink and purple hues is rounded out with *Torenia* 'Summer Wave Amethyst'. The 'Summer Wave' series of *Torenia*, also called wishbone flower, is a trailing type with good heat tolerance. 'Amethyst' has reddish purple flowers and light-colored foliage. It's an abundant trailer that's great in hanging baskets.

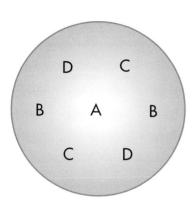

A = *Fuchsia* 'Ballerina Blau'
B = *Torenia* 'Summer Wave Amethyst' (2)
C = *Pelargonium* 'Blue Blizzard' (2)
D = *Pelargonium* 'White Blizzard' (2)

Container Personalities

Moss baskets are my personal favorites when it comes to planting hanging baskets. I simply love their natural look. Even when your plants have not covered the entire basket yet and you can see part of the moss, it's beautiful and natural looking. The downside is that they dry out fast once the temperatures rise, so you'll have to make sure that you water them frequently. Don't be surprised if you have to water them daily during hot summer months. Some moss baskets are available with built-in water reservoirs. The reservoirs are not visible once the basket is planted, but they help keep them moist longer. This particular basket is fourteen inches in diameter.

Care Clues

Fuchsias develop dark seedpods, which you might want to remove regularly if you don't like their look. It also encourages more continuous blooms. The ivy geraniums also benefit from regular deadheading. Other than that and the watering, this basket is very low-maintenance.

Plant Personalities

As if it was taken right out of an English cottage garden, this design let's you bring Old World charm right into your own garden.

The tallest plant is in the back, giving the planter a distinct angle from which it looks its best. The beautiful magenta flowers belong to *Anisodontea* 'Elegant Lady', an African mallow that's a traditional English cottage garden plant. While some might consider it too tall for containers, I love its airy height. The flowers of this variety are slightly larger than some others and have beautiful, dark magenta veins. Next to it is another plant that was used to add height, but it's barely visible from this angle. It's an ornamental grass, *Pennisetum messiacum* 'Red Bunny Tails'. Its green leaves have subtle burgundy accents, especially during cool temperatures. Its true attraction is its flowers, which are soft to the touch, like a bunny's tail.

On the second tier is *Nemesia* 'Safari Pink'. Its lavender-pink color builds a visual transition from the magenta blooms of the African mallow to the lavender flowers of the trailing plants. On the shortest tier are two plants with lavender flowers. *Sutera* 'Bermuda Sky' is commonly known as bacopa. This new variety has an airy, semi-trailing habit. If you can't find this particular variety, look for a similar one with the same colored blooms. As a blooming trailing element, I added *Petunia* 'Supertunia Priscilla'. This variety from the U.K. has very large, double flowers that are soft lavender with dark purple veins, echoing the color of the *Sutera*. A special bonus: its fragrant flowers have a sweet grape scent.

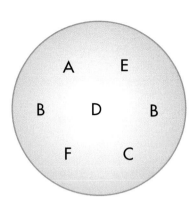

A = *Anisodontea* 'Elegant Lady'
B = *Muehlenbeckia* (creeping wirevine) (2)
C = *Petunia* 'Supertunia Priscilla'
D = *Nemesia* 'Safari Pink'
E = *Pennisetum messiacum* 'Red Bunny Tails' (barely visible)
F = *Sutera* 'Bermuda Sky' (bacopa)

Muehlenbeckia is a trailing foliage element and is, in fact, one of my favorite foliage accents to use. With its wiry growth habit, it weaves through container gardens and cascades over the edges with small, round, emerald green leaves.

Container Characteristics

Although this elegant urn looks like it's made of stone or clay, it's actually made of plastic, so it's easy to move and very break- and chip-resistant. If you use one that is hollow all the way to the bottom like this one was, it's especially important that it has drainage holes. Otherwise you could accumulate a foot of standing water in the bottom, which can breed fungi and bacteria. If it doesn't come with pre-drilled drainage holes, drill some yourself—another advantage of using plastic containers rather than clay. This urn had a sixteen-inch diameter. For different sized urns, adjust the number of plants accordingly.

Care Clues

Deadhead the petunia regularly to keep it looking tidy. Besides that, this design requires very little maintenance. If you live in a frost-free climate, you can plant all plants in the garden at the end of the season. This is especially valuable with the *Anisodontea* because it will turn into a shrub and you'll be able to enjoy it for many years.

Plant Personalities

The combination of two such vibrant colors as red and yellow creates a
cheerful summer look. One look and you'll want to have this container
garden for your summer parties. It's also not completely symmetrically
planted, which keeps the arrangement casual.

The fountain grass in the center adds height without being obtrusive.
It is so airy that you barely notice it, yet it adds texture and interest. The
second foliage accent is an ornamental sage, *Salvia* 'Icterina', or golden
sage. It has a mounding growth habit and beautifully variegated, fragrant
foliage. You can even use its leaves for cooking.

Simply using two colors can create such a stunning contrast. The
vibrant red is *Verbena* 'Tukana Scarlet', a trailing selection with large flower
heads that starts to bloom very early in the year. Three yellow flowering
varieties were used: *Bidens*, *Lantana*, and a marguerite daisy. All three have
a similar shade of yellow but different growth habits, which means that
you can find yellow flowers at different heights in the container. This effect
leads the eye from one plant to the other.

All of the flowering selections are very heat tolerant and start blooming
early in the year, so you'll be able to enjoy this container garden from early
spring until late fall.

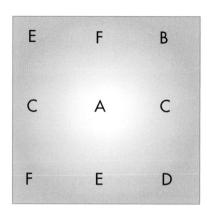

A = *Pennisetum messiacum* 'Red Bunny Tails'
B = *Argyranthemum* 'Butterfly'
C = *Salvia* 'Icterina' (sage) (2)
D = *Bidens* 'Peter's Gold Carpet'
E = *Verbena* 'Tukana Scarlet' (2)
F = *Lantana* 'New Gold' (2)

Container Characteristics

To stay with the warm color scheme but provide a contrasting backdrop at the same time, I chose a dark brown glazed container. It is square with inside dimensions of twelve inches. If you use larger or smaller containers, adjust the number of plants accordingly.

Care Clues

To assure continuous blooms, deadhead the *Argyranthemum* regularly. It also results in a tidier look. The verbenas and lantanas may also be dead-headed, but they don't benefit from it quite as much as the daisy. None of the other plants need any special care. If *Bidens* gets too big, cut it back liberally. The fountain grass flowers can be used in fresh or dried arrangements, and sage leaves are a popular culinary herb.

Plant Personalities

Annuals and perennials work beautifully together in this composition in cool colors. The heavy use of foliage makes this container garden very rich in texture. It's great for any time of the year, but especially for the early months of spring and the late months of fall, when plant selections are often limited because the blooming varieties flower early and late in the year independent of daylength. All of the plants used here can even withstand some frost.

Although *Carex*, commonly called sedge, is, botanically speaking, not categorized as a grass, it's handled and known as an ornamental grass. This selection, also called weeping brown New Zealand sedge, adds movement and texture with its needle-thin leaves. It brings height to the plant composition without overpowering it because its fine, flowing texture is open and airy. Since this sedge grows slower that the other plants in the container, you will want to look for nice, full plants. If you can't find a well-developed four-inch pot, look for a six-inch pot or even a gallon to make sure that its companions won't overgrow it.

The other two strong foliage components are *Salvia* 'Purpurascens' (purple sage) and *Heuchera* 'Amethyst Myst' (coral bells). The silver sheen that's characteristic to both of these contributes to the overall cool appeal of the plant composition. Their coloring is especially intense during the cooler months of the year. By using the same purplish silver twice—once in purple sage and once in *Heuchera*—the plants are brought together for a

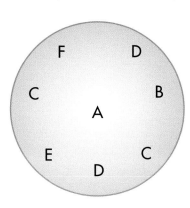

A = *Carex flagellifera* 'Toffee Twist'
B = *Heuchera* 'Amethyst Myst'
C = *Hedera* 'Ritterkreuz' (English ivy) (2)
D = *Calibrachoa* 'Million Bells Cherry Pink' (2)
E = *Salvia* 'Purpurascens' (sage)
F = *Nemesia* 'Blue Bird'

very well-balanced look. This effect is called color echoing. English ivy (*Hedera*) was added as a trailing foliage accent. Its subtle green keeps the container garden from getting too busy.

Cool blue *Nemesia* and vibrant pink *Calibrachoa* provide the splashes of color. Both varieties start flowering early in the year and will continue throughout the summer. Without their brilliant colors, the composition would be too subtle for most tastes.

Container Characteristics

This fourteen-inch container is a fairly inexpensive pot made of plastic. It has a textured finish, which makes it look almost like stone or coarse clay. Because the effect of the plants is so powerful, the container doesn't need to be elaborate, especially because the trailing plants cover most of it.

Care Clues

This container garden is very easy to care for. None of the plants needs to be deadheaded or trimmed back. At the end of the growing season, you may take the plants apart and plant the *Carex*, *Heuchera*, English ivy, and sage in the garden. They are perennial in USDA Hardiness Zone 5 and warmer. *Carex* might need some additional frost protection. Plant them early enough so that they have time to establish themselves before winter sets in. Areas with little or no frost can also plant the *Nemesia* and *Calibrachoa* in the garden.

Plant Personalities

This combination is rich in texture and color due to its many foliage and flowering plants.

Two ornamental grasses add texture to the design. The wispy one in the back is *Carex flagellifera* 'Toffee Twist'. For such a relatively small container garden, an airy and weeping grass like this is just right because a taller growing one would get too tall and one with a fuller growth habit could get too dominant. In the front center is *Hakonechloa macra* 'Aureola', an ornamental grass with gold and green variegation. Once this plant gets bigger, it will start cascading out of the container. Its bright golden leaves brighten the otherwise dark foliage.

Two dark-leaved plants, *Trifolium* 'Dark Dancer', frame the plants in the center. Its foliage is almost black with a very slim green margin. It's a very unusual plant that is sure to draw attention.

The two flowering plants have mostly red flowers. To add some moderate height in the back, I used *Pelargonium* 'Fireworks Red-White Bicolor', a geranium with beautiful, star-shaped flowers that fade from red to white in the center and with enticing foliage with dark zones. The second flowering plant that echoes the more intense shades of red in the geranium flowers is *Verbena* 'Temari Patio Red'. It has a mounding growth habit, broad leaves, and large flower clusters. I chose not to use strictly trailing plants in this design, but if you can't find a verbena that fits, you could use a moderately trailing variety because the verbena are positioned at the edge of the planter and have room to cascade.

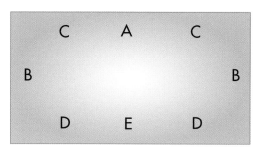

A = *Carex flagellifera* 'Toffee Twist'
B = *Trifolium* 'Dark Dancer' (2)
C = *Pelargonium* 'Fireworks Red-White Bicolor' (2)
D = *Verbena* 'Temari Patio Red' (2)
E = *Hakonechloa macra* 'Aureola'

Container Characteristics

This rectangular stone planter shows two different colors—it's darker where moisture has seeped through its porous sides. That's one of the charming characteristics of these types of planters. This particular example has inside dimensions of approximately nine by fifteen inches.

Care Clues

Deadhead the *Pelargonium* flowers regularly to ensure continuous and profuse blooms. None of the other varieties need any special attention. *Carex*, *Hakonechloa*, and *Trifolium* can be planted in a perennial bed at the end of the season. *Trifolium* and *Hakonechloa* are hardy to USDA Zone 5, whereas *Carex* is hardy to USDA Zone 6.

Plant Personalities

This beautiful basket in pink hues brightens any summer patio. It thrives best in full sun.

The eye is drawn to *Bracteantha* 'Sundaze Pink' in the center, a strawflower with an upright but fairly compact habit. Its star-shaped flowers show different tints of pink in their petals, ranging from vibrant pink at the tips over soft pink to almost white in the center, where the petals meet the deep golden yellow eye. Its darkest shade of pink is echoed in the flowers of *Calibrachoa* 'Million Bells Cherry Pink', an excellent hanging basket plant with hundreds of small, miniature petunia-like flowers. Unlike some *Calibrachoa* varieties, this one doesn't close its flowers on gloomy days, but the strawflowers will close in the rain to protect themselves.

The most trailing element is 'Supertunia Mini Blue Veined', a fast-growing trailer with white flowers and dark blue veins. It echoes the white portions of the strawflowers so that your eye travels from one plant to the next.

Finally, to the front right you can see an ivy geranium (*Pelargonium*) variety called 'Blue Blizzard', with flowers that are actually more lavender than blue. It's an excellent hanging basket plant with a trailing but compact habit. Its large, lavender flowers are accented with dark purple veins.

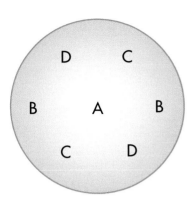

A = *Bracteantha* 'Sundaze Pink'
B = *Calibrachoa* 'Million Bells Cherry Pink' (2)
C = *Petunia* 'Supertunia Mini Blue Veined' (2)
D = *Pelargonium* 'Blue Blizzard' (2)

Container Personalities

Moss baskets are my personal favorites when it comes to planting hanging baskets. Even when your plants have not covered the entire basket yet and you can see part of the moss, it's beautiful and natural looking. Their downside is that they dry out fast once the temperatures rise, so you'll have to make sure that you water them frequently. Don't be surprised if you have to water them daily during hot summer months. Some moss baskets are available with built-in water reservoirs. The reservoirs are not visible once the baskets are planted, but they help keep them moist longer. This particular basket is fourteen inches in diameter.

Care Clues

The strawflower benefits from regular deadheading. Not only will it flower more profusely, but discarding spent flowers also keeps the plant from developing seeds, which can be untidy. The ivy geranium also flowers more continuously if it's deadheaded regularly. The other two plants don't need deadheading, but you can trim the petunias if they get too big. The plants used in this basket have quite a healthy appetite, so make sure that you fertilize them regularly.

Plant Personalities

This design uses a lot of foliage plants for a lush, tropical look accented by specks of flowering plants.

Phormium, also known as New Zealand flax, gives the design height and texture. It's an excellent plant for the center of planters because it adds height without dominating the entire design. It's still hard to find in certain parts of the country, but many nurseries have recognized its potential, and its availability is increasing. There are many different colors available, so you can substitute if needed. *Phormium* grows more slowly than do the other plants in the design, so use a larger plant, ideally one in a six-inch or gallon pot. For more foliage texture, I added two coleus varieties, 'Pineapple' and 'Super Sun Plum Parfait'. Coleus is experiencing a comeback, with many new varieties coming to the market. The newer varieties are also often more sun-tolerant, which is what you need for this design. 'Pineapple' has chartreuse leaves with maroon centers, and 'Super Sun Plum Parfait' has foliage in different shades of pink and burgundy. Both echo the color of the *Phormium.* The chartreuse leaves of *Coleus* 'Pineapple' are echoed in *Ipomoea* 'Terrace Lime', an ornamental sweet potato with trailing habit. 'Terrace Lime' is very similar to a variety called 'Margarita', which can be substituted. Finally, this color is echoed one more time in *Lysimachia* 'Outback Sunset', a variegated *Lysimachia* with yellow and green leaves, yellow flower clusters, and a trailing growth habit.

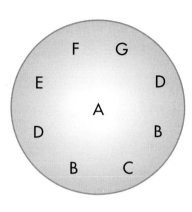

A = *Phormium* (New Zealand flax)
B = *Coleus* 'Pineapple' (2)
C = *Kalanchoe* 'Elves' Bells'
D = *Petunia* 'Supertunia Mini Blue' (2)
E = *Lysimachia* 'Outback Sunset' (not visible)
F = *Coleus* 'Super Sun Plum Parfait'
      (barely visible)
G = *Ipomoea* 'Terrace Lime' (sweet potato)
      (not visible)

The kalanchoe in this design is likely to be different from what you are familiar with. Compared to the popular kalanchoe flowering pot plant, 'Elves' Bells' has narrower leaves and individual, bell-shaped flowers. The burgundy blooms echo the color of the *Phormium*. 'Elves' Bells' flowers only in spring if it's under natural light conditions, but you can enjoy its olive-green, succulent, glossy foliage for the rest of the year. Finally, to add a few more color specks, I used *Petunia* 'Supertunia Mini Blue'. It provides a trailing element and intensifies the color impact with its deep blue flowers.

Container Characteristics

This classic terra cotta container emphasizes the warm colors of many of the plants in this design. With its bellied design, it holds a larger potting mix volume, which makes it easier to provide an adequate moisture and fertilizer supply. This pot is sixteen inches in diameter.

Care Clues

This is a low-maintenance design. None of the plants requires special care. If the sweet potato or any of the other vigorous plants tries to outgrow the others, trim them back. Most plants in this design are heat lovers, so don't plant them too early in the spring.

Plant Personalities

For this design, I chose a monochromatic theme with yellow foliage and flowers. In addition, all of the foliage and flowers are small, which creates a fine-textured look. The repetition of many different yellow flowers leads the eye from one plant to the next and connects the design visually.

Starting with the flowering plants, there is *Calibrachoa* 'Million Bells Yellow' in the front right corner. This miniature petunia-like flower produces an abundance of blooms that cascade over the edges. Its earthy tone of yellow subdues the more vibrant yellows in the other flowers. In the front left corner is *Bidens* 'Goldie', a compact variety of *Bidens* with cheery yellow flowers and a sweet, honeylike scent. Of the different varieties of *Bidens* available, 'Goldie' seems to be the most compact. An alternative with a compact habit but larger flowers is 'Peter's Gold Carpet'. The small, button-shaped flowers in the back left corner belong to *Chrysocephalum* 'Baby Gold'. It's a good "filler" plant for mixed container gardens. Its silver-green foliage is soft to the touch. Sometimes it's still labeled under its previous botanical name, *Helichrysum* 'Baby Gold'. Finally, in the back right corner is a strawflower, *Bracteantha* 'Golden Beauty'. Where many strawflowers grow upright, 'Golden Beauty' has a trailing habit. Its golden yellow flowers feel like straw and are excellent as dried flowers. It can also sometimes be found under its previous botanical name, *Helichrysum bracteatum*.

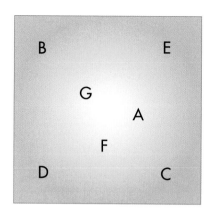

A = *Plectranthus coleoides* 'Variegata'
B = *Chrysocephalum* 'Baby Gold'
C = *Calibrachoa* 'Million Bells Yellow'
D = *Bidens* 'Goldie'
E = *Bracteantha* 'Golden Beauty'
F = *Lamium* 'Golden Anniversary'
G = *Phormium* (New Zealand flax)

For more texture, I added three foliage plants. The one in the middle is a yellow and green striped *Phormium*. *Phormium* is excellent for mixed containers, as it provides height and texture without dominating. There are many varieties available today, although their quantities are often limited. Just look for a yellowish or greenish color, ideally a variety with variegation. This design would look even better had I used a larger *Phormium* plant. *Phormium* grows quite slowly, so it's best to start with a larger plant compared to the other plants in the design.

The two other foliage plants are *Lamium* 'Golden Anniversary' and *Plectranthus* 'Variegata'. *Lamium* 'Golden Anniversary' has a mounding growth habit and yellow and green variegated foliage. It is very self-branching and builds a thick tuft of leaves. *Plectranthus* 'Variegata', also known as trailing Swedish ivy, builds long, fountainlike branches with cream and green variegated leaves.

Container Characteristics

This twelve-inch, square, brown glazed planter completes the earthy look of this design. Glazed containers evaporate water more slowly than non-glazed ones do, which can be especially helpful during hot summer months.

Care Clues

The only plant that really benefits from deadheading is the strawflower—its seed heads are not very attractive if they remain on the plant. All of the other plants are very low-maintenance varieties. If any of them gets too big, they respond well to a trim.

Plant Personalities

This lovely design uses purple tones that are complemented by the cool gray of a stone planter. An ornamental grass, *Stipa tenuissima*, gives the design height, texture, and movement. Commonly known as Mexican feather grass, it has needle-thin leaves that sway in the slightest breeze. The emerald green leaves are so thin they are almost iridescent. It can also be found labeled as *Nassella tenuissima*.

Although used primarily for its flowers, *Osteospermum* 'Dandenong Daisy Variegated Pink' also adds intriguing foliage accents with its cream and green variegated leaves. Even when the flowers give in to the heat of the summer, it will still look good. The flower petals are medium pink and fade to a lighter tone toward the center, where they meet a dark eye. Because it has so many tints in its flowers, it echoes several of the other flowers in this design.

The pink and lavender shades are continued with *Scaevola* 'Pink Fanfare' and *Sutera* 'Glacier Blue'. The *Scaevola,* also known as fan flower, has lavender-pink flowers that trail over the edges. *Sutera* 'Glacier Blue', commonly called bacopa, has tiny, round, lavender-blue blooms. It develops a trailing habit as it gets bigger.

Purple is present in several different shades and growth habits. In the back right is *Verbena* 'Superbena Large Lilac Blue'. This variety has multi-toned flowers that start out as deep lilac before they fade to a soft lavender shade. This makes it look as if there were multiple plants where in fact

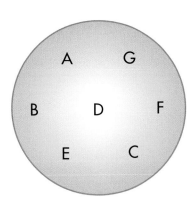

A = *Stipa tenuissima* (Mexican feather grass)
B = *Osteospermum* 'Dandenong Daisy Variegated Pink'
C = *Scaevola* 'Pink Fanfare'
D = *Ageratum* 'Artist Blue'
E = *Calibrachoa* 'Superbells Blue'
F = *Sutera* 'Glacier Blue' (bacopa)
G = *Verbena* 'Superbena Large Lilac Blue'

there's only one. It also echoes several of the other flower colors in the design. The 'Superbena' series has a semi-upright growth habit. If you can't find this particular variety, try to match color and growth habit. Somewhat hiding in the center is *Ageratum* 'Artist Blue', an ageratum grown from cuttings with purple-blue flower clusters. It seems to withstand heat better than seed-grown varieties. Finally, another trailing element is *Calibrachoa* 'Superbells Blue', with miniature petunia-like flowers in dark purple-blue with yellow centers.

Container Characteristics

You can see how this stone planter has started to age at the bottom, which makes it more interesting over time. The porous material permits air circulation, which is important for good plant performance. This planter is ten inches in diameter and not as heavy as it might seem. If you use plants in four-inch pots, loosen the potting mix to fit them all in.

Care Clues

Deadhead the *Osteospermum* regularly to encourage new bloom production, but expect it to go out of bloom once the summer temperatures get hot. The verbena also benefits from regular deadheading. If you don't care for the flowers that the Mexican feather grass produces in summer, simply cut them off.

Plant Personalities

The focus is definitely on foliage in this design. It combines culinary herbs with ornamental plants. The variety of textures and colors results in a rustic look.

The design gets its height from an ornamental grass in the center, *Pennisetum* 'Red Riding Hood', also sold under the names 'Dwarf Rubrum' and 'Eaton Canyon'. This dwarf form of purple fountain grass is the often-preferred variety over regular purple fountain grass for small- to medium-size container gardens, as it only grows to thirty inches tall. Its foxtail flower plumes start out in purple-pink before they mature to soft beige. Its purple foliage is popular for container gardens.

The trailing element in the front is 'Santa Cruz' oregano. It can be used like regular oregano in the kitchen, but is also beautiful as an ornamental. Its arching branches and dark green textured leaves work great in this design.

Although hard to see, two more foliage plants add more color tones to the design. One is *Salvia* 'Icterina', also known as golden sage. Its mounding habit and bicolored leaves are as versatile as an ornamental as they are in the kitchen. Its yellow variegation is echoed in the leaves of the English ivy, which adds another trailing element.

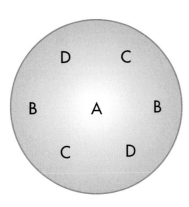

A = *Pennisetum setaceum* 'Red Riding Hood'
B = *Salvia* 'Icterina' (sage) (2)
C = *Hedera* 'Yellow Ripple' (English ivy) (2)
D = *Origanum* 'Santa Cruz' (oregano) (2)

Container Characteristics

Although this container garden is used as an upright pot, it was actually planted in a fourteen-inch moss hanging basket, which adds to the rustic look of the design. Simply take the hangers off and you have a beautiful pot. You can also resort to this creative use of hanging baskets if the hanging baskets that you planted didn't turn out to be as trailing as you had envisioned. The base that you can see is an attractive plant stand used to give it some more height.

Care Clues

Other than enjoying the herbs in your kitchen, there's not much you need to do with this container garden—it's very low-maintenance. If the oregano gets too big, cut it back liberally. Moss baskets dry out quite fast, especially in hot climates and once the plants get big, so make sure to keep them watered well.

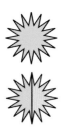

Plant Personalities

Instead of using foliage to accent the flowers, the roles are reversed in this design. It's a composition in cool colors that is completed by the look of the container. All of the varieties used tolerate cool temperatures, even a slight frost. It's a great container garden for spring and summer, or for winter in climates with little or no frost.

Since this pot had a fairly small inside diameter of ten inches, there was not enough room to place an upright plant in the center with mounding and/or trailing plants around it. Instead, I placed two upright plants in the back. The flowering variety is *Argyranthemum* 'Harvest Snow', a compact marguerite daisy with white flowers and yellow centers and fleshy, silver-green leaves that are almost succulent looking. Its companion on the other side is Mexican feather grass, botanically known as *Stipa* or *Nassella*. It has needle-thin leaves that sway in the slightest breeze—it provides movement to the container garden. In summer it produces beige flowers similar in color to the variegation of this English ivy.

The cool purple foliage accents are *Heuchera* 'Amethyst Myst', with its metallic sheen, and *Ajuga* 'Burgundy Glow'. The gray, white, and purple variegation of ajuga is especially intense during cooler months of the year. In spring, it produces cornflower-blue flowers that go very well with this color scheme.

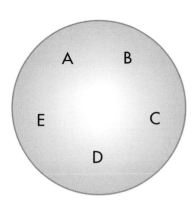

A = *Stipa tenuissima* (Mexican feather grass)
B = *Argyranthemum* 'Harvest Snow'
C = *Ajuga* 'Burgundy Glow'
D = *Hedera* 'Yellow Ripple' (English ivy)
E = *Heuchera* 'Amethyst Myst'

Container Characteristics

I love these stone planters for their rustic character. Their color turns darker when they are wet, as here in the picture. They also age beautifully—the older they get, the more interesting they become. They are not as heavy as they look, which makes them fairly easy to handle. This particular one has a ten-inch diameter.

Care Clues

This is a very low-maintenance container garden. You can deadhead the marguerite daisy, but that's really all you have to do besides watering and fertilizing. It provides great impact with minimal effort!

Plant Personalities

By using several different foliage plants and flowering plants, this design becomes very rich in texture.

The foliage plants dominate in this planter, but some of them also have attractive flowers. In the center is *Carex flagellifera* 'Toffee Twist', with needle-thin, bronze-colored leaves. Although sedge is botanically speaking not a grass, it is commonly referred to and treated as an ornamental grass. As its leaves get tall, the sedge takes on a weeping habit, which is great for the center of such a relatively shallow planter. *Muehlenbeckia,* also known as creeping wirevine, is the most trailing element. It has small, emerald green, glossy leaves that cascade over the rim. Next to it is *Ajuga* 'Mahogany'. Although this plant was selected for its large, glossy, mahogany leaves, it also charms with bright blue flower panicles that appear in spring. The flowers add height, and without them ajuga grows very low. Right behind it is *Erysimum* 'Variegatum'. This variegated wallflower grows compact upright. The yellow and green variegated leaves are topped with lavender pink flowers in spring. But again, it was primarily selected for its foliage.

Two flowering plants add playful splashes of color. *Diascia* 'Strawberry Sundae' has medium pink, twinspur flowers that tie in with the flowers of *Erysimum.* The foliage stays low and compact. There are many varieties of *Diascia* available today, and you can use a different one with a similar color. The vibrant blue flowers of *Nemesia* 'Blue Bird' echo the color of the

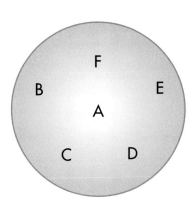

A = *Carex flagellifera* 'Toffee Twist'
B = *Nemesia* 'Blue Bird'
C = *Muehlenbeckia* (creeping wirevine)
D = *Ajuga* 'Mahogany'
E = *Erysimum* 'Variegatum'
F = *Diascia* 'Strawberry Sundae'

ajuga flowers. All of the flowers in this design are small, which contributes to the fine texture of this container garden.

Container Characteristics

Because none of the plants in this design is very tall, a shallow planter like this is best. Otherwise the pot might dominate over the plants and distract from them. I used a simple plastic pot, but you could very well use an ornate terra cotta planter. If you use four-inch plants, look for a pot with a diameter of about twelve inches.

Care Clues

If the *Nemesia* sets seed, cut them off to keep the plant looking neat. Also trim the spent flowers of ajuga and *Erysimum* once their blooming period is over. Most of the plants are quite frost hardy. At the end of the season, you may take the plants apart carefully and plant them in the garden, provided you give them enough time to get established before the first frost. The hardiness varies by plant: Ajuga is hardy to USDA Zone 3, *Carex, Diascia,* and *Erysimum* to Zone 6, *Muehlenbeckia* to Zone 7, and *Nemesia* to Zone 8.

Plant Personalities

Here is a design that combines warm summer tones with different shades of pink—a cheerful combination.

The basket gets wispy height and texture from *Plectranthus* 'Variegata', also known as trailing Swedish ivy. I like using this plant in container gardens because of its specific growth habit. At first it grows quite compact, but once it gets a bit bigger, it develops long, fountain-like branches that spill over the entire design.

The focus is definitely on flowering plants, starting with 'Million Bells Cherry Pink' in the center, a *Calibrachoa* with miniature petunia-like flowers in reddish pink with a bright yellow eye. Its compact but trailing habit makes it a good candidate for hanging baskets. Its sister variety, 'Million Bells Terra Cotta', is much more visible with its multicolored flowers. Its color ranges from almost pure, earthy yellow to almost red, with other warm, Mediterranean colors in between. You might even see a color fluctuation throughout the season because its flowers are often more red in early spring while it's still cool but almost completely yellow in the middle of summer when the mercury rises. The remaining flowering plant in the front is *Pelargonium* 'Blue Blizzard', a very trailing type of ivy geranium that is also quite heat- and sun-tolerant. Admittedly, its name is deceiving, because its flowers are actually lavender-pink with dark veins, but the dark veins echo the color of 'Million Bells Cherry Pink' and tie the design together visually.

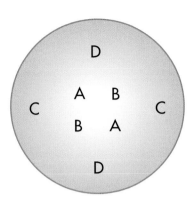

A = *Plectranthus coleoides* 'Variegata' (2)
B = *Calibrachoa* 'Million Bells Cherry Pink' (2)
C = *Calibrachoa* 'Million Bells Terra Cotta' (2)
D = *Pelargonium* 'Blue Blizzard' (2)

Container Characteristics

Moss baskets add a natural look to container gardens while also providing good growing conditions due to their good air circulation. Their only disadvantage is that they dry out quickly, which can be counteracted by using baskets with a built-in water reservoir. The plants used in this design have medium growth vigor and are not particularly fast. That means that parts of the basket will be visible for quite some time. If you don't like that, you can use more plants and/or plant along the sidewalls, or use the same amount of plants in a smaller basket. In this example, I used a sixteen-inch basket.

Care Clues

This is a very low-maintenance design. Deadheading the ivy geranium regularly promotes continuous bloom, but other than that, you don't need to give it any special attention.

Plant Personalities

Here is a trendy design with black plants in a stone planter. This is anything but ho-hum!

To add height in the back, I used *Coleus* 'Dark Star', an upright but
compact variety with nearly black foliage. Coleus has experienced a renaissance over the last few years, and today you can find an abundance of different varieties on the market. With its many colors and rich textures,
coleus is excellent for mixed containers. If you can't find 'Dark Star', look
for a dark-leaved variety. The second upright variety in the back is
Plectranthus 'Zulu Wonder'. It has dark green foliage with black veins and
purple undersides. Although it produces soft blue flowers, it is mainly used
for its richly textured foliage. There are many different species of
Plectranthus on the market, but try to find this particular one, which
belongs to *Plectranthus ciliatus*.

The two plants in the front carry on the dark-leaved theme. In the
center you can see *Ipomoea* 'Black Heart', an ornamental sweet potato with
heart-shaped, almost black leaves. If you can't find 'Black Heart', look for a
similar variety such as 'Blackie', a variety with similar color but deeply
lobed leaves, or 'Ace of Spades', a variety that is very similar—if not identical to—'Black Heart'. The sweet potato is framed by two plants of
Persicaria 'Red Dragon' with nearly black foliage with silver accents. On
the left you can see one of its creamy white flower clusters, which definite-

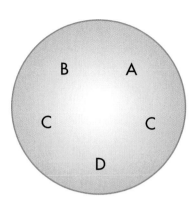

A = *Plectranthus ciliatus* 'Zulu Wonder'
B = *Coleus* 'Dark Star'
C = *Persicaria* 'Red Dragon' (2)
D = *Ipomoea* 'Black Heart' (sweet potato)

ly play second fiddle to the foliage. You might even want to cut them off to emphasize the black theme. *Persicaria* is actually a hardy perennial, but it is used with frost-tender plants in this design.

Container Characteristics

The light gray color of this heavy-duty stone planter really accents the black foliage. Its majestic shape emphasizes the impressive design. The only downside of this beautiful piece is that it's very heavy, so make sure to put it in place before you plant it; otherwise, it might be too heavy to move after planting. The inside diameter of this particular planter was about fourteen inches. I used larger sized plants to fill it more quickly. If you have only four-inch plants available, you can either use a smaller planter, accept that it'll take longer to fill out, or increase the number of plants.

Care Clues

Because there aren't any flowers to deadhead, this is a very low-maintenance design. All plants are also quite vigorous, so you shouldn't have any problems with any of the plants trying to take over. If you do, simply trim the aggressive plants back. If you wish, you can plant the *Persicaria* in the garden at the end of the season—it's quite frost hardy.

Plant Personalities

Lush foliage creates a tropical look in this container garden. Also, note that this design is an excellent example of color echoing, which visually connects the design by leading the eye from one plant to where the color is used to the next.

Instead of placing the tallest plant in the center, I placed it in the back to give the design a distinct angle from which it looks its best. *Phormium*, or New Zealand flax, is an excellent plant for this purpose. Its multicolored foliage gives a rich, tropical look. It's often still hard to find, but availability is increasing. *Phormium* grows slower than the other plants in the design, so choose a well-developed plant in a six-inch or gallon pot. This variety with yellow and green stripes sets the tone for the color theme. Its yellow color is echoed in the foliage of *Ipomoea* 'Terrace Lime', an ornamental sweet potato with a trailing habit. An almost identical variety is called 'Margarita', which you can substitute if you can't find 'Terrace Lime'. The yellow is echoed once more in *Coleus* 'Pineapple', a variety with lemon-yellow leaves and maroon centers, which echoes the maroon in the foliage of *Coleus* 'Sun Fire'. Both coleus varieties are sun-tolerant selections of medium height. There are many new coleus varieties available today, and you're likely to be able to choose from a considerable selection.

One more trailing element completes the design. *Lysimachia* 'Outback Sunset' is a variegated variety with yellow and green leaves and yellow flower clusters. It echoes both *Phormium* colors.

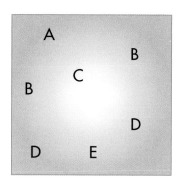

A = *Phormium* (New Zealand flax)
B = *Coleus* 'Sky Fire' (2)
C = *Coleus* 'Pineapple'
D = *Ipomoea* 'Terrace Lime' (sweet potato) (2)
E = *Lysimachia* 'Outback Sunset'

Container Characteristics

This dark brown glazed container makes the yellow and light green foliage stand out. Glazed containers have lower air circulation and water evaporation than planters that are more porous. The reduced evaporation can be especially helpful in hot weather. This pot's inside dimensions are twelve inches square.

Care Clues

All of the plants in this design love warm temperatures, so don't plant this container garden too early in spring. Once it gets hot, the sweet potato might try to outgrow some of the other plants. If this happens, just give it a generous trim.

Plant Personalities

An unusual planter like this puts special demands on the plant selection. While the container shouldn't be hidden by trailing plants too much, it's more important to add height to the design. This plant composition in pink and purple tones accomplishes that goal.

Instead of placing the tallest plant in the center, I put it in the back to balance the shape of the container. The ornamental grass is *Pennisetum setaceum* 'Rubrum', also known as purple fountain grass. Its stately four-foot height and airy growth habit give the needed vertical aspect without becoming overpowering. Its purple foliage is echoed in 'African Blue' basil, a versatile plant that is as valuable for its culinary aspects as it is for its aesthetic value. It's a good middle-height plant with lavender-pink flowers that attract hummingbirds. The lavender-pink of its flowers is echoed in *Lantana* 'Lavender Popcorn', a truly fun plant that develops nonedible, bright lavender-pink seeds the size of popcorn kernels.

As we move toward the front of the container, the plants become lower in height. In the center is *Verbena* 'Temari Patio Rose', a vibrant magenta verbena with an upright growth habit. Low-growing and trailing plants frame the front edges. The flowering one in the center is *Diascia* 'Little Charmer', a compact variety that is part of a fairly new and more heat-tolerant series from the late *Diascia* breeder Hector Harrison. Two foliage plants add more texture to the design. *Muehlenbeckia*, also known as creeping wirevine, is an excellent container garden plant with its wiry growth

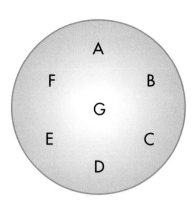

A = *Pennisetum setaceum* 'Rubrum'
B = *Ocimum* 'African Blue' (basil)
C = *Hedera* 'Glacier' (English ivy)
D = *Diascia* 'Little Charmer'
E = *Muehlenbeckia* (creeping wirevine)
F = *Lantana* 'Lavender Popcorn'
G = *Verbena* 'Temari Patio Rose'

and small, round, emerald green leaves. Finally, variegated trailing English ivy spills off the edges to the right.

Container Characteristics

This container is certain to make your neighbors do a double take! Put it on your front lawn and it'll look as if it's partially buried in the ground. Its Roman-inspired, antique look looks superb wherever you put it. It's best showcased in a prominent spot.

It's taller in the back than in the front, which makes it a little trickier to plant. The actual planting surface is about fourteen inches in diameter. Fill it with soil to the lower rim and accept that there will be room in the back that you won't be able to fill, but that space will be hidden if you place tall plants in the back. A planter of this size gets quite heavy once planted. It's best to plant it in its final spot, or have several pairs of strong hands available to move it.

Care Clues

You can use the foxtail plumes of purple fountain grass as cut flowers or enjoy them as they mature to soft beige. While verbena benefits from regular deadheading, leave spent lantana flowers so that they can develop into seedpods. You can snip and use the basil leaves in the kitchen. Many of the plants used enjoy warm temperatures, so don't plant it too early in spring.

Plant Personalities

Cool colors are always popular, which is no surprise when they come in the form of a hanging basket as beautiful as this one.

Instead of using a truly upright variety in the center, I chose *Dianthus* 'Devon Cottage Rosie Cheeks'. Its flower stems grow upright at first, but as the blooms open, they weigh down the stems and start to cascade in elegant arches, which makes them a great candidate for hanging baskets. This large-flowered variety has vibrant pink blooms with a sweet scent and elegant, silver foliage. Its pink flowers look great with the bright blue flowers of *Nemesia* 'Blue Bird', which has a mounding growth habit and—if planted at the edge of a hanging basket—trails slightly once it gets bigger. Its white-flowered counterpart, *Nemesia* 'Compact Innocence', has a similar growth habit, but slightly smaller flowers in pure white. Both have a yellow center and a faint fragrance. Finally, the last flowering variety is *Calibrachoa* 'Million Bells Cherry Pink' with small, miniature petunia-like flowers in deep pink with a yellow center. Its growth habit is moderately trailing, which complements the other varieties.

To add texture to the design, I used *Ipomoea* 'Tricolor', an ornamental form of sweet potato. Its foliage is a beautiful, multicolored composition of silver-green, pink, and white. The pink accents are especially prominent on new growth, while older growth loses most of its pink tinge. Compared to other sweet potatoes, 'Tricolor' is not as fast growing, which fits right in

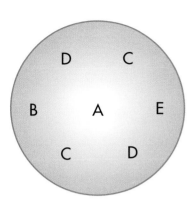

A = *Dianthus* 'Devon Cottage Rosie Cheeks'
B = *Nemesia* 'Blue Bird'
C = *Calibrachoa* 'Million Bells Cherry Pink' (2)
D = *Ipomoea* 'Tricolor' (sweet potato) (2)
E = *Nemesia* 'Compact Innocence'

with the growth vigor of the other plants in the basket. Its leaves are also smaller, which once again complements the texture of the remaining plants.

Container Characteristics

With exception of the sweet potato, the plants in this design are not very trailing. It's important to select the basket carefully because for a good portion of the season significant parts of the basket will be visible. Moss baskets are attractive enough that you can incorporate them into the design rather than feeling the need to hide them. This particular design used a fourteen-inch moss basket. If you use a smaller or larger basket, adjust the number of plants accordingly.

Care Clues

Deadhead the dianthus regularly to ensure a steady production of new blooms. In case the sweet potato gets too big in the heat of the summer (when sweet potatoes truly thrive), trim it back liberally. But since 'Tricolor' is not as aggressive as other *Ipomoea* varieties, you might not have to worry about that. The rest of the plants don't need any special care.

Plant Personalities

You can create a beautiful design without any flowering plants, as this texture-rich combination of annuals and perennials shows. Use it in a partially shady location.

The tallest plant in the back is *Strobilanthes*, also called Persian shield. It has stunning purple foliage with a metallic sheen. It can get three feet tall in the landscape, but it stays shorter in containers and in cool weather. Both its purple and silver colors are echoed in the begonias and the *Heuchera*, connecting the plants visually, leading the eye from one plant to the next. I used two four-inch plants, but you may need only one if it's well developed.

Next to it are two rex begonias, which are wonderful foliage plants. This particular variety is from the 'Great American Cities' series, but there are several series on the market and you can substitute a variety with similar colors. They need warm temperatures because temperatures below 45°F halt growth and temperatures below 40°F cause damage. In hot, dry climates, shade is important. Because they grow slower than the other varieties in the design, use begonias in five- or six-inch pots and the remainder of the plants in four-inch pots.

Heuchera 'Amethyst Myst' in the front center repeats the colors of the begonias and Persian shield. It's a mounding plant grown primarily for its beautiful foliage, though it does produce small, creamy white flowers on long stems.

The remaining two foliage plants are trailing, which is perfect for the front of this window box. They both have similar textures with their perfectly round, glossy leaves. *Muehlenbeckia* has emerald green leaves and a wiry growth habit, whereas *Lysimachia* 'Goldilocks' has soft, golden leaves and a flat, trailing growth.

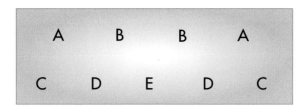

A = *Begonia rex* 'Savannah Pink Parfait' (2)
B = *Strobilanthes* (Persian shield) (2)
C = *Muehlenbeckia* (creeping wirevine) (2)
D = *Lysimachia* 'Goldilocks' (2)
E = *Heuchera* 'Amethyst Myst'

Container Characteristics

This redwood window box measures eight by twenty-seven inches. Its rustic appeal looks great with this texture-rich design. Wooden window boxes usually have good drainage, but make sure that they have drainage holes before you plant them, drilling some if not already there.

Care Clues

There are no flowers to deadhead, which makes this a very low-maintenance design. *Strobilanthes* and the rex begonias are heat lovers, so make sure that the temperatures don't drop too low. You can use the begonias as houseplants in winter. *Lysimachia*, *Heuchera*, and *Muehlenbeckia* are hardy perennials and can be planted in the garden in fall.

Plant Personalities

If pink is one of your favorites, this easy design is right for you.

The plant in the center is *Osteospermum* 'Dandenong Daisy Rose'. It has low-growing foliage and daisy-shaped flowers that are held high above the leaves on long stems. The vibrant pink flowers are accented by yellow centers. In very hot climates, it tends to stop blooming in the heat of the summer. It closes its flowers at night and under low light conditions and displays silver-tinged undersides.

A similar vibrant pink is found in *Petunia* 'Supertunia Mini Pastel Pink' in the front of the container. In this picture it is not fully-grown and not in full bloom yet, but you can see its bright pink flowers with almost white centers. The flower size is small, which harmonizes with the other small-flowered plants in this design. Once it gets larger, it will easily cover the side of the planter box and reach the ground.

The third plant in this design is *Sutera* 'Lilac King', which billows out each side of the planter. Commonly known as bacopa, this plant can most frequently be found in white, but lavender and pink varieties have become increasingly popular over the last years. 'Lilac King' is covered with small, soft lavender-colored flowers, but you can substitute a different variety in a similar color if you can't locate this particular selection.

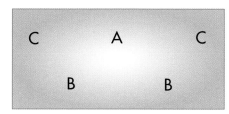

A = *Osteospermum* 'Dandenong Daisy Rose'
B = *Petunia* 'Supertunia Mini Pastel Pink' (2)
C = *Sutera* 'Lilac King' (bacopa) (2)

Container Characteristics

This rectangular planter can either be used as a window box or as a planter on the ground. It's a simple design made of plastic, but because the plants are so trailing, they will cover the sides eventually, and you can get away with using a low-budget planter. For this design, a seven-by-sixteen-inch planter is sufficient.

Care Clues

Deadhead the *Osteospermum* regularly to ensure continuous bloom production. If the trailing varieties get too big, simply trim them back.

Plant Personalities

This beautiful combination of foliage and flowers is perfect for a partially shady location. It uses different hues of pink and purple with lush green foliage accents. It combines frost-hardy perennials with heat-loving plants for an unconventional design.

There are two types of flowering plants in this design, although one is hidden for the most part. Your eye is drawn to *Fuchsia* 'Lohn der Liebe', a small-flowering selection with single flowers and an upright growth habit. It's a fairly rare variety, but you may simply substitute another variety with an upright growth habit if you can't find this particular selection at your garden retailer. Its pink is repeated in the margins of *Ajuga* 'Burgundy Glow' and in the eyes of *Torenia* 'Summer Wave Amethyst', which shows a glimpse of its beauty in the lower right corner. The 'Summer Wave' series is a trailing and heat-tolerant type of *Torenia*, also called wishbone flower.

This container garden emphasizes the use of foliage. The purple-hued colors are represented with *Ajuga* 'Burgundy Glow', *Ajuga* 'Mahogany' (not visible), and *Ipomoea* 'Blackie', a dark-leafed form of ornamental sweet potato. To brighten the design, I added lush green foliage with fiber-optic grass, which got its name from its iridescent, hairlike leaves that are capped with small flower spikes, giving it the appearance of fiber optics. Botanically speaking, it's not a grass but belongs to the rush family, but it's known and handled as an ornamental grass. It seems botanists still disagree about the correct naming of it. You can find fiber-optic grass in stores under the

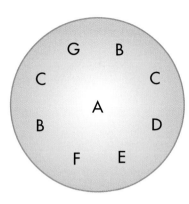

A = *Fuchsia* 'Lohn der Liebe'
B = *Scirpus cernuus* (fiber-optic grass) (2)
C = *Torenia* 'Summer Wave Amethyst' (2)
D = *Ipomoea* 'Blackie' (sweet potato)
E = *Heuchera* 'Splish Splash'
F = *Ajuga* 'Burgundy Glow'
G = *Ajuga* 'Mahogany' (not visible)

botanical names *Eleocharis cernuus, Scirpus cernuus, Isolepis cernua*, and possibly others.

Finally, the bright green foliage speckled with white that you can see in the center front belongs to *Heuchera* 'Splish Splash', a small-growing variety that sports pink flowers in spring and summer.

Container Characteristics

Stone planters like this one have a beautiful, rustic look. Their color turns darker when they are wet. They also age beautifully—the older they get, the more interesting they become. They are not as heavy as they look, which makes them fairly easy to handle. This shallow bowl with a fifteen-inch diameter looks particularly good with these specific plants because it keeps the eye focused on the plants while its color fits perfectly with the color scheme of the plants.

Care Clues

You can pinch off the spent fuchsia flowers if you wish, but it's not necessary to maintain flowering. The sweet potato has a tendency to take over once it gets warm, but it can be trimmed back liberally. At the end of the season, you can take the plants apart carefully and plant the two ajugas and the *Heuchera* in the garden. They are frost hardy to USDA Hardiness Zone 4 and warmer. The rest of the plants are not frost hardy.

Plant Personalities

This combination is easy to plant, rich in foliage texture, and has abundant blooms at the same time.

In the center is *Strobilanthes,* commonly called Persian shield, a heat-loving foliage plant with deep purple and silver leaves. It has greatly gained in popularity over the last few years. It performs best in warm temperatures but tolerates cooler climates as well—it just grows slower. Use a well-developed plant in a five- or six-inch pot so that it can keep up with the other plants, which should be in four-inch pots when you buy them.

As a mounding component I used *Coleus* 'Amora'. Its leaves are butter-yellow and green variegated, with the green being most prominent along the margins and on the older foliage that's exposed to less sun. Its special surprise is the undersides of the leaves, which are purple, echoing the color of *Strobilanthes.* Coleus is another heat lover that has become widely available over the last few years. You can choose from many different colors and may substitute a variety with similar colors if you can't find 'Amora'.

As a blooming and trailing element, I used *Petunia* 'Supertunia Blushing Princess'. This vigorous trailer has white flowers with a blush of lavender-pink, which again repeats the color theme of *Strobilanthes,* although only in a slight hint. The large flowers are usually abundant, covering most of the foliage.

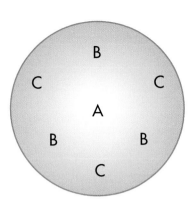

A = *Strobilanthes* (Persian shield)
B = *Coleus* 'Amora' (3)
C = *Petunia* 'Supertunia Blushing Princess' (3)

Container Characteristics

This shallow, blue-glazed container looks good with the cool colors of this design. The glazing reduces water evaporation, which is helpful in summer when container gardens tend to dry out fast. This particular pot is sixteen inches in diameter.

Care Clues

Make sure you start with a well-developed *Strobilanthes* when planting. *Strobilanthes* and coleus need warm temperatures to maintain growth. Temperatures below 45°F stall growth. None of the plants need any special care. If the petunias cascade too much and cover too much of the container for your taste, simply trim them back.

Plant Personalities

I planted this planter in purple tones with taller plants in the back and trailing ones in front. This technique gives the design a distinct angle from which it looks its best and is ideal if you want to place it against a wall or fence.

I love using *Angelonia* in mixed container gardens because it provides height, but has an airy habit so that it's not overpowering. This variety is 'Angelface Blue Bicolor' with white flowers accented by blue markings. *Angelonia* loves the heat and excels even when the temperatures rise beyond the comfort level. In this picture, the plant had just started to bloom and not reached its peak yet. I used a six-inch *Angelonia* compared to the other plants, which were all in four-inch pots.

Verbena 'Superbena Pink Shades' surrounds the *Angelonia*. It has a semi-upright growth habit and large flower clusters that display different shades of purplish pink over time. It's a vigorous grower that will start to drape over the edges as it gets bigger. In the center is *Nemesia* 'Blue Bird', a heat-tolerant selection with large blue flowers accented by yellow in the centers. It has a mounding growth habit and is perfect for this spot in the center, where is builds a transition from the upright plant in the back to the trailing ones in front.

The two trailing elements are *Scaevola* 'New Wonder' and *Sutera* 'Cabana'. *Scaevola* has blue, fan-shaped blooms that gave it its common name, fan flower. It's an excellent choice for the edges of mixed containers,

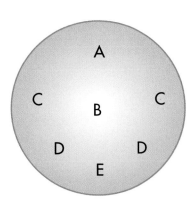

A = *Angelonia* 'Angelface Blue Bicolor'
B = *Nemesia* 'Blue Bird'
C = *Verbena* 'Superbena Pink Shades' (2)
D = *Scaevola* 'New Wonder' (2)
E = *Sutera* 'Cabana' (bacopa)

where it can cascade with clusters of blue flowers. Once the plants are bigger, they show much more color than in this picture. To brighten the design, I added *Sutera* 'Cabana' with its dainty, snow-white flowers. 'Cabana' is more compact and less trailing than many other white *Sutera*, but you could substitute another white variety if needed. *Sutera* is commonly known as bacopa.

Container Characteristics

This blue glazed container completes the color theme. It's sixteen inches in diameter and has ample potting mix volume for the plants. The glazing reduces evaporation, which is especially beneficial during hot weather.

Care Clues

This is a low-maintenance design that's perfect for the busy gardener. The verbena benefit from regular deadheading, but it's not required for good bloom production.

Plant Personalities

This basket was designed for a partially shady spot, where it can be tricky to find the right plant varieties. This design focuses on foliage and uses flowers solely as accents.

The center showcases *Coleus* 'Kingswood Torch', a beautiful, deep red coleus variety with burgundy to maroon edges. Coleus is experiencing a comeback in the early 2000s with an immensely broadened color palette and better availability in garden retail stores. 'Kingswood Torch' builds the centerpiece in this design and draws the eye immediately to its bold colors. The color of its foliage is partially echoed in the flowers of *Fuchsia* 'Golden Marinka', a compact trailing variety with beautiful flowers and variegated foliage that plays anything but second fiddle to the blooms. Its leaves are bright yellow and lime-green variegated, and its growth is trailing, which was important for this particular design. Its foliage color is echoed in the leaves of *Lamium* 'Golden Anniversary' with golden-yellow, green, and silver variegation. It has a very compact, mounding habit and builds a tight cushion of foliage. As an added bonus, small, purple flowers adorn the plant for almost all but the hottest times of the year.

Container Characteristics

Once the plants are fully grown, you can hardly see the basket. But these plants are not particularly fast growing, so parts of the container are visible

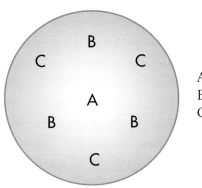

A = *Coleus* 'Kingswood Torch'
B = *Lamium* 'Golden Anniversary' (3)
C = *Fuchsia* 'Golden Marinka' (3)

during the earlier months after planting. That's why I chose a moss basket, which has a natural look and fits right into the design. The only downside of moss baskets and those made of coco fiber is that they dry out fairly quickly, but since this mixed basket was designed for a partially shady spot, this won't be as much of a problem as if it were a design for full sun. I used a fourteen-inch basket, but if you use a larger or smaller basket, adjust the number of plants accordingly.

Care Clues

If the coleus gets too tall, you can cut it back. Also, if the *Lamium* tries to outpace the fuchsia, you can give it a trim. While these plants don't require any special care, the coleus and the fuchsia like warm temperatures, so wait to plant this basket until the temperatures have warmed. Temperatures below 40°F can cause damage. The *Lamium*, on the other hand, is quite cold tolerant and can be planted in a perennial bed in the garden in fall.

Plant Personalities

If you're looking for a dramatic color composition, this might very well be the one for you! Black foliage is not something you see every day, which is one of the reasons why it's so incredibly impressive. The good news is that this black plant, *Ipomoea* 'Black Heart', is fairly easy to find in well-stocked garden centers. If you can't locate it, use its sister variety, 'Blackie', which has foliage of the same color but with lobed leaves. Whichever one you choose, the black foliage really makes the yellow tones jump. 'Black Heart' can also be found under the name 'Ace of Spades'.

The second foliage component is leatherleaf sedge. It's certainly a lot subtler than the sweet potato, but it adds movement and texture with its needle-thin leaves.

The dark foliage serves as a backdrop for the flowering plants, which are dominantly from the yellow and orange tones. The window box gets height from *Argyranthemum* 'Butterfly', a cheery yellow marguerite daisy with excellent heat tolerance. The orange tones are represented by *Osteospermum* 'Orange Symphony'. While many *Osteospermum* grow upright, the 'Symphony' series is a mounding type, which is perfect for this use. It's also a lot more heat tolerant than many older introductions, which is important so that you get flowers throughout the summer. The yellow and orange tones of these two plants are echoed in *Calibrachoa* 'Terra Cotta'. It's an exquisite variety with earthy colors. Its multitone flow-

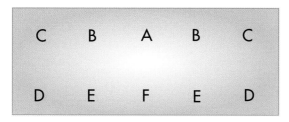

A = *Argyranthemum* 'Butterfly'
B = *Carex buchananii* (leatherleaf sedge) (2)
C = *Osteospermum* 'Orange Symphony' (2)
D = *Verbena* 'Babylon Lilac' (2)
E = *Calibrachoa* 'Million Bells Terra Cotta' (2)
F = *Ipomoea* 'Black Heart' (sweet potato)

ers actually vary in color, ranging from almost yellow to almost red. As the finishing touch, the violet flowers of *Verbena* 'Babylon Lilac' add lively specks of color.

Container Characteristics

The plants were planted in a redwood window box, although you can't see it in the picture. Its warm tones complement the yellow and orange flowers nicely. This box measures eight by twenty-seven inches. If you choose a larger or smaller container, adjust the number of plants accordingly.

Care Clues

Although deadheading is not required for any of these varieties, both the *Argyranthemum* and the *Osteospermum* benefit from it. They will reward your extra work with more abundant and continuous blooms. Occasional deadheading can also keep the verbena more colorful. Once it gets hot in the summer, the sweet potato might get too vigorous. If that's the case, you can trim it back to the desired size.

Plant Personalities

Instead of putting the tallest plant in the center, I chose two tall plants for the back and worked my way toward the front with steadily decreasing plant heights. This gives the container garden a preferred side from which it should be viewed and is a good choice for placement near a wall or fence. The earthy colors of the plants complement the rustic, earthy look of the planter.

The ornamental grass in the back is *Carex flagellifera* 'Toffee Twist', a sedge with a weeping growth habit and needle-thin, bronze leaves. Since many ornamental grasses grow slower than the rest of the plants in this design, it's best if you start with a well-developed plant because it won't grow as much after it's planted. It's often best to start with a grass in a six-inch pot and buy the rest of the plants in four-inch pots.

To its left is Coleus 'Dipt in Wine', one of the many wonderful coleus varieties available today. Its rich colors make coleus a superb plant for container gardens. This variety with its multicolored leaves echoes many of the other colors in the design, which captures the eye and leads it from one plant to the next. There is a second coleus in this pot, 'Texas Parking Lot', a very tough and heat-tolerant variety, as the name implies. 'Texas Parking Lot' gets quite a bit bigger than what you see in the picture. If you want to keep the plant in this spot shorter, you can trim it regularly or use a smaller-growing variety with similar colors.

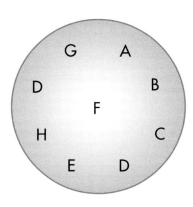

A = *Carex flagellifera* 'Toffee Twist'
B = *Coleus* 'Texas Parking Lot'
C = *Vinca minor* 'Illumination'
D = *Verbena* 'Tukana Scarlet' (2)
E = *Persicaria* 'Red Dragon'
F = *Osteospermum* 'Orange Symphony'
G = *Coleus* 'Dipt in Wine'
H = *Ipomoea* 'Terrace Lime' (sweet potato)

Three more foliage plants are in this texture-rich combination. *Vinca* 'Illumination' is a trailing vinca vine with golden yellow foliage and deep green margins. It's excellent for the edge of a pot, where it can spill over the rim like liquid gold. *Persicaria* 'Red Dragon' is a vigorous, bushy plant with burgundy and silver variegated foliage. It echoes the deep color of coleus. Finally, the last foliage plant is *Ipomoea* 'Terrace Lime', an ornamental sweet potato with chartreuse leaves. Its spreading growth cascades over the rims of planters and its color echoes that of vinca vine.

For flowering accents I added *Osteospermum* 'Orange Symphony' and *Verbena* 'Tukana Scarlet'. 'Orange Symphony' is a low-growing variety with bright orange flowers and dark eyes. It's excellent for the middle of this particular design. 'Tukana Scarlet' has vibrant red flowers that cascade over the rim of the pot.

Container Characteristics

This decorative, ornate planter with an earthy, rustic look goes beautifully with the warm colors of the plants in this design. A pot like this is not cheap, but its appeal makes more than up for the expense. Since it's clay, make sure to handle it with care so that you can enjoy it for many years. This round planter is fourteen inches in diameter. If you use a larger or smaller pot, increase or decrease the number of plants or the plant size accordingly.

Care Clues

Because this design uses mainly foliage rather than flowers, you don't need to spend much time on maintenance. Both flowering plants benefit from occasional deadheading. Some of the foliage plants vary in temperament, so if some try to outgrow the others, simply trim them back.

Plant Personalities

It can be difficult to find the right plant selections for partial shade, but this design with primarily foliage plants is a good example.

The dominant plant is *Coleus* 'Super Sun Plum Parfait', with red and burgundy leaves. Coleus is an outstanding plant for shade and partial shade. Coleus is experiencing a well-deserved comeback, so you will be able to find more and newer varieties in the stores. If you can't find this particular variety, substitute a similar one. There are so many coleus varieties on the market today that you shouldn't have a problem finding the right color. There is also a second coleus variety in this planter, but it's barely visible, as it's hiding behind 'Super Sun Plum Parfait'. It's called 'Dark Star' and has very dark purple, almost black, foliage and a more compact growth habit than 'Super Sun Plum Parfait'.

The color of the coleus is complemented by *Lysimachia* 'Goldilocks', with its small, round, golden yellow leaves. It's excellent for container gardens in the shade, where it cascades over the edges. Another foliage component is *Lamiastrum* 'Herman's Pride', which is not visible in the picture. It has a very low-growing habit and white and green variegated foliage. It is also sold as *Lamium* 'Herman's Pride'.

Although it was not in bloom at the time the picture was taken, there is a flowering variety in the design. It's an ivy geranium called 'White Blizzard', a white-flowering variety with a cascading growth habit. You may

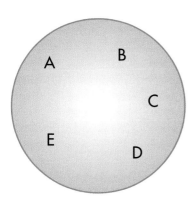

Planter in Back (p.154)

A = *Coleus* 'Super Sun Plum Parfait'
B = *Coleus* 'Dark Star' (barely visible)
C = *Lamiastrum* 'Herman's Pride' (not visible)
D = *Pelargonium* 'White Blizzard' (geranium)
E = *Lysimachia* 'Goldilocks'

substitute a different color if you wish, or you might choose not to use any flowering plants at all, as this photo proves that an all-foliage design can be beautiful.

Container Characteristics

Stone planters like these have a beautiful, rustic look. Their color turns darker when they are wet. They also age beautifully—the older they get, the more interesting they become. They are not as heavy as they look, which makes them fairly easy to handle. The pots in the back and front right are tall round pots with ten-inch diameters, while the one in the front left is a shallow bowl with a fourteen-inch diameter. Using containers of different heights in a grouping like this allows you to create several visual tiers.

Care Clues

This is a very low-maintenance design because none of the plants needs to be trimmed back. If you don't like the coleus flowers that may appear on older plants, simply cut them off. At the end of the season, you may take the plants apart carefully and use the *Lysimachia* and *Lamiastrum* as perennials in the garden.

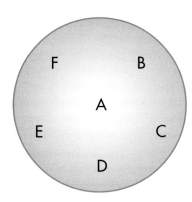

Planter in Front Left (p.154)
A = *Stipa tenuissima* (Mexican feather grass)
B = *Hosta* 'Golden Prayers' (not visible)
C = *Heliotropium* 'Atlantis'
D = *Hedera* 'Goldstern' (English ivy)
E = *Heuchera* 'Purple Petticoats'
F = *Heuchera* 'Amethyst Myst' (not visible)

Plant Personalities

Once again, flowers are used to accent foliage rather than the other way around. It's a beautiful combination of purple shades and lush green. The only plant selected for its bloom is *Heliotrope* 'Atlantis', a compact and early-blooming selection with dark purple flowers with the sweet scent of vanilla. If you need to substitute with another variety, look for a compact-growing one.

The purple color of the heliotrope is echoed in the dark foliage of *Heuchera* 'Purple Petticoats' and *Heuchera* 'Amethyst Myst' (the latter is not visible in the picture). They are beautiful foliage plants that also produce delicate, tall, soft-colored flowers, but flowers were not a considering factor in this design.

Green and chartreuse are represented in three foliage plants. Mexican feather grass, also sold under the botanical names *Stipa* and *Nassella*, has needle-thin leaves that sway in the slightest breeze—it provides movement to the container garden. In summer, it produces beige flowers. The English ivy in the front provides bright chartreuse accents that are especially prominent in the younger growth. Its new leaves echo the color of the *Lysimachia* in the pot in the back, which connects the planters visually. Yellowish foliage was used a third time with *Hosta* 'Golden Prayers', although not visible here. It's a compact growing, slug-resistant variety.

Care Clues

The heliotrope benefits from deadheading. It will bloom more continuous-ly and look tidier if you cut off the spent flowers regularly. None of the other varieties require any special care. At the end of the season, you may take the plants apart carefully and plant the *Heuchera* and English ivy in the garden. They are frost hardy in USDA Zone 4 and warmer.

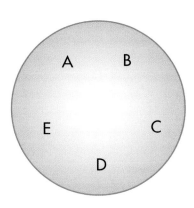

Planter in Middle Right (p.154)
A = *Pennisetum setaceum* 'Red Riding Hood'
B = *Lantana* 'Lavender Popcorn'
C = *Ipomoea* 'Tricolor' (sweet potato)
D = *Nemesia* 'Blue Bird'
E = *Pelargonium* 'Blue Blizzard' (geranium)

Plant Personalities

Unlike the other two pots in the picture, this container garden can also be used in a full sun application.

The tall ornamental grass in the background, dwarf purple fountain grass, adds height without being overpowering. Its airy, foxtail-like, burgundy flowers and purple leaves repeat the color of the coleus in the planter in the back and that of the *Heuchera* in the planter on the left, which visually connects the three. The tall flowering plant in the back is *Lantana* 'Lavender Popcorn', a heat-tolerant selection discovered by Dr. Allan Armitage from the University of Georgia. Once its lavender-colored flowers mature, they develop nonedible, lavender-pink seeds the size of popcorn kernels—a fun addition to your garden. The lavender/blue theme is continued with *Nemesia* 'Blue Bird' and a lavender-colored flowering ivy geranium called 'Blue Blizzard'. Although it was not in bloom when the picture was taken, it has lovely, lavender-blue flower clusters.

The white eyes of the *Nemesia* flowers are echoed in the white margins of *Ipomoea* 'Tricolor', an ornamental sweet potato with silver-green, white, and pink variegated foliage. It's smaller than most of the other ornamental sweet potatoes on the market.

Care Clues

None of the varieties here require deadheading, but the flowers of the purple fountain grass can be used in fresh or dried flower arrangements. If the sweet potato gets too big during summer, trim it back as desired.

Plant Personalities

It's a shame that the lobelia on the left is not in full bloom. Otherwise, this design in pink and purple with dark foliage accents would be a true knockout. In time, though, it will look gorgeous.

The dominant color in the back of the planter is *Nemesia* 'Blue Lagoon', a variety with lavender-blue flowers. Its compact growing habit is perfect for smaller-sized containers like this. To its left is the first foliage accent, *Stipa tenuissima*, although its needle-thin leaves are very subtle. This Mexican feather grass can also be found under the botanical name *Nassella tenuissima*. Its spring-green, almost iridescent foliage sways in the slightest breeze. In summer, it produces wheat-colored flowers and its foliage turns to a soft beige color. If you wish to emphasize its effect, choose a larger plant than in the picture because it won't grow much in just one season. Next up is a flowering accent, *Diascia* 'Strawberry Sundae'. The medium pink flowers of this twinspur sit atop long flower stems and compact foliage. The cheerful color is a welcome accent in this pink-and-purple theme. Finally, the last plant in the back was chosen for its flowers as well as its foliage. Although only the trained eye can see it, *Gaura* 'Perky Pink' holds up a long flower stem that's not quite in bloom yet. Once in bloom, the medium pink flower spikes will add just the right height for this size planter. *Gaura*'s foliage is deep maroon, which makes the flowers stand out even more.

The biggest color splash in the front is *Calibrachoa* 'Million Bells Trailing Pink'. Its dark pink flowers are accented by yellow centers. With

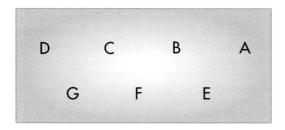

A = *Nemesia* 'Blue Lagoon'
B = *Stipa tenuissima* (Mexican feather grass)
C = *Diascia* 'Strawberry Sundae'
D = *Gaura* 'Perky Pink' (barely visible)
E = *Calibrachoa* 'Million Bells Trailing Pink'
F = *Ipomoea* 'Blackie' (sweet potato)
G = *Lobelia* 'Laguna Pink'

its trailing habit, it cascades over the edge of the planter. When the picture was taken, it had just started to trail, but it'll soon cascade all the way down. To its left is another foliage accent, *Ipomoea* 'Blackie', an ornamental sweet potato with deeply lobed leaves. Its dark color echoes that of *Gaura*'s foliage. On the very right you can see *Lobelia* 'Laguna Pink', a lovely variety that unfortunately doesn't show its beauty in this picture yet. When in full bloom, it is covered with soft pink—almost white—flowers with dark pink veins.

Container Characteristics

Even a small planter like this can be brimming with flowers, as this example shows. You can also see that this nine-by-fifteen-inch stone planter has started to age, with subtle accents of sediments and algae that give it character. Because this planter is porous, it provides good air circulation, which is important for good plant performance. It's also not as heavy as it might look, not only because it's small, but also because of the material it's made of. This stone planter is manufactured by Braun Horticulture.

Care Clues

This is a very low-maintenance design. Just keep an eye on the sweet potato—it loves warm temperatures and can get quite vigorous once the mercury rises. Trim it back if needed.

Plant Personalities

"Foliage and flowers" is the theme of this mixed basket, which incorporates perennials into the design.

The focal point is *Nemesia* 'Blue Bird' with its vibrant blue flowers. Its compact, semi-upright growth habit is perfect for the center of hanging baskets, where you want plants that don't get too tall. If you would use 'Blue Bird' in a large, upright planter, you would likely use it as a mounding component. 'Blue Bird' has large flowers dotted with yellow centers, and it has a faint fragrance.

The two foliage plants build a stunning contrast due to their light and dark foliage. *Ajuga* 'Mahogany' has extremely dark, almost black, foliage, which is actually a very trendy color among some container garden designers. Its low-growing, creeping habit works well in hanging baskets. In spring, ajuga produces whorls of bright blue flowers, which echo the color of *Nemesia*. Once ajuga reaches the edges of the moss basket, you can use pins to train it to grow close to the basket. It develops roots at the leaf nodes if it's given close contact with the moss and adequate moisture.

The second foliage plant is *Hedera* 'Glacier', a variegated English ivy. English ivies can be found in countless varieties and color schemes, but I chose this particular variety for its silvery green and white variegation to complement the color theme. If you can't find this particular variety, look for one with a similar color. English ivies are very trailing and excellent for

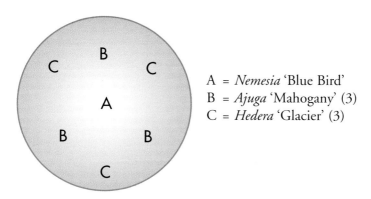

A = *Nemesia* 'Blue Bird'
B = *Ajuga* 'Mahogany' (3)
C = *Hedera* 'Glacier' (3)

hanging baskets. Like ajuga, English ivies can be trained to "hug" the basket, as they root very freely when given the opportunity.

Container Characteristics

The moss that you can see at the bottom and lower left corner of the basket adds to the texture-rich design. This particular example used a fourteen-inch moss basket, but one made of coco fiber would achieve a similar effect. Although a cedar basket would also look nice with these plants, you wouldn't have the opportunity to train the ajuga and English ivy along the sides.

Care Clues

If you deadhead spent flowers of the *Nemesia*, it will respond with more abundant blooms, but *Nemesia* blooms quite freely even without deadheading. Ajuga and *Hedera* can be planted in the perennial garden in the fall—they are quite frost hardy.

This romantic grouping of container gardens in predominantly pink hues creates a look reminiscent of
English cottage gardens.

Plant Personalities

If you love an abundance of color, try this combination that consists of
only flowering plants without any foliage accents. This particular pot is
fairly large and was planted using six-inch pots. You can use the same
amount of four-inch plants in a smaller container or use more four-inch
plants if you want to plant a large container like this.

The plant in the center is *Nemesia* 'Candy Girl', a soft pink variety
with a mounding growth habit. Its romantic, blush pink color brightens
the design. Two varieties of *Calibrachoa* add vibrant pinkish red and purplish blue, 'Million Bells Cherry Pink' and 'Million Bells Trailing Blue'.
These petunia relatives have hundreds of small, petunia-shaped flowers
with yellow eyes. The two varieties have different growth habits. While
'Cherry Pink' is mounding and starts flowering early in spring, 'Trailing
Blue' has—as the name suggests—a very trailing growth habit and starts
flowering mid-spring. Its flowers close during rainy, low-light weather.

The purple blue of the trailing *Calibrachoa* is echoed in *Brachyscome*
'New Amethyst'. It's barely visible in the picture, but it has hundreds of
small, purple, daisy-shaped flowers with yellow centers and a trailing
growth habit with dense, lacy leaves. Finally, a vibrant pink verbena adds

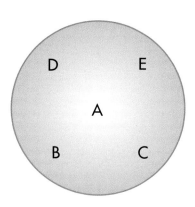

Planter in Center (p.162)
A = *Nemesia* 'Candy Girl'
B = *Calibrachoa* 'Million Bells Trailing Blue'
C = *Verbena* 'Tapien Pink' or 'Babylon Pink'
D = *Calibrachoa* 'Million Bells Cherry Pink'
E = *Brachyscome* 'New Amethyst'

even more lively color. The particular variety in the picture is 'Tapien Pink', but you may substitute 'Babylon Pink' or a similar pink variety with a trailing habit.

Container Characteristics

This trio consists of the same pot design in three different sizes. The pot in the front left shows the attractive rim design nicely. Classy terra cotta planters like these are always a great choice for container gardens. If you handle them with care so that they don't chip or break, you'll enjoy them for many years and will be able to admire how they age over the years into beautiful, antique-looking planters rich in character. These pots range in sizes from ten- to fourteen-inch inside diameters. Although they all have the same number of plants, I used different plant sizes to fill the different pots. If you want to work with only one plant size, you can adjust the number of plants per pot or accept the fact that some pots will look sparser until the plants completely fill the pot.

Care Clues

All of the varieties in this design have a healthy appetite, so make sure that you fertilize them regularly. If you tend to forget about fertilizing, use a generous amount of slow-release fertilizer.

Nemesia tends to set seed, but deadheading will keep it looking tidy and will keep the flowers coming all summer. Verbenas generally also flower more continuously if they are deadheaded regularly. None of the other plants require any special care. If you live in a frost-free climate, you can either keep the container for more than one season or plant the plants in the garden in the fall.

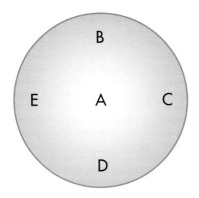

Planter on Left (p.162)
A = *Dianthus* 'Devon Cottage Rosie Cheeks'
B = *Calibrachoa* 'Million Bells Cherry Pink'
(not visible)
C = *Hedera* 'Glacier'
D = *Verbena* 'Babylon Purple'
E = *Diascia* 'Little Charmer'

Plant Personalities

Once again, cool pinks and purples dominate this design of flowers accented by foliage. In the center, a variety of dianthus, or garden pinks, adds height without being overpowering. The flowers of 'Devon Cottage Rosie Cheeks' are not only vibrant, but also very fragrant. As the flowers open up, the stems start to cascade under the weight of the flowers. While its silver foliage is echoed in the variegation of the English ivy (the foliage accent), its flower color is echoed in the delicate flowers of *Diascia* 'Little Charmer'. 'Little Charmer' is part of a new series of diascia from England, which has greatly improved heat tolerance compared to some of the earlier introductions. Its dainty flowers and neat growth habit are wonderful for container gardens.

The two other color accents are *Verbena* 'Babylon Purple' and *Calibrachoa* 'Million Bells Cherry Pink'. While 'Million Bells Cherry Pink' is not visible in the container, you can see it in the large pot right behind it. The verbena is a trailing selection with large purple flower clusters.

Care Clues

Deadhead the dianthus and verbena regularly to assure continuous bloom. None of the other varieties need special care, but make sure that you fertilize regularly, as all of these benefit from a good dose of fertilizer. *Diascia* and dianthus are frost hardier than you might think. They can withstand temperatures to 0°F, so you might be able to use them as perennials in your garden. This verbena and *Calibrachoa* tolerate temperatures into the mid-teens if they are well established in the ground.

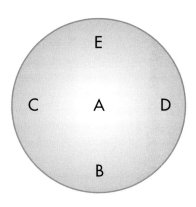

Planter on Right (p.162)
A = *Barleria* 'Amethyst Lights'
B = *Torenia* 'Summer Wave Amethyst'
C = *Diascia* 'Little Charmer'
D = *Sutera* 'Snowstorm' (bacopa)
E = *Nemesia* 'Compact Innocence'

Plant Personalities

Here's a beautiful example of color harmony in pink, reddish purple, and white. Because the planter is bigger than the one on the left and the plants are not as trailing as in the planter in the back, I chose a taller plant in the center to give it the necessary height. The center plant is *Barleria* 'Amethyst Lights', a beautiful, heat-loving plant with foliage in green, pink, and dark plum. It even makes two-tone pink flowers in late summer, but I usually use it for its exquisite foliage. The darkest shades of its leaves are echoed in *Torenia* 'Summer Wave Amethyst', another heat lover, this time with a trailing habit and light green foliage. The pink tinge of *Barleria* can also be found in *Diascia* 'Little Charmer', the same lovely plant as used in the planter on the left.

White flowers always look elegant and brighten the design. Here whites were used on two levels, once in an upright mounding plant, *Nemesia* 'Compact Innocence', and once as trailing component, *Sutera* 'Snowstorm'. *Nemesia* is a wonderful plant for container gardening due to its tidy habit and floriferous nature. It's especially great for a spot near the house, where you can enjoy its sweet fragrance. *Sutera* is one of the biggest container garden blockbusters of the last years. Its thousands of small, white flowers that appear in abundance from spring through fall have made it very popular. It's best known as bacopa, but its correct botanical name is *Sutera*.

Care Clues

The only plant that benefits considerably from deadheading is *Nemesia*. None of the others have any special care requirements. *Barleria* prefers warm temperatures, so it's best if you wait until temperatures warm up in spring before you plant this particular combination.

Plant Personalities

A pot as majestic as this one requires an equally impressive plant, which it found in *Pennisetum setaceum* 'Rubrum'. Purple fountain grass is perfect for large container gardens. It keeps its burgundy foliage all summer long, and its graceful foxtail flowers, which can be used as cut flowers, start out in a deep purple color but fade to soft beige as they mature. Purple fountain grass is a warm-season grass that thrives as the temperatures rise.

The second foliage accent is provided by *Vinca* 'Illumination', a yellow variegated vinca vine. Its slender branches cascade over the rim of the pot like liquid gold. It softens the dominance of the pot by visually breaking its color dominance. Since yellow is complementary to blue, it builds a stunning contrast.

This pot demonstrates that you don't need flowers for a stunning container garden. As a matter of fact, the beautiful foliage and the majestic container create a very elegant sight. This container garden is perfect for a front entrance or any place where you want to make an impression.

Container Characteristics

This container is so impressive that it doesn't need much color added. The focus is definitely on the container itself. At the same time it presents

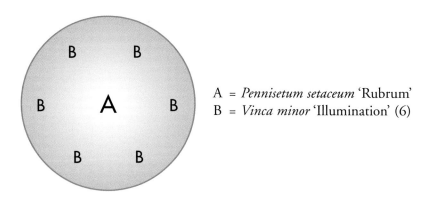

A = *Pennisetum setaceum* 'Rubrum'
B = *Vinca minor* 'Illumination' (6)

somewhat of a challenge because it is about three feet tall but has an opening for planting of only about eleven inches. That makes appropriate plant selection extremely important.

Care Clues

After placing the large purple fountain grass in the container—it was in an eight-inch pot when I planted it—there was hardly any room for other plants, so the extremely cascading vinca was an excellent choice. But when you buy vinca in four-inch pots, you often get multiple plants that you can carefully take apart and plant around the fountain grass. If you can't find four-inch pots with multiple plants, buy the smallest pots you can find and carefully remove enough potting mix so that you can fit the plants in.

If you live in an area that gets very little or no frost, you can plant the fountain grass in your garden in fall. Otherwise, use it as an annual. *Vinca* 'Illumination' is frost hardy to USDA Zone 4.

Plant Personalities

Bright, cheerful summer colors dominate this design for a sunny spot on your patio.

The plant in the center is *Erysimum* 'Variegatum', also known as variegated wallflower. I used it for its attractive foliage, but its lavender-purple flowers, which appear mainly in spring, are also quite nice. It gives the needed height in the basket without getting too tall. While its foliage color—a nice variegation in yellow and green—ties in with the orange flowers of *Osteospermum*, the lavender-purple flowers of *Erysimum* tie in with the purple flowers of the petunia, which brings the entire design together visually.

The two flowering plants are *Osteospermum* 'Orange Symphony' and *Petunia* 'Supertunia Mini Purple'. 'Orange Symphony' is a semi-trailing variety of *Osteospermum;* most varieties grow upright and would not fit into this particular spot. The 'Symphony' series is also more heat tolerant than some other varieties, which ensures a longer bloom time. In fact, in most climates they flower throughout the summer. As you can see in the picture, the flower color varies slightly based on the stage the flower is in. They open up bright orange, but mature to a softer shade over time, while their center always stays dark purple.

The second flowering plant is *Petunia* 'Supertunia Mini Purple', a trailing petunia that is excellent for hanging baskets. While some

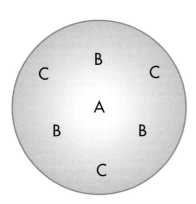

A = *Erysimum* 'Variegatum'
B = *Osteospermum* 'Orange Symphony' (3)
C = *Petunia* 'Supertunia Mini Purple' (3)

'Supertunia' are extremely cascading and can reach three feet or more in total length, the 'Mini' series is a bit more compact, which in this case looks better with the moderately trailing *Osteospermum*, creating a more symmetrical basket. 'Supertunia Mini Purple' has small, deep magenta flowers with dark eyes. Their color builds a strong contrast to the *Osteospermum* flowers.

Container Characteristics

I used moss baskets for most hanging baskets in this section because I like their looks as well as the plant performance in them, but since the plants in this design—the petunia in particular—are very trailing, they cover the basket quickly and leave no parts of it visible. For that reason, you could get away with using a lower-priced alternative. This design used a fourteen-inch moss basket. If you use a larger basket, adjust the number of plants accordingly. I advise against using a smaller moss basket because the plants grow quickly and have significant needs for water and fertilizer, which are easier to maintain in baskets of fourteen-inches or larger.

Care Clues

Deadhead the *Osteospermum* regularly for a more continuous flower show, and cut off spent *Erysimum* flowers after they stop blooming. The petunia doesn't require special care except that you need to make sure to provide an adequate supply of fertilizer, as it is considered a "heavy feeder."

Plant Personalities

Imagine this warm-colored, harvest-themed container garden on your patio. Make it a part of your autumn decoration and you will enjoy it well into the fall. All plants can tolerate a slight frost.

The tallest plant in the center adds subtle height. It's *Carex buchananii*, commonly called leatherleaf sedge. Its bronze, thin leaves are slightly curly at the top. They look and feel dry, even when they're fresh. Some people even go as far as to humorously call it "dead grass."

The other two foliage plants include mounding and trailing elements. *Salvia* 'Icterina' is a golden variegated sage. It has a compact, mounding habit, and its leaves are tremendous as a culinary herb. *Ajuga* 'Chocolate Chip' is a variety with a very low-growing, spreading habit. If placed along the edges of a container garden, as done here, it develops trailing growth as it gets bigger. 'Chocolate Chip' has very small, almost black leaves. In spring, it surprises with bright blue flower panicles.

There are two flowering components in the design. *Osteospermum* 'Cream Symphony' is a very compact variety with a semi-trailing growth habit. *Osteospermum* traditionally grows taller, so careful variety selection is important. The 'Symphony' series is also more heat tolerant and flowers longer, which is important if you want to use this container garden in late summer and fall. *Bracteantha* 'Bronze Orange' is partially hidden. It's an

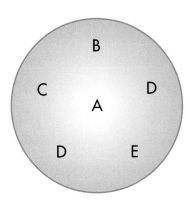

A = *Carex buchananii* (leatherleaf sedge)
B = *Bracteantha* 'Sundaze Bronze Orange'
C = *Osteospermum* 'Cream Symphony'
D = *Ajuga* 'Chocolate Chip' (2)
E = *Salvia* 'Icterina' (sage)

upright-growing strawflower with dark orange flowers. When this picture was taken, the plant was still small, but it grows taller until it reaches a mature height of twelve to fourteen inches.

Container Characteristics

This twelve-inch clay container has an attractive design that looks like a woven basket, which is a perfect fit for this harvest-themed design. Due to its porosity, you can see how it has started to age, which gives it more character. The porous material also provides for good air circulation, which improves plant performance.

Care Clues

Deadhead the *Osteospermum* and *Bracteantha* regularly to keep them looking tidy and to encourage continuous flower production. *Carex*, salvia, and ajuga can be treated as perennials. They are hardy to USDA Zone 6 (*Carex*), Zone 5 (salvia), and Zone 3 (ajuga).

Plant Personalities

I love this combination in pink and purple colors and the neutral stone
planter. Besides the color and texture composition, I adore the tall spikes
of flowers in the center.

The center plant is *Anisodontea* 'Elegant Lady'. Some gardeners consider this African mallow from South Africa to be too "wild" with its tall,
open growth habit, but I enjoy using it in container gardens. It provides
height and flowers without being overpowering. Besides, its pink flowers
with burgundy are charming and remind me of English cottage gardens. Its
pink flower color is echoed in *Dianthus* 'Devon Cottage Rosie Cheeks' to
the right. This dianthus variety's flowers reach two inches in diameter and
are delightfully fragrant. Its flower stems grow upright at first, but as the
bloom clusters begin to open, the stems cascade gracefully. Its foliage is elegantly silver. The dark veins of *Anisodontea* are echoed in the flowers of
Verbena 'Superbena Burgundy', which, if you look closely, you can see
peaking through from the back. The 'Superbena' series has large flower
clusters and a semi-upright growth habit. If you can't find this particular
variety, try to match the color because this design allows for both trailing
as well as upright plants. *Ageratum* 'Artist Alto Blue' builds the transition
from pink to purple tones with its warm purple flowers. It has a compact,
upright growth and better heat tolerance compared to some seed-grown
varieties. Finally, the last flowering variety is *Nemesia* 'Safari Plum', with
deep purple flowers accented by soft yellow centers. Although its color is

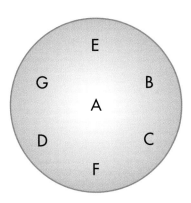

A = *Anisodontea* 'Elegant Lady'
B = *Dianthus* 'Devon Cottage Rosie Cheeks'
C = *Persicaria* 'Red Dragon'
D = *Nemesia* 'Safari Plum'
E = *Verbena* 'Superbena Burgundy'
F = *Ageratum* 'Artist Alto Blue'
G = *Calibrachoa* 'Million Bells Trailing Pink'

similar to its sister variety 'Blue Bird', 'Safari Plum' has larger flowers and a slightly more purple tone. But if you can't locate it, 'Blue Bird' would certainly be an appropriate substitution.

Persicaria 'Red Dragon' is an excellent texture plant that complements the colors of this design. Its burgundy leaves have silver accents. Although it produces small, round, creamy white flowers, they definitely play second fiddle to the beautiful foliage. Its sprawling growth provides mounding and semi-trailing elements.

Container Characteristics

This large stone container with a fourteen-inch diameter has a neutral color, which keeps the focus clearly on the plants. Its porous surface allows water to seep through, which gives it a different, darker color when it's wet and as it ages. Because of its porosity, it's also not as heavy as you might think.

Care Clues

Deadhead the verbena and dianthus regularly for more continuous bloom production. If the *Anisodontea* gets out of hand and becomes too tall for your taste, simply trim it back as desired. *Persicaria* can get quite vigorous. If it tries to take over, give it a liberal trim.

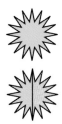

Plant Personalities

I chose to combine annuals and perennials for an unusual, texture-rich container garden. Each color is used several times, which visually connects the plants.

The plant that gives the design height is *Phormium*, also known as New Zealand flax. It's one of my favorite plants for container gardens because it adds subtle height and color. Unfortunately, availability is still somewhat limited, but nurseries realize its value and popularity and are starting to bring more varieties and higher quantities to the market. *Phormium* comes in many different colors. Make sure to look for one in red, purple, or pink tones to carry through the color theme.

The color of the *Phormium* is echoed in the stems and flowers of *Bergenia* 'Autumn Glory'. This hardy perennial has beautiful flowers in spring and early summer. The very large, fleshy, glossy leaves are deep green during warm weather but turn to an attractive bronze in fall when the temperatures drop. Even after the flowers are gone, this is a beautiful plant.

Lotus vine is an excellent texture plant with its fine, silver foliage that reminds of pine needles, just much shorter. Although used for its foliage, 'Amazon Sunset' produces flaming orange flowers in early spring that last for as long as the night temperatures are cool. In this design, I used it for its foliage and accepted the flowers as a welcome bonus in spring.

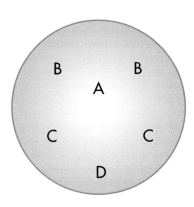

A = *Phormium* (New Zealand flax)
B = *Bergenia* 'Autumn Glory' (2)
C = *Lotus* 'Amazon Sunset' (2)
D = *Heuchera* 'Amethyst Myst'

The silver color of lotus is echoed in *Heuchera* 'Amethyst Myst'. This is another plant that I used for its foliage, but it produces whitish flowers on long stems in summer. The flowers are a lot subtler than those of lotus are. 'Amethyst Myst' also echoes the color of *Phormium* and *Bergenia* in the undersides of its leaves.

Container Characteristics

This stone planter completes the cool color theme with its neutral gray. While many stone planters are quite heavy, this one is more porous, which reduces its weight. It also allows for water and nutrients to seep through, which gives it a beautiful, aged look. This particular planter has an inside diameter of twelve inches.

Care Clues

Cut off the spent flowers of *Bergenia* to keep it blooming for as long as possible and to keep it looking neat. If you find the flowers of *Heuchera* distracting, you may cut them as soon as they appear and can use them in flower arrangements. *Bergenia* and *Heuchera* are frost hardy to USDA Zone 4. At the end of the season, you can take the plants apart carefully and plant the perennials in the garden.

Plant Personalities

This basket is very rich in texture, which is true in part because the moss of the basket itself was incorporated into the design. While most baskets in this book were planted so that they eventually cover the moss, this one was intentionally planted so that some of the moss is always visible.

The main color theme is purple, with three different purple plants in the top part of the basket. The flowering variety is *Heliotropium* 'Atlantis', a compact heliotrope with deep purple flowers and a sweet vanilla scent. Its foliage is dark green, which goes nicely with the other dark foliage in the basket. Right next to heliotrope in the center is *Coleus* 'Dark Star', a compact-growing variety that is perfect for hanging baskets, whereas many other coleus varieties would get too tall. Its dark mahogany, almost black, leaves look good next to the rich flowers of heliotrope and echo some of their deepest tones. Both the coleus and the heliotrope have a compact upright habit. Finally, the last of the more upright plants on the top is *Salvia* 'Purpurascens', a purple-leaved ornamental form of sage that has not only beautiful foliage, but also an aromatic fragrance. Its leaves can even be used in cooking. 'Purpurascens' has a mounding growth habit and will eventually drape over the edges slightly. It can also be found labeled as purple sage.

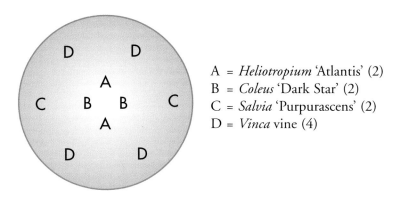

A = *Heliotropium* 'Atlantis' (2)
B = *Coleus* 'Dark Star' (2)
C = *Salvia* 'Purpurascens' (2)
D = *Vinca* vine (4)

The trailing foliage element is variegated vinca vine, which is an excellent hanging basket plant. Its strictly trailing habit cascades over the edges for several feet. With its light-colored foliage in silver-green and white, it brightens the design and provides a welcome contrast to the otherwise rich, dark colors.

Container Characteristics

Part of the character of this design comes from the moss basket. Its natural look adds a rustic character and texture to the design. Plant performance is also excellent in moss baskets because the natural fibers allow for good air circulation. Their only downside is that the potting mix dries out faster than in plastic pots, which can be a problem in hot weather and once the plants are big. Some moss baskets come with a water reservoir in the bottom, which slows the water loss. In this design, I used a sixteen-inch basket. If you use smaller or larger baskets, adjust the number of plants accordingly.

Care Clues

This is a very low-maintenance design. Deadhead the heliotrope regularly to ensure continuous bloom, but none of the other plants need special care. If the vinca vine gets too long, you may trim it back liberally. All of the plants used here like warm temperatures, so don't plant this combination too early in the year.

Plant Personalities

Here is a seasonal specialty container for those of you who are lucky to live in a frost-free climate. It's a way to enjoy the holiday season with a festive container garden in patriotic colors.

Start with a bright red poinsettia, such as 'Orion Red' or any other bright red variety that you like. Depending on your container size, use, for example, a good-sized poinsettia in an eight-inch pot and three four-inch plants of each of the other varieties. The poinsettia won't grow any more once it is planted; that's why it's important that you start with a good-sized poinsettia so that you can keep the holiday red as the dominant color.

For the patriotic holiday theme, use deep blue, trailing *Petunia* 'Supertunia Royal Velvet'. Be careful if you make substitutions, as not all petunias flower in the winter. Many petunias need longer days to bloom, but the majority of the 'Supertunia' line was selected for its ability to bloom even when the days are short. Another plus is that 'Royal Velvet' has a full, almost mounding growth, which is perfect for its particular place in the container.

The pure white flowers of *Verbena* 'Tukana White' complete the patriotic theme. As with petunias, not all verbenas flower during the short days of the year, but the 'Tukana' series does. Its large flower clusters and ferny foliage provide a trailing element.

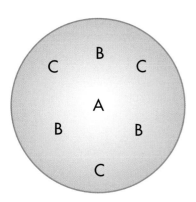

A = Poinsettia
B = *Petunia* 'Supertunia Royal Velvet' (3)
C = *Verbena* 'Tukana White' (3)

Container Characteristics

This sixteen-inch stone planter look-alike is made of plastic, which makes it very easy to handle and durable. Its casual design keeps the focus on the plants, and the trailing plants show very little of the container, so you can get away with using a lower-budget container.

Care Clues

Clearly, this is a regional, seasonal item. It is designed for frost-free climates, where it can be placed on a patio or at the front entrance. Expect it to last for about as long as you expect your indoor poinsettias to last. After that, you can plant the petunias and verbenas in the garden and enjoy them throughout the following seasons.

Plant Personalities

If you're looking for a monochromatic container garden, you might like this cheery one in yellow. By using yellow not only in flowers but also in foliage, it gets more texture and interest. Monochromatic designs are great if you want to create a uniform look on your patio or complement the color of your patio furniture or house.

Argyranthemum 'Butterfly', a marguerite daisy, dominates this design. It's a very heat-tolerant selection with large flowers and is used for height in the center. Other flowering varieties are *Bidens* 'Peter's Gold Carpet', which has fragrant, five-petaled flowers; *Calibrachoa* 'Million Bells Terra Cotta', which is barely visible here but has a more earthy tone than its companions; and *Osteospermum* 'Lemon Symphony', a mounding, heat-tolerant daisy.

Lamium 'Golden Anniversary' and fiber-optic grass are the foliage components. This *Lamium* (also known as deadnettle) has a very compact, self-branching habit and beautifully variegated foliage in yellow and green. If you can't locate this variety and wish to substitute, make sure that you use a selection with yellow variegation rather than white or silver so you can preserve the color scheme. The second foliage element, fiber-optic grass, got its name from its iridescent, hairlike leaves that are capped with small flower spikes, giving it the appearance of fiber optics. Botanically speaking, it's not a grass but belongs to the rush family, but it's known and handled as an ornamental grass. It is great for container gardens where it

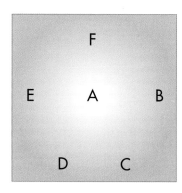

A = *Argyranthemum* 'Butterfly'
B = *Osteospermum* 'Lemon Symphony'
C = *Lamium* 'Golden Anniversary'
D = *Bidens* 'Peter's Gold Carpet'
E = *Scirpus cernuus* (fiber-optic grass)
F = *Calibrachoa* 'Million Bells Terra Cotta'

can cascade over the edges. Botanists still disagree about the correct scientific name. You can find fiber-optic grass in stores under the botanical names *Eleocharis cernuus*, *Scirpus cernuus*, *Isolepis cernua*, and possibly others.

Container Characteristics

To stay with the warm color scheme but provide a contrasting backdrop at the same time, I chose a dark brown glazed container; its inner dimensions are ten inches square. If you use larger or smaller containers, adjust the number of plants accordingly.

Care Clues

To assure continuous blooms, deadhead the *Argyranthemum* and *Osteospermum* regularly. It also results in a tidier look. None of the other plants needs any special care. If *Bidens* gets too big, cut it back liberally.

Plant Personalities

Even though some of the plants in this container garden produce flowers eventually, I selected all of them for their foliage. The dark purple leaves really jump out visually when underplanted with yellow. This foliage combo for a shady spot uses annuals and perennials together.

The most dominant dark-colored foliage plant is *Heuchera* 'Amethyst Myst'. Its dark purple leaves are overlaid with silver. It also produces small, soft pink flowers that are displayed on long spikes, but they play second fiddle to the stunning leaves. The second dark-colored foliage plant is *Ajuga* 'Mahogany' with its almost black leaves. Its low-growing habit looks its best along the edges of the container. In spring and early summer, ajuga produces bright blue bloom whorls that also look stunning with the yellow foliage of the companion plants.

Yellow foliage builds a striking contrast to the dark plants. The only annual is *Lysimachia* 'Outback Sunset', a great container garden plant for the shade. It has gold and green variegated foliage and develops deep golden yellow flower clusters. It's a good trailer, so it should always go around the edges of containers. In the front center of the picture is *Saxifraga* 'Harvest Moon'. Its round leaves curl slightly, and it develops small plantlets on long, trailing stems as it gets more mature. It's also best used along the edges, where the plantlets can trail over the rim. Although not visible, I used a third trailing plant with yellow foliage. It's *Lysimachia* 'Goldilocks', which has small, round, glossy golden foliage and very trail-

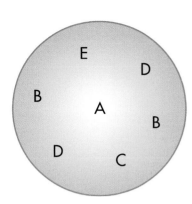

A = *Heuchera* 'Amethyst Myst'
B = *Lysimachia* 'Outback Sunset' (2)
C = *Saxifraga* 'Harvest Moon'
D = *Ajuga* 'Mahogany' (2)
E = *Lysimachia* 'Goldilocks' (not visible)

ing growth. Both 'Goldilocks' and 'Outback Sunset' come from the *Lysimachia* genus, but they belong to different species and look quite different. That means that even though the names are similar, the effects that both achieve are different.

Container Characteristics

Stone planters like this one have a beautiful, rustic look. Their color turns darker when they are wet. They also age beautifully—the older they get, the more interesting they become. You can even see part of the aged look in the front of the picture. They are not as heavy as they look, which makes them fairly easy to handle. This shallow bowl with a fifteen-inch diameter looks particularly good with these specific plants. It keeps the eye focused on the plants while its color fits well with the color scheme of the plants.

Care Clues

None of the plants in this design need any pruning or other special care. With exception of *Lysimachia* 'Outback Sunset', all plants are perennials and can be planted in a partially shady perennial bed at the end of the season.

Plant Personalities

Purple flowers and foliage compose the theme of this design. In order to get several different plants into this small planter, I used smaller plants and removed part of the potting mix. You can also use well-developed plants and a larger pot.

The most visible flowering plant is *Nemesia* 'Blue Bird'. Its clusters of blue flowers are accented by creamy yellow centers. It's a quite heat-tolerant selection with a compact, mounding growth habit that's perfect for such a relatively small planter. The pink flowers belong to *Calibrachoa* 'Million Bells Trailing Pink'. Its miniature petunia-like flowers are vibrant pink with yellow centers. Its growth habit is very trailing and will eventually cascade over the edges of the pot. In the front is *Scaevola* 'New Wonder', also known as fan flower. Although it wasn't in full bloom yet when the picture was taken, it develops sizeable flower clusters with lovely, fan-shaped flowers. *Scaevola* is a true heat lover and is excellent for mixed containers due to its trailing growth. The fourth flowering plant is not visible. It's *Lobelia* 'Laguna Pink', which builds a dense tuft of blush pink flowers with dark pink veins.

Strobilanthes, also known as Persian shield, is an excellent foliage plant for mixed containers. Its purple foliage has a metallic sheen. Although it can get three to four feet tall in the landscape in warm climates, it stays shorter in container plantings. It's definitely a heat lover, so you won't want to plant it too early in spring. A second foliage plant is *Ipomoea* 'Blackie',

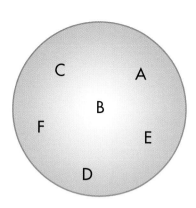

A = *Strobilanthes* 'Persian Shield'
B = *Nemesia* 'Blue Bird'
C = *Lobelia* 'Laguna Pink' (not visible)
D = *Scaevola* 'New Wonder'
E = *Calibrachoa* 'Million Bells Trailing Pink'
F = *Ipomoea* 'Blackie' (sweet potato)

an ornamental sweet potato with dark purple—almost black—deeply lobed leaves. Its dark foliage color echoes that of *Strobilanthes*, and, like *Strobilanthes*, it thrives under warm temperatures. Once it gets bigger, it will cascade over the edge of the planter.

Container Characteristics

This stone planter with a ten-inch diameter has a porous surface, which allows water to seep through. This causes the planter to age over time, which adds to its character. Because of its porosity, it is not as heavy as many other stone planters. Overall, these types of stone planters are great choices for medium-budget container gardens.

Care Clues

This is a low-maintenance design. None of the plants require pruning or deadheading. Once the temperatures rise, the sweet potato might grow more vigorously than the other plants. If this becomes the case, simply trim it back.

Plant Personalities

Cheerful spring colors like these brighten any sunny spot on your patio.
This hanging basket uses only flowering plants to create a colorful impact.

The center plant is *Nemesia* 'Blue Bird', with its vibrant blue flowers.
Its compact, semi-upright growth habit is perfect for the center of hanging
baskets, where you'll want to look for plants that don't get too tall. 'Blue
Bird' has large flowers dotted with yellow centers and a faint fragrance.

The yellow flowers of *Osteospermum* 'Lemon Symphony' complement
the blue color of the *Nemesia*. 'Lemon Symphony' is a semi-trailing variety
of *Osteospermum*, while most varieties grow upright and would not fit into
this particular spot. The 'Symphony' series is more heat tolerant than some
other varieties, which ensures a longer bloom time. In fact, in most climates they flower throughout the summer. Its cheerful yellow blooms
dominate this design and make it so lively.

The third plant is *Pelargonium* 'White Blizzard', a trailing ivy geranium that withstands heat and sun quite well. Dark reddish purple veins
accent its white flowers. White flowers can be used in almost any design to
brighten its overall appearance.

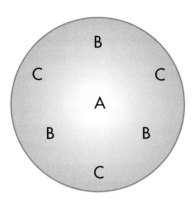

A = *Nemesia* 'Blue Bird'
B = *Osteospermum* 'Lemon Symphony' (3)
C = *Pelargonium* 'White Blizzard' (3)

Container Characteristics

Moss baskets are my personal favorites when it comes to planting hanging baskets. I just love their natural look. Even when your plants have not covered the entire basket yet and you can see part of the moss, it's beautiful. Their downside is that they dry out fast once the temperatures rise, so you'll have to make sure that you water them frequently. Don't be surprised if you have to water them daily during hot summer months. Some moss baskets are available with built-in water reservoirs. The reservoirs are not visible once the basket is planted, and they help keep them moist longer. This particular basket is fourteen inches in diameter.

Care Clues

To ensure continuous blooms, deadhead the *Osteospermum* and *Pelargonium* regularly. *Nemesia* also benefits slightly from deadheading, although it's not required. Overall, this is a fairly low-maintenance design.

Plant Personalities

Here's a classic combination in red, white, and blue that looks great not only for Memorial Day and Independence Day, but any time of the year. All varieties in this design start flowering early in the year, so you can start this planter as soon as the weather is frost free.

To give the design height, I started with a marguerite daisy in the center, *Argyranthemum* 'Summer Angel'. Its pure white flowers with bright yellow centers range from single to semi-double petals. Its fine, silvery foliage adds elegance and texture. If you can't find this particular variety, look for a fairly tall-growing, white variety.

I added two shades of blue, although only one is visible. The one hidden behind the daisy is *Nemesia* 'Blue Bird', a medium purple-blue with a mounding growth habit. The more prominent blue in the front is *Petunia* 'Supertunia Royal Velvet'. It has very rich, deep blue flowers and a trailing habit, which is just right for the edge of the planter. Its flowers look and feel like velvet, and it starts blooming early in the year.

Two verbena varieties add more trailing elements. 'Babylon White' to the right repeats the pure white flower color of the *Argyranthemum* on the lower trailing level with its brilliant white flower clusters. 'Babylon Red' from the same series represents the red element in our patriotic design. Its vibrant red flower clusters are very vigorous and cascading.

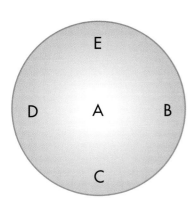

A = *Argyranthemum* 'Summer Angel'
B = *Verbena* 'Babylon White'
C = *Petunia* 'Supertunia Royal Velvet'
D = *Verbena* 'Babylon Red'
E = *Nemesia* 'Blue Bird' (not visible)

Container Characteristics

Because the plants in this design are so trailing, they cover the majority of the planter quite quickly. I chose a clay look-alike made of plastic. Although not quite as attractive as real clay, it was less expensive, which is acceptable since it's mostly hidden. Plastic containers are also more light-weight and chip resistant compared to clay. This particular planter had an inside diameter of twelve inches.

Care Clues

Although not necessary, deadheading the marguerite daisy and verbena regularly encourages more profuse flower production. None of the other plants need any special care, but all of them are heavy feeders, which means you have to ensure an adequate fertilizer supply.

Plant Personalities

This lush, tropical design in earthy colors is perfect for a sunny patio in summer.

Phormium, also called New Zealand flax, provides height and color. It's one of my favorites to use in mixed containers because it grows tall but is not overpowering. Its availability used to be—and still might be in some areas—limited, but nurseries are beginning to realize its value and versatility, and it's becoming easier to find. There are many different varieties available, so look for one that has reddish colors. *Phormium* grows slowly, so start with a well-developed plant in a larger pot than the other plants so that it doesn't get outgrown.

The colors of *Phormium* are echoed in *Coleus* 'Sky Fire', which visually connects the two plants. Coleus is one of the best foliage plants for container gardens, and it's experiencing a renaissance with more and more colorful varieties coming to the market. Many of today's coleus varieties are sun tolerant, with 'Sky Fire' being just one example. Its red and maroon leaves have thin, lime-green margins, which reflect the color of the third plant in the design, *Ipomoea* 'Terrace Lime'.

Ipomoea 'Terrace Lime' is an ornamental sweet potato with chartreuse leaves. Like the other plants in this design, it loves warm temperatures and can get quite vigorous in summer. Its trailing habit is ideal for the edges of planters. A variety that is very similar to 'Terrace Lime' is 'Margarita', which you may use instead.

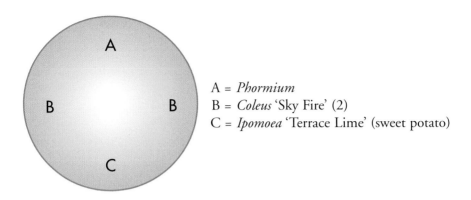

A = *Phormium*
B = *Coleus* 'Sky Fire' (2)
C = *Ipomoea* 'Terrace Lime' (sweet potato)

Container Characteristics

To emphasize the earthy tones of the plants, I used a simple terra cotta pot. This particular one has an inside diameter of twelve inches. It's decorated around the rim, which is partially hidden by the *Ipomoea*, but visible around the rest of the pot.

Care Clues

Since this design doesn't use any flowers, there's nothing that you have to deadhead. If the coleus or *Ipomoea* ever get too big, simply trim them back. All of the plants in this design are heat lovers, so make sure that you don't plant this combination too early in spring.

Plant Personalities

A tall urn like this is excellent for a prominent spot, such as the front entrance. It uses a variety of different plant heights and growth habits to create a dramatic impact with colors. Its cool, purple color theme complements the color theme of this front entrance.

The container garden gets height through the use of an ornamental grass in the center. This particular variety is *Pennisetum setaceum* 'Rubrum', also called purple fountain grass. It provides height without being overpowering because of its airy, see-through structure. For a container of this size, you should definitely use 'Rubrum' rather than the dwarf form of purple fountain grass.

The purple foliage of the fountain grass is echoed in 'African Blue' basil, an ornamental but edible form of basil. As if its purple-black foliage wasn't beautiful enough, it produces lavender pink flowers in summer that are true hummingbird magnets. It shows you how beautiful herbs can get if you decide not to cut them. Basil is a warm-season herb whose growth stalls during cool conditions. Therefore it's best if you don't plant this container garden too early, but wait until the temperatures have warmed.

Another foliage accent is 'Tricolor' sage in the front left. Its multicolored leaves in gray-green, white, and pink echo several of the colors used in this design. Its mounding habit builds a nice transition from upright plants to trailing plants. Finally, although hard to see, an English ivy on the right adds a trailing foliage element with green and white variegated leaves.

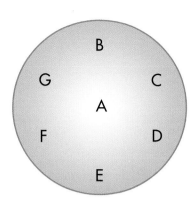

A = *Pennisetum setaceum* 'Rubrum'
B = *Ocimum basilicum* 'African Blue' (basil)
C = *Nemesia* 'Blue Bird'
D = *Hedera* 'Glacier' (English ivy)
E = *Petunia* 'Supertunia Mini Blue Veined'
F = *Salvia* 'Tricolor' (sage)
G = *Verbena* 'Babylon Purple'

Besides the basil, there are three flowering plants evenly distributed throughout the design. A second mounding element is *Nemesia* 'Blue Bird', a profuse bloomer with purple-blue flowers. The two trailing flowering components are *Verbena* 'Babylon Purple', a low-growing variety with ferny leaves and dark purple flower clusters, and *Petunia* 'Supertunia Mini Blue Veined', a trailing petunia with white flowers accented with dark blue veins that echo the color of the verbena flowers.

Container Characteristics

Although this elegant urn looks like it's made of stone or clay, it's actually made of plastic. That makes it easy to move and very chip resistant. If you use one that is hollow all the way to the bottom, as this one was, it is especially important that it has drainage holes; otherwise, you could accumulate a foot of standing water in the bottom, a breading ground for fungi and bacteria. If your urn doesn't come with pre-drilled drainage holes, drill some yourself—another advantage of using plastic containers versus clay. This urn had a sixteen-inch diameter. For different sized urns, adjust the number of plants accordingly.

Care Clues

You can use the foxtail flower plumes of purple fountain grass as cut flowers or discard them when they mature if you don't like their light beige color in the mature state. You can snip the basil leaves and use them in cooking. Besides that, you might want to deadhead the verbena regularly to assure continuous reblooming. Other than that, this container garden requires little maintenance.

Plant Personalities

A simple, but effective design that uses one flowering plant in the center surrounded by foliage plants.

The focal point is *Bracteantha* 'Sundaze Golden Yellow'. It's an upright-growing strawflower with rich, golden yellow flowers. Strawflowers are excellent as fresh or dried cut flowers. In fact, even when the flowers are fresh, they are crinkly and feel like paper—people usually can't resist touching them. The color of the flowers sets the warm-toned theme, which looks great for summer and fall patios.

All of the other plants are foliage plants. The tallest one in the back is *Carex buchananii*, also called leatherleaf sedge. Although botanists don't consider sedges to be "grasses," we commonly handle them as ornamental grasses. This variety has tall, upright growing leaves with curlicue tips. The thin leaves are bronze and look very dry, even when they are fresh. As a mounding foliage accent I chose *Salvia* 'Icterina', commonly known as golden sage. With its golden yellow and green variegated leaves, it continues the warm-colored theme.

There are two trailing foliage elements, *Lamium* 'White Nancy' and *Lysimachia* 'Goldilocks'. This *Lamium* variety has green and white variegated foliage and a cascading habit. The reason why the foliage has a reddish tinge in this picture is because the picture was taken in early spring, when the cold temperatures turned the leaves reddish. In order to make the warm color theme more prominent, you could use a yellow and green vari-

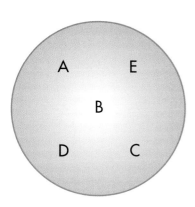

A = *Carex buchananii* (leatherleaf sedge)
B = *Bracteantha* 'Sundaze Golden Yellow'
C = *Salvia* 'Icterina' (sage)
D = *Lamium* 'White Nancy'
E = *Lysimachia* 'Goldilocks' (not visible)

ety instead, such as 'Golden Anniversary'. The second trailing plant is not visible. It's *Lysimachia* 'Goldilocks' with small, round, glossy golden leaves that echo the color of the strawflowers.

Container Characteristics

This design is planted in a slightly ornate, twelve-inch diameter plastic container. The advantage is that plastic containers are lightweight and chip resistant. Because only two of the plants are trailing and a good portion of the container is visible, it would also look very attractive in a more ornate clay container.

Care Clues

Deadhead the strawflower regularly to keep it looking neat and to keep the flowers coming in abundance. Spent strawflowers turn brown and unsightly. The other four plants can be planted in the perennial garden at the end of the season. Sage, *Lamium*, and *Lysimachia* are hardy to USDA Zone 5, and *Carex* to Zone 6. Sage leaves can be used as culinary herb, making it practical as well as decorative.

Plant Personalities

The scarlet red geranium flowers are the eye-catchers of this warm-colored design with flowering and foliage plants.

Pennisetum setaceum 'Rubrum', also know as purple fountain grass, adds height in the center. This ornamental grass is excellent for mixed containers because it is tall but airy and doesn't overpower the other plants. Purple fountain grass is one of the most popular ornamental grasses for container gardens, so you should have no problems finding it at your retailer.

On the next level are medium-height plants with *Pelargonium* 'Fireworks Scarlet'. This fancy-leafed geranium has star-shaped flowers in scarlet red and gingko-shaped leaves with dark zoning. The vibrant blooms are truly the attraction of this design. Just slightly shorter are the yellow flowering varieties. *Osteospermum* 'Lemon Symphony' is in the front. It has lemon-yellow flowers and a mounding growth habit, whereas many *Osteospermum* grow more upright. Once it gets bigger, it'll cascade over the rims of the pot. It also has great heat tolerance. The second yellow flowering variety is barely visible. It's *Bidens* 'Peter's Gold Carpet' with small, five-petaled flowers that have a sweet, honeylike scent. It is one of the more compact *Bidens* varieties on the market and a popular choice for mixed containers. Some *Bidens* varieties can get quite big and try to outgrow other plants, so beware. If you can't find this particular variety, 'Goldie' is a good substitute.

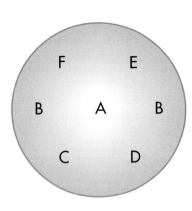

A = *Pennisetum setaceum* 'Rubrum'
B = *Pelargonium* 'Fireworks Scarlet' (2)
C = *Muehlenbeckia* (creeping wirevine)
D = *Osteospermum* 'Lemon Symphony'
E = *Hedera* 'Yellow Ripple' (English ivy)
    (barely visible)
F = *Bidens* 'Peter's Gold Carpet'

Two foliage plants add texture to the design. *Muehlenbeckia*, also known as creeping wirevine, is one of my favorite plants for mixed containers because it has a wiry growth that weaves between the other plants. Its small, emerald green leaves are round and shiny. The second foliage plant is a true classic. This English ivy variety, 'Yellow Ripple', has yellow and green variegated leaves that carry on the color theme. If you can't find it, look for one of the many ivy varieties with yellow variegation.

Container Characteristics

A planter can't get much more classic than this simple but elegant terra cotta pot. It's a natural for this plant design. Due to its porous sides, water evaporation and air circulation are possible, which can improve plant performance, but it will dry out more quickly than a glazed pot would. This pot is fifteen inches in diameter and accommodates the grass in a five-inch pot and six plants in four-inch pots, with room to grow.

Care Clues

Deadhead the *Pelargonium* and *Osteospermum* regularly for more profuse bloom production. Other than that, this is a fairly low-maintenance design. You can use the flowers of purple fountain grass in flower arrangements.

Plant Personalities

I designed this mixed basket to be hanging at or above eye level. That's why I didn't use any upright or mounding plants, only trailing varieties. The color theme in pink, blue, and white is an upbeat color choice that's ideal for summer.

The dominant, white flower is *Petunia* 'Supertunia Mini White'. It differs from the regular 'Supertunia' series in its smaller flower size and slightly more compact habit. Where 'Supertunia' can trail up to three feet or more, 'Mini' doesn't get quite as long, which allows the other plants in the basket to keep up. 'Supertunia Mini White' has pure white flowers that flower from early spring until fall.

The second flowering plant in this basket is *Monopsis* 'Royal Flush', a fairly new discovery. It has rich blue flowers that are intriguingly shaped. Its growth habit is strictly trailing with almost no upright growth at all, which makes it an excellent candidate for hanging baskets. It's a bit late to flower in spring, so don't lose your patience, but its delicate foliage is also quite nice. Its deep blue color builds a nice contrast to the pure white petunia flowers. If you can't find this variety in the store, substitute with a trailing blue *Calibrachoa*, which has a very similar growth habit and similar color.

Finally, we have *Diascia* 'Red Ace' as the third element. Compared to many other *Diascia*, 'Red Ace' is more trailing and more vigorous. I chose these traits so that it would complement the growth habit of the other two

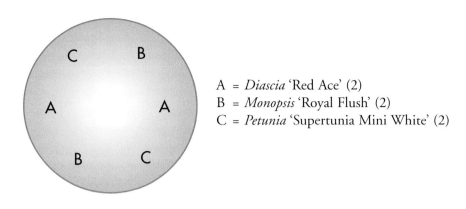

A = *Diascia* 'Red Ace' (2)
B = *Monopsis* 'Royal Flush' (2)
C = *Petunia* 'Supertunia Mini White' (2)

plants used and so that it could keep up with the vigor of the other varieties. If you use less-vigorous *Diascia* varieties, increase the number of *Diascia* in relation to the other plants—especially the 'Supertunia'—so that the *Diascia* doesn't get overpowered and outgrown by its companions.

Container Characteristics

All of the varieties used are very trailing and covered the basket quickly. I used a fourteen-inch moss basket because I like the look and the plant performance in it. But since the basket isn't visible for very long, you could use a lower-priced alternative with little lost in aesthetics. If you use larger or smaller baskets, adjust the number of plant accordingly.

Care Clues

Space the plants close enough together so that there is no hole in the center of the container. This is a very low-maintenance design that doesn't require any deadheading or special care. Just make sure that you fertilize these heavy feeders regularly.

Plant Personalities

This design in pink and purple tones uses primarily foliage plants, with a few flowering plants as accents. It's rich in texture due to the heavy use of foliage.

There are two rex begonias in the design. Both are from the 'Great American Cities' series, but there are many different varieties available today, and you may substitute some with similar colors. They need warm temperatures because temperatures below 45°F halt growth and temperatures below 40°F cause damage. In hot, dry climates, shade is important. Because they grow more slowly than the other varieties in the design, use begonias in five- or six-inch pots and the remainder of the plants in four-inch pots.

The other foliage plant in purple shades—echoing the colors of the begonias—is an ornamental sweet potato, *Ipomoea* 'Blackie'. Its deeply lobed leaves add to the texture of the design. It's a heat lover and can get quite vigorous once it's warm. There's also a foliage plant in silver, *Helichrysum* 'Petite Licorice'. This fine-textured plant has leaves that are velvety to the touch. Its silver color echoes one of the colors found in the begonias.

Fuchsia 'Sun Ray' was used for its flowers as well as for its foliage. It's an unusual variety with a semi-upright growth habit. Its leaves are white and silver-green variegated with pink veins. The flowers have bright pink sepals and purple corollas, which again echo the begonias' colors. Finally, *Diascia* 'Strawberry Sundae' is a pure flower accent. The medium pink flowers sit atop compact, mounding foliage.

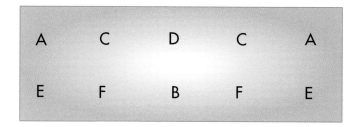

A = *Begonia rex* 'Houston Fiesta' (2)
B = *Begonia rex* 'Albuquerque Midnight Sky'
C = *Fuchsia* 'Sun Ray' (2)
D = *Ipomoea* 'Blackie' (sweet potato)
E = *Helichrysum* 'Petite Licorice' (2)
F = *Diascia* 'Little Charmer' (2)

Container Characteristics

What looks like a stone planter is actually made of plastic, so it's light-weight and resistant to chipping. Its gray color goes well with this particular plant selection. This window box is nine-by-twenty-nine inches. If it doesn't have drainage holes, drill some yourself before you plant it.

Care Clues

This is a very low-maintenance design. If the sweet potato gets too big during the heat of the summer, simply trim it back.

Plant Personalities

Here is a colorful combination that uses an abundance of flowering plants with a few foliage accents.

In the center is *Osteospermum* 'Lemon Symphony', a compact variety with good heat tolerance. Because of this location in the design, you could also use a taller variety, but make sure you use one that flowers throughout the summer. Its color is echoed in *Lysimachia* 'Goldilocks', a trailing foliage plant that spills over the edges of the barrel to the left. Its small, glossy golden leaves are popular for container gardens.

Pink and red tones are represented in *Calibrachoa* 'Million Bells Cherry Pink' and *Diascia* 'Strawberry Sundae'. *Calibrachoa* has miniature petunia-like flowers and trailing growth habit. With its hundreds of flowers, it builds a waterfall of color. This particular variety has reddish pink flowers with yellow eyes. *Diascia* 'Strawberry Sundae' is barely visible. Only one flower peeks out from the back. It has medium-pink blooms and grows semi-trailing.

There are two blue plants, but only one is visible. *Nemesia* 'Blue Bird' has bright blue flowers with yellow centers. It grows upright, but when planted along the edges like it is here, it drapes over the sides. *Scaevola* 'New Wonder' is hidden. Also known as fan flower, it cascades over the sides of the planter.

White flowers and silver foliage accent the plant composition. *Nemesia* 'Compact Innocence' has fragrant white flowers with yellow eyes and a

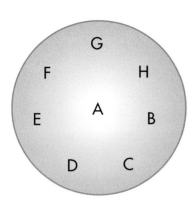

A = *Osteospermum* 'Lemon Symphony'
B = *Nemesia* 'Compact Innocence'
C = *Calibrachoa* 'Million Bells Cherry Pink'
D = *Santolina* (lavender cotton)
E = *Nemesia* 'Blue Bird'
F = *Lysimachia* 'Goldilocks'
G = *Diascia* 'Strawberry Sundae'
H = *Scaevola* 'New Wonder'

similar growth habit as 'Blue Bird'. *Santolina,* commonly called lavender cotton, is a Mediterranean native with very fine, fragrant, silver foliage. Its cushionlike growth habit is noninvasive.

Container Characteristics

An old barrel is getting a second chance as rustic planter. Wooden barrels like this make charming planters. If you recycle an old barrel, make sure that it hadn't been treated with chemicals that could be harmful to the plants. You can also buy new barrels that were made specifically as planters and have not been treated. This barrel is about two feet in diameter and was planted with large plants.

Care Clues

Containers of this size get heavy once they're planted. It's best if you plant it in its final spot. Deadhead the *Osteospermum* regularly to keep it looking neat and to encourage continuous bloom production. None of the other plants require special care, but most of them are heavy feeders, so make sure that you fertilize regularly.

Plant Personalities

Although I always say that you don't need to use a symmetrical planting pattern, that doesn't mean that using one couldn't result in a beautiful container garden—this example proves it.

This window box is perfect for the fall, not only because of its warm harvest colors, but also because that's when *Ajania* blooms naturally. If you can't find the variety 'Bea' at your garden retailer, feel free to substitute a similar variety. *Ajania* is sometimes still sold under its previous name, *Chrysanthemum pacificum*. If you still can't find it or want to grow this container earlier in the year, you might want to substitute *Chrysocephalum* 'Baby Gold' (see plant profiles section, page 59), which also has small, button-shaped flowers.

The other flowering plant here is *Bracteantha* 'Sundaze White', a strawflower. Its pure white, papery petals brighten the arrangement, while the rich golden centers echo the color of the *Ajania*.

Plants selected for their foliage frame the flowering varieties. The ornamental grass in the background is Mexican feather grass, botanically known as *Stipa* or *Nassella*. It has needle-thin leaves that sway in the slightest breeze, providing movement to the container garden. In summer, it produces beige flowers that complement the other plants in the planter very well. Finally, *Lysimachia* brings in a trailing element with its small, round, lush golden yellow leaves.

A = *Stipa tenuissima* (Mexican feather grass) (3)
B = *Ajania* 'Bea' (2)
C = *Bracteantha* 'Sundaze White' (2)
D = *Lysimachia* 'Goldilocks' (3)

Container Characteristics

The warm glow of this redwood window box complements the harvest-colored plant selections. It's attractive enough that you'll want to see part of it instead of having it covered by plants completely. Its dimensions are eight by twenty-seven inches. For larger or smaller containers, adjust the number of plants accordingly.

Care Clues

Strawflowers bloom more continuously if you deadhead them regularly. Cut of spent flowers of *Ajania*, as they become unsightly. Other than that, this window box is fairly carefree. Although the Mexican feather grass looks its best under cooler temperatures, its golden hot-weather foliage also looks very charming with its companions.

Plant Personalities

This friendly design in pastel colors utilizes the brilliant colors and trailing habit of verbena.

In the center of the basket is *Chrysocephalum* 'Baby Gold', a great filler plan with small, golden, button-shaped flowers. It has a very open, unobtrusive habit, which makes it a great container garden plant. As a bonus, its silver leaves and stems are velvety to the touch. In this design, it adds just enough height and color specks without taking the attention away from the verbena varieties. Sometimes you can still find *Chrysocephalum* under its previous botanical name, *Helichrysum* 'Baby Gold'.

Verbenas are a great choice for hanging baskets if you choose the trailing kind. They are easy to care for and have tremendous flower power. This design in pink and lavender shades uses *Verbena* 'Babylon Light Blue', a very trailing type with delicate, feathery foliage and good tolerance to mildew. Its large flower clusters consist of many individual, large blooms in a color that goes well with many others and is one of my favorites to use in combinations due to its versatility. The second verbena variety is 'Tukana Salmon'. Its huge flower clusters are brilliant salmon-pink in a shade that's not as dominant as some other purer and more vibrant shades of pink might be. Its foliage is more broad-leafed compared to the 'Babylon' series.

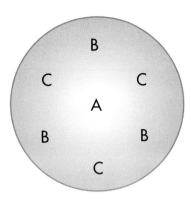

A = *Chrysocephalum* 'Baby Gold'
B = *Verbena* 'Babylon Light Blue' (3)
C = *Verbena* 'Tukana Salmon' (3)

Container Characteristics

Because of the vigorous and trailing nature of the plants in this basket, you could use an inexpensive basket, but I like using those made of natural fiber. Instead of moss—my most frequent choice—I used a coco-fiber basket in this design. Both provide good air circulation and drainage, which is important for good plant performance. This basket was fourteen inches in diameter. If you use a larger or smaller basket, adjust the number of plants accordingly.

Care Clues

This is a very low-maintenance design that requires no special care, although the verbena might benefit from regular deadheading. Make sure to supply enough fertilizer for the fast-growing verbena.

Plant Personalities

What's special about this pink-and-purple-themed design is that the planter is a topiary frame filled with moss and planted with English ivy. You could call this a "living planter."

The dominant purple flowers belong to *Petunia* 'Supertunia Royal Velvet', an early-flowering, trailing petunia with deep purple flowers that look and feel like velvet. Although it starts flowering early in spring, it continues to bloom throughout the summer, provided it's given sufficient water and fertilizer. What's nice is that where many trailing petunias can get really leggy, this variety stays nice and full in the center, where it continues to produce new growth. Its color is repeated in a lighter shade in *Nemesia* 'Blue Bird', which adds a semi-upright component to the design. The purple-blue flowers of 'Blue Bird' are accented by soft yellow centers. There are two pink flowering plants in the design, but only one is visible, *Verbena* 'Tapien Pink'. Its bright pink flower clusters trail abundantly. It's a variety that roots quite freely, so you could even pin it to the planter and let it root. The second pink flowering plant—*Diascia* 'Little Charmer'—is not visible. It's a compact variety with medium pink flowers. *Sutera* 'Snowstorm' is also not visible in this picture. It has small, five-petaled, white flowers and a cascading growth habit. It's commonly known as bacopa.

Two foliage plants add texture to the container. *Carex buchananii* is an upright-growing sedge with thin, bronze leaves that look almost as if they were dried. Even though a sedge is, botanically speaking, not a grass, it's

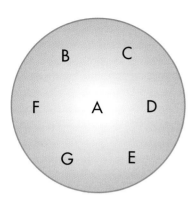

A = *Carex buchananii* (leatherleaf sedge)
B = *Diascia* 'Little Charmer' (not visible)
C = *Nemesia* 'Blue Bird'
D = *Muehlenbeckia* (creeping wirevine)
(barely visible)
E = *Petunia* 'Supertunia Royal Velvet'
F = *Sutera* 'Snowstorm' (bacopa) (not visible)
G = *Verbena* 'Tapien Pink'
Also needed: *Hedera* (English ivy)

commonly considered an ornamental grass. The second foliage plant is barely visible. It's *Muehlenbeckia*, also known as creeping wirevine. It has small, round, emerald green leaves and a wiry growth habit, which makes it excellent for mixed containers, where it intertwines with other plants.

Considering that three plants are barely or not at all visible, you can imagine that this design looks quite different from the other side, giving it several view angles.

Container Characteristics

This container is actually a topiary frame from Green Piece Wire Art. It was completely filled with moss, but I took some of the moss out to create a planting cavity. The base of this urn-shaped planter is still filled with moss, and so are its sides. After filling the planter with potting mix and planting the plants on top, I planted English ivy along the edges and pinned its branches with bobby pins very tightly to the moss walls. Repeat this process as the ivy continues to grow until the planter is covered.

Care Clues

The only plant that benefits from regular deadheading is the verbena. All plants are fairly vigorous, so make sure that you fertilize regularly. If you plant English ivy along the moss, as in this example, make sure that you moisten the moss well before planting. For the first few weeks, you'll need to water the sides of the planter where the ivy is growing because it won't yet have sufficient roots to retrieve water from the core. Once it's well established, watering only from top should be sufficient, but check periodically to be sure, especially during hot weather.

Plant Personalities

Even without bold flowers, this is one of my favorite container gardens! It combines hardy perennials selected for their attractive foliage with an ornamental grass. With such beautiful foliage, who needs flowers anyway?

The design combines two color schemes—different shades of purple and different shades of green. The center height plant is dwarf purple fountain grass, a wonderful ornamental grass for container gardens. Where its "cousin," regular purple fountain grass, would get too tall, the dwarf version is just the right height. Besides 'Red Riding Hood', it can also be found in garden centers under the names 'Dwarf Rubrum' or 'Eaton Canyon'. Its soft, foxtail flower plumes mature from deep burgundy to soft beige over time. Its purple color is echoed in *Heuchera* 'Amethyst Myst', a selection with a metallic sheen, and *Ajuga* 'Burgundy Glow' with gray, white, and purple variegated leaves that become more intense in color as the temperatures drop. Ajuga's white variegation is echoed again in the *Lamiastrum* and *Heuchera* 'Splish Splash'. Both of these have green and white variegated leaves, which makes them part of the green color scheme.

The last two foliage accents are *Muehlenbeckia* and English ivy. *Muehlenbeckia* is one of my favorite container plants because of its wiry growth. Its small, emerald green foliage weaves between the other plants and trails at the same time. English ivy is always a classic foliage plant. It's so easy to grow and available in so many different colors that you're bound to find the perfect selection.

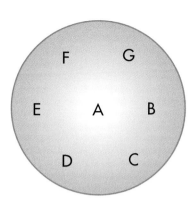

A = *Pennisetum setaceum* 'Red Riding Hood'
B = *Lamiastrum* 'Herman's Pride'
C = *Muehlenbeckia* (creeping wirevine)
D = *Ajuga* 'Burgundy Glow'
E = *Hedera* 'Goldstern' (English ivy)
F = *Heuchera* 'Amethyst Myst'
G = *Heuchera* 'Splish Splash' (not visible)

Container Characteristics

I love these stone planters for their rustic character, and they turn darker when they are wet. They also age beautifully—the older they get, the more interesting they become. They are not as heavy as they look, which makes them fairly easy to handle. This shallow bowl with a fourteen-inch diameter looks particularly good with these specific plants because it keeps the eye focused on the plants, while its color fits perfectly with the color scheme of the plants.

Care Clues

This is a very low-maintenance container garden, since there are no flowers to deadhead. The flowers of the fountain grass can be used in fresh or dried arrangements. If the English ivy, *Muehlenbeckia*, or *Lamiastrum* get too big, cut them back as desired.

At the end of the season, take the plants apart carefully and plant them in the garden, except the fountain grass, which is not frost hardy. All of the other varieties are hardy perennials that you can enjoy for more than one season. Frost-free climates can also plant the fountain grass in the garden or keep the entire container garden over winter.

Plant Personalities

This simple but elegant terra cotta container is brimming with warm colors in different shades of red and yellow. It's a welcoming summer combo that even includes herbs.

The bronze-colored grass in the center, *Carex buchananii*, adds texture and height to the design. Its needle-thin leaves curl at the top. Because it grows more slowly than the other plants in the design, look for a well-developed plant. It's often best to use a six-inch *Carex* and the rest of the plants in four-inch pots.

There are two red flowering varieties in the planter. One of them is *Verbena* 'Babylon Red', which you can see trailing to the right with large, bright red flower clusters—one of the most trailing elements in the design. The second red flowering variety is *Tropaeolum* 'Red Wonder', a nasturtium variety that is much more compact than most, with double, fragrant, vibrant red flowers. Both the flowers and leaves of nasturtium are edible. The flowers can be used in salads or as edible decoration, and the leaves are delicious in cream cheese and egg dishes.

Osteospermum 'Orange Symphony' builds the transition from red to yellow with its lively orange flowers. While most *Osteospermum* varieties grow upright, the 'Symphony' series is mounding and semi-trailing, which makes it an excellent choice for the edge of a pot, where it can cascade over time.

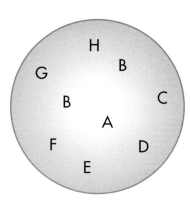

A = *Carex buchananii* (leatherleaf sedge)
B = *Tropaeolum* 'Red Wonder' (nasturtium) (2)
C = *Verbena* 'Babylon Red'
D = *Bracteantha* 'Sundaze Lemon Yellow'
E = *Bidens* 'Goldie'
F = *Salvia* 'Icterina' (sage)
G = *Osteospermum* 'Orange Symphony'
H = *Thymus* 'Golden King' (thyme) (not visible)

The two yellow flowering plants are *Bidens* 'Goldie' and *Bracteantha* 'Sundaze Lemon Yellow'. *Bidens* is a popular plant for container gardens because there aren't many yellow blooming plants that trail. Another benefit is its sweet, honeylike fragrance. 'Goldie' is one of the most compact varieties on the market. If you can't find it, look for one called 'Peter's Gold Carpet'. *Bracteantha* 'Sundaze Lemon Yellow' is a strawflower with an upright but compact growth habit. It has lemon-yellow flowers with orange centers.

To add more texture, I included two foliage plants, both of which are herbs and can be used in the kitchen. One is *Salvia* 'Icterina', also known as golden sage. The second one is *Thymus* 'Golden King', a low-growing thyme with gold and green variegated leaves.

Container Characteristics

The warm color of the terra cotta planter completes the color theme of this design. This large pot with a sixteen-inch diameter is simple but elegant, with subtle decoration around the rim that's quickly covered by plants. Its bellied shape leaves room for a larger potting mix volume, which makes watering easier, as the larger volume doesn't dry out as quickly.

Care Clues

Deadhead *Bracteantha* and *Osteospermum* flowers regularly for more profuse bloom production. Since there are a lot of plants in this container, make sure that you water and fertilize sufficiently.

Plant Personalities

This composition of annuals and perennials is very rich in texture because four foliage plants were used. It's great for any time of the year, even for the early months of spring and the late months of fall, when plant selections are often limited—these varieties flower early in the year.

The container garden gets height through the use of an ornamental grass in the center. This particular variety is *Pennisetum setaceum* 'Red Riding Hood', also called dwarf purple fountain grass. Some nurseries sell it under the name 'Dwarf Rubrum' or 'Eaton Canyon'. For container gardens, it is an often-preferred selection over *Pennisetum* 'Rubrum' because 'Rubrum' gets too tall for most uses. The deep burgundy flowers turn a light beige color as they mature.

Three other foliage plants add even more texture and movement. The variegated foliage of the sage adds an additional color element. If you decide to use 'Icterina' (golden sage), you'll repeat the color of the daisy flowers, which is a desired effect called color echoing. The use of one color in two plants creates a flow of movement between the two.

The two subtle greens are *Muehlenbeckia* and English ivy. *Muehlenbeckia* is a wonderful container plant because of its wiry growth. It weaves between the other plants and trails at the same time. Its small foliage is in harmony with the other plants, which are also fairly small-leafed. English ivy adds a classic, trailing element. Using a yellow variety of English ivy adds more character than using a green-leafed form would.

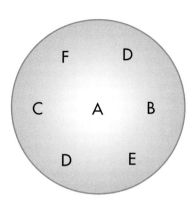

A = *Pennisetum setaceum* 'Red Riding Hood'
B = *Salvia* 'Tricolor' or 'Icterina' (sage)
C = *Hedera* 'Goldstern' (English ivy)
D = *Osteospermum* 'Lemon Symphony' (2)
E = *Muehlenbeckia* (creeping wirevine)
F = *Nemesia* 'Blue Bird'

The flowering focal points of this container garden are *Nemesia* and *Osteospermum*. The blue and yellow colors build a strong contrast. The soft yellow eye of the *Nemesia* even echoes the color of the *Osteospermum* flowers. Variety selection is crucial in this composition. Most *Osteospermum* grow quite tall and would not look good in this design. But this particular variety grows more mounding and fits perfectly into this spot.

Container Characteristics

This fourteen-inch container is a fairly inexpensive pot made of plastic. It has a textured finish, which makes it look almost like stone or coarse clay. Because the effect of the plants is so powerful, the container doesn't need to be elaborate, especially because the trailing plants cover most of it.

Care Clues

Outside of the general care described in an earlier chapter, this container garden is very easy to care for. *Osteospermum* benefits from regular deadheading; it will respond by producing flowers more continuously and in abundance. At the end of the growing season, you may take the plants apart and plant the *Muehlenbeckia*, English ivy, and sage in the garden. They are perennial in USDA Hardiness Zone 5 and warmer. Plant them early enough so that they have time to establish themselves before winter sets in. Areas with little or no frost can also plant the fountain grass, *Nemesia,* and *Osteospermum* in the garden.

Plant Personalities

The cool-colored flowers harmonize nicely with the neutral gray planter.

The tallest plant is an ornamental grass, *Stipa tenuissima*, also known as Mexican feather grass. (It can also be found under the name *Nassella*.) It builds the backbone of the design with its needle-thin, lush green leaves that sway in the slightest breeze. It's a wonderful ornamental grass, and few people can resist touching its soft foliage. Because it grows more slowly than most of the other plants in the design, I used a well-developed plant to start with.

The many flowering plants in this design create a lush color splash. Going clockwise and starting in the back right, you can see *Brachyscome* 'City Lights', a compact, trailing variety with lavender-colored flowers. It builds a thick carpet of finely textured foliage. Next is *Oxalis* 'Alba', a perennial with clover-like leaves and pure white flowers that close under low light conditions. It stays mounding and compact all season. In the front center is *Nemesia* 'Blue Lagoon'. It has a compact, mounding habit and lavender-blue flowers. As you can see when you compare it with the *Nemesia* to the left, you can see that 'Blue Lagoon' stays shorter, but you could substitute a different blue variety if you wish. The variety on the left, 'Safari Pink', is taller growing with medium pink flowers and yellow centers. In the back is a trailing variety that's not visible from this angle: *Calibrachoa* 'Superbells Coral Pink' has miniature petunia-like flowers that trail in abundance over the edge of the planter. The last flowering plant is

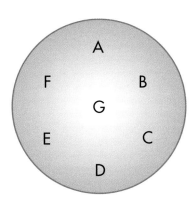

A = *Stipa tenuissima* (Mexican feather grass)
B = *Brachyscome* 'City Lights'
C = *Oxalis* 'Alba'
D = *Nemesia* 'Blue Lagoon'
E = *Nemesia* 'Safari Pink'
F = *Calibrachoa* 'Superbells Coral Pink' (not visible)
G = *Verbena* 'Superbena Purple'

Verbena 'Superbena Purple'. This new variety of verbena has very large flowers and a vigorous habit. If you wish to substitute, look for a variety with semi-trailing growth habit. Or, if you wish to use a strictly trailing variety, switch its position with that of *Nemesia* 'Safari Pink'.

Container Characteristics

This neutrally colored pot in gray keeps the focus on the plants and draws little attention to itself. Although it looks like stone, it's actually made of plastic, which makes it easy to handle and chip resistant. This pot is fourteen inches in diameter. For smaller or larger pots, you may adjust the number or size of plants used accordingly.

Care Clues

This is a low-maintenance design that requires little special care. In general, verbena benefits from regular deadheading and responds with a more abundant and continuous show of blooms. If the *Nemesia* varieties set unsightly seeds, you may want to deadhead them as well.

Plant Personalities

Here's a beautiful, exotic design that combines many different plant types, colors, and textures.

Since some of the flowering plants were also used for their foliage, I can't divide them into those two groups, so instead I'll describe them from A through I.

Saxifraga 'Harvest Moon' is one of the many perennial *Saxifraga* types. It is very low growing and develops runners that will cascade over the rim. In high light levels and under cool temperatures its foliage turns an attractive bronze. It's a slow grower, so plant it next to plants that aren't invasive. Next to it is *Diascia* 'Summer Celebration Coral Belle'. This *Diascia* variety has coral-colored flowers, a color that can be found in other plants in the design. It stays nice and compact, a quality that is desired in this combination, where all plants are of moderate height. *Begonia* 'Maribel Pink Shades' is hard to see, but it has beautiful mahogany leaves and blush pink flowers. The higher the light levels and the cooler the temperatures, the more intense the foliage and flower colors. In the heat of the summer, expect the foliage to be mostly green and the flowers almost white, especially if you live in an area with high night temperatures. If you can't locate this variety, look for *Begonia* 'Richmondensis'.

For texture, I added *Acorus gramineus* 'Ogon', a variegated sweet flag. Its gold and green variegated leaves continue the warm color theme. *Osteospermum* 'Orange Symphony' provides an abundance of color with its

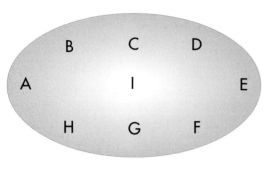

A = *Saxifraga* 'Harvest Moon'
B = *Diascia* 'Summer Celebration Coral Belle'
C = *Begonia obliqua* 'Maribel Pink Shades'
D = *Acorus gramineus* 'Ogon'
E = *Osteospermum* 'Orange Symphony'
F = *Sutera* 'Gold 'n' Pearls' (bacopa)
G = *Thymus* 'Goldem King' (thyme)
H = *Yucca*
I = *Heuchera* 'Purple Petticoats'

daisy-shaped flowers. It's a very compact, semi-trailing variety compared to many other *Osteospermum*, which is important for this location in the design. It's a heat-tolerant selection that flowers all summer. *Sutera* 'Gold 'n' Pearls' is a specialty selection of a popular plant. Commonly known as bacopa, *Sutera* has become a popular plant that is most often found with white flowers and green foliage, but pink and lavender varieties are also available. 'Gold 'n' Pearls' is special because of its variegated leaves in gold and green. Its trailing habit is best utilized where it can drape over the edges. In the front center is *Thymus* 'Golden King', a variegated thyme with yellow and green leaves and a trailing growth habit. It's a culinary herb used here for its aesthetic value. The yucca is definitely a specialty plant, and you might have trouble locating one like it. This dwarf form has striped foliage, which reflects several of the colors found in other plants in the design. It's important to use a dwarf form to fit into the overall design. Good dwarf varieties are 'Golden Sword' and 'Color Guard'. Finally, *Heuchera* 'Purple Petticoats' in the center echoes the foliage color of the begonia with its deep purple leaves. And since purple is complementary to yellow, it stands out against the other plants in the design.

Container Characteristics

I used a bronze-colored metal trough that works very well with this color design. It didn't have drainage holes, so I drilled some in the bottom. The dimension is approximately nine by sixteen inches.

Care Clues

Deadhead the *Osteospermum* regularly to keep the flowers coming in abundance and to keep the plant looking neat. None of the other plants need any special care. You can snip the thyme branches and use them for cooking.

Plant Personalities

You don't need a lot of different colors for an impressive hanging basket. This elegant design in all white is always a favorite among friends and fellow gardeners.

In the center is *Nemesia* 'Compact Innocence', with pure white flowers with yellow centers and a subtle, sweet fragrance. *Nemesia* is a good choice as an upright component in a hanging basket because it doesn't get too big. If you'd use the same plant in an upright container, you would use it as a mounding component. 'Compact Innocence' stays fairly low with a dense growth. Its cousin, *Nemesia* 'Innocence', has the same colored flowers, but it gets bigger, the flowers are larger, and it's more fragrant. But you could substitute one for the other.

The second pure white flower is *Verbena* 'Tukana White', a trailing verbena with large, brilliant flower clusters. It has a full but trailing growth habit and broad leaves. Verbena varieties have tremendously improved in their disease tolerance over the last several years—especially against mildew—and the 'Tukana' series is one example of that.

Finally, the most trailing element is *Petunia* 'Supertunia Mini Blue Veined'. It is part of a small-flowered series of trailing petunias. Its flowers are almost white with a soft blush of lavender and dark blue veins. It gives the design a subtle hint of color to add just enough interest without changing the all-white color theme.

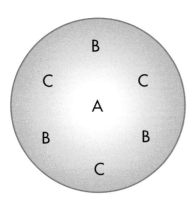

A = *Nemesia* 'Compact Innocence'
B = *Verbena* 'Tukana White' (3)
C = *Petunia* 'Supertunia Mini Blue Veined' (3)

Container Characteristics

Once again I used my favorite—a moss basket—with a fourteen-inch diameter. But since these plants are so trailing, they quickly cover the basket, which allows you to use a lower-priced alternative. But if you want a great look from the get-go, a natural looking basket such as one made of moss or cedar is more than worth it. Since the verbenas and petunias grow rapidly, baskets made of natural fiber can dry out quickly once the plants are big. If this is a concern, look for baskets with built-in water reservoirs.

Care Clues

All of the plants in this design require little maintenance. Just make sure that you supply enough fertilizer because the verbenas and petunias are heavy feeders. Deadhead the verbenas regularly to encourage continuous, abundant blooms.

Plant Personalities

This fairly small container uses a mix of ornamental grasses and vibrant flowering varieties. The ornamental grass in the center is Mexican feather grass, also sold under the botanical names *Stipa* or *Nassella*. It has needle-thin leaves that sway in the slightest breeze. It looks lush green in spring and for as long as the temperatures are moderate, but turns a golden beige color in hot and dry summer conditions—both phases are very attractive. The small black plant in the front center with the arching leaves is black mondo grass. It grows quite slowly, so I used three plants. Although it looks quite shy in the picture, it is a beautiful grasslike plant with a dramatic effect.

Cool-colored flowering varieties look great with the blue container. The pink flowers belong to *Diascia* 'Little Charmer', which is part of a fairly new, more heat-tolerant series from England. The bright pink flowers look especially spirited next to the dark foliage of the mondo grass and the blue pot. The white flowers are *Sutera* 'Giant Snowflake'. Its small flowers and trailing habit are excellent for container gardens. Although it's commonly known as bacopa, its correct botanical name is *Sutera*. The third flowering plant is not visible in the picture. It's *Verbena* 'Babylon Blue Carpet', a very low-growing variety with deep purple blue flowers.

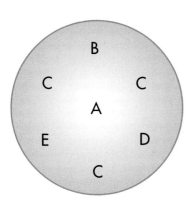

Planter on Left (p. 222)

A = *Stipa tenuissima* (Mexican feather grass)

B = *Verbena* 'Babylon Blue Carpet' (not visible)

C = *Ophiopogon* (black mondo grass) (3)

D = *Sutera* 'Giant Snowflake' (bacopa)

E = *Diascia* 'Little Charmer'

Container Characteristics

The calm and serene blue of this glazed planter looks not only great with the cool-colored flowering plants, but it also fits with this poolside setting. This pot is only eight inches in diameter, but I used smaller plants to fit more variety into it.

Care Clues

The verbena benefits from regular deadheading. It responds with more continuous blooms. None of the other plants need deadheading or pruning, but may be cut back if they get too big. *Diascia* and Mexican feather grass are frost hardy to USDA Hardiness Zone 7. If you live in Zone 7 or above, you can plant them in the garden at the end of the season.

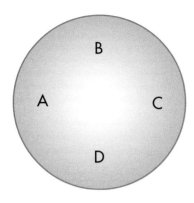

Planter on Right (p. 222)
A = *Cleome* 'Linde Armstrong'
B = *Verbena* 'Temari Patio Blue'
C = *Petunia* 'Supertunia Mini Blue Veined'
D = *Verbena* 'Temari Patio Rose'

Plant Personalities

This larger of the two pots pictured complements the smaller pot on the left. It carries through the theme of cool-colored flowering plants. It uses only flowering plants and no foliage plants for high-impact color.

The tallest and most dominant plant on the left is *Cleome* 'Linde Armstrong'. It is a very compact form of *Cleome* with a mature height of only thirty inches. Its lovely pink flowers are in proportion to the overall plant height, which is not always the case with *Cleome*. Dr. Allan Armitage of the University of Georgia discovered this variety. It is an especially heat-tolerant selection.

I also used two broad-leaved verbenas in this container. Both are from the 'Patio Temari' series, a vigorous, semi-upright series that works very well in container gardens. The variety in the back is 'Temari Patio Blue', a purple-blue selection with a lighter colored eye. In the front is 'Temari Patio Rose', a vibrant rose-pink variety. Both colors harmonize with the pink flowers of *Cleome*, as they are all from the cool color range.

Finally, a trailing element is provided by 'Supertunia Mini Blue Veined', a vigorous variety of trailing petunia with small, white flowers with dark blue veins.

Container Characteristics

This container is the same glazed blue style as the smaller pot on the left, just much bigger. It looks beautiful with the cool-colored flowers in the poolside setting. I used large plants for this sixteen-inch-diameter pot, but you could also use smaller plants and use more of each.

Care Clues

If you deadhead the verbenas regularly, they will reward you with a continuous display of flowers from spring through fall. None of the other plants need any trimming or pruning. All of the plants used benefit from above-average fertilizer doses, so make sure that you fertilize regularly.

Plant Personalities

This is a wonderful combination of foliage and flowering plants. It can be grown any time of the year, even in early spring and fall, because all of the plants used can withstand slight frost. With its earthy colors, it's especially nice for fall decorating.

In the center is *Carex buchananii*, also called leatherleaf sedge. If you want to nitpick, a sedge is not considered a "grass," but nurseries and gardeners commonly refer to it as one. This variety grows upright with thin, bronze-colored leaves that curl slightly at the top. The foliage is stiff and almost feels like it's been dried. It's wonderful for autumn-themed designs and picks up the color of the container. Because it grows slowly, it's best if you start with a well-developed *Carex* plant so that it can keep up with the other plants. It won't grow much after it's been planted. The mounding foliage plants are *Salvia* 'Purpurascens', commonly called purple sage. Its color is especially intense under high light levels and once the temperatures start to cool off. The cool temperatures also make it stay more compact. As a popular culinary herb, you can use it for flavoring dishes. The lowest growing and most trailing foliage plant is *Ajuga* 'Chocolate Chip'. This popular perennial has very small, almost black leaves. Again, the color intensifies under high light and cool temperatures. In spring, it's adorned with bright blue flower panicles. As it gets bigger, it starts cascading over the edges.

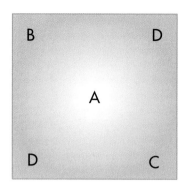

A = *Carex buchananii* (leatherleaf sedge)
B = *Osteospermum* 'Lemon Symphony'
C = *Ajuga* 'Chocolate Chip'
D = *Salvia* 'Purpurascens' (sage) (2)

The only plant that was selected for its flowers is *Osteospermum* 'Lemon Symphony'. Compared to some other *Osteospermum* varieties, it's very compact and semi-trailing. It is also heat tolerant and flowers even in mid- and late summer after some varieties cease blooming. As it gets big, it cascades over the rim, balancing the cascading element of ajuga in the opposite corner.

Container Characteristics

This look-a-like terra cotta container is actually made of plastic, which makes it lightweight and chip resistant. The air circulation and water evaporation are lower than in terra cotta and clay planters, which has advantages and disadvantages. Simply from a design perspective, you could substitute a clay or terra cotta planter. This pot is twelve inches square.

Care Clues

Deadhead the *Osteospermum* regularly to promote continuous bloom production. Ajuga, *Carex*, and salvia are perennials to USDA Zone 3 (ajuga), Zone 6 (*Carex*), and Zone 5 (salvia). At the end of the season, you can take them apart carefully and plant them in the perennial bed or overwinter them and replace the *Osteospermum* in spring.

Plant Personalities

While most of the time foliage is used to accent flowers, I reversed that concept for this planter. The result is just as beautiful!

The center plant that draws attention first is *Coleus* 'Amora'. Coleus are fantastic container garden candidates. They come in a wide array of colors, sizes, and shapes, so you'll likely find the right variety for your specific design. 'Amora' has cream-colored leaves with green edges, but the special appeal is its bright pink undersides. That pink is echoed twice in the container. It first appears in the flowers of *Fuchsia* 'Lohn der Liebe', an upright-growing variety from Germany with small, single flowers. If you have trouble locating this specific variety, look for a similar one with an upright habit. The pink tones are repeated once more in the foliage of *Ajuga* 'Burgundy Glow' in the front of the container. This low-growing variety is excellent for the edges of container gardens. The pink tinges are especially prominent during cooler temperatures.

The cream-colored leaves of *Coleus* 'Amora' are echoed in the margins of vinca vine. Vinca vine is a popular plant for container gardens with a strictly trailing growth habit. Creamy white can again be found in the tips of fiber-optic grass on the left. Its needle-thin leaves are topped with tiny inflorescences, giving it the appearance of fiber optics. It's best used where it can drape over the edges of containers.

Other foliage accents in this design are *Ipomoea* 'Blackie', an ornamental sweet potato with dark purple foliage, and *Muehlenbeckia,* also known

D	E	F	D
	C	A	G
B	E	H	F

A = *Coleus* 'Amora'
B = *Scirpus cernuus* (fiber-optic grass)
C = *Nemesia* 'Compact Innocence'
D = *Fuchsia* 'Lohn der Liebe' (2)
E = *Vinca* vine (2)
F = *Muehlenbeckia* (creeping wirevine) (2)
G = *Ipomoea* 'Blackie' (sweet potato)
H = *Ajuga* 'Burgundy Glow'

as creeping wirevine, a fine-textured plant with small, emerald green, glossy leaves. It's an exceptional container garden plant due to its wiry growth.

Container Characteristics

This beautiful, rectangular stone planter complements the textures of the plants well. Stone planters like this one are not as heavy as you might think. They add a lot of character to a container garden because they not only turn darker when they are wet, but they also age beautifully, giving the entire design even more personality. This particular one has inside measurements of ten by sixteen inches.

Care Clues

This is a very low-maintenance design that doesn't require any special care. If any of the plants get too big, you may trim them back as desired. The plant most likely to get a little too big is the sweet potato. It loves warm temperatures and thrives once the mercury rises. But if temperatures remain moderate, so will its growth.

This container garden is best suited for a partial shade location, but if you live in an area with moderate sun intensities during the summer, you may place it in full sun.

Plant Personalities

Black foliage has become popular among professional container garden designers. It builds an especially nice contrast against the white pillar and fence in this setting.

The most visible plant with black foliage is *Ipomoea* 'Black Heart', an ornamental sweet potato with heart-shaped, olive green to black foliage. Its vigorous foliage will cover the hanging basket in no time at all. If you can't find this particular variety, look for one called 'Blackie', which has the same color, but loped leaves, or 'Ace of Spades', which is very similar if not identical to 'Black Heart'.

The foliage shape and color of the sweet potato are repeated in *Coleus* 'Dark Star' in the center. It's a small-growing selection that is just right for the center of hanging baskets. Its oval, pointed foliage is deep mahogany, almost black.

To add contrast to the black foliage, I added a white verbena as another trailing element. The brilliant white flowers really stand out against the dark foliage. Without it, the entire design would be too dark for most tastes.

Container Characteristics

Moss baskets are my personal favorites when it comes to planting hanging baskets. Even when your plants have not yet covered the entire basket and

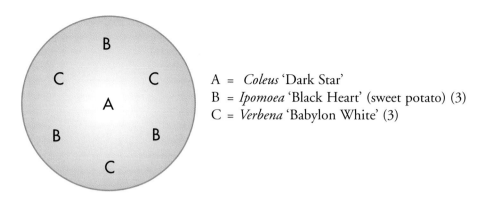

A = *Coleus* 'Dark Star'
B = *Ipomoea* 'Black Heart' (sweet potato) (3)
C = *Verbena* 'Babylon White' (3)

you can see part of the moss, it's beautiful and natural looking. Their downside is that they dry out quickly once the temperatures rise, so you'll have to make sure that you water them frequently. Don't be surprised if you have to water them daily during hot summer months. Some moss baskets are available with built-in water reservoirs. The reservoirs are not visible once the basket is planted, but they help keep them moist longer. This particular basket is fourteen inches in diameter.

Care Clues

This is a very low-maintenance basket that requires very little care. Once the temperatures rise in summer, the sweet potato can get quite vigorous and might try to outgrow some of the other plants. If this is the case, simply trim it back. The coleus and the sweet potato both like warm temperatures and don't do well when it's still cold, so it pays off to wait until the temperatures have warmed before you plant this basket.

Plant Personalities

There's always room for a shallow bowl like this, maybe even on your patio table. This design combines pinks and purples with attractive foliage accents.

In the center is *Gaura* 'Perky Pink', a perennial with deep maroon foliage and wispy, bright pink flowers. While the foliage stays low, the flowers stand up on long stems. 'Perky Pink' gives the design height while still being airy enough so that it won't block the view if you decided to use it as a centerpiece on your patio table.

To its left and right is *Nemesia* 'Blue Lagoon', a compact *Nemesia* with a canopy of large, soft blue flowers. As with most *Nemesia* varieties that came to the market over the last few years, this variety is quite heat tolerant.

The flowers that partially echo the color of the *Gaura* blooms belong to *Calibrachoa* 'Million Bells Cherry Pink', a petunia relative with flowers that resemble a miniature petunia. It provides the trailing element in this design. But since this bowl is so shallow, I chose a moderate trailer like 'Million Bells Cherry Pink', whereas some other *Calibrachoa* varieties are more trailing.

For more texture, I added *Heuchera* 'Green Spice', a perennial that's prized for its beautiful foliage, although it produces wispy, delicate, almost white flowers in summer. Its leaves are overlaid with silver and are accented by dark green veins.

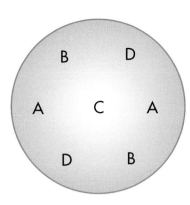

A = *Nemesia* 'Blue Lagoon' (2)
B = *Calibrachoa* 'Million Bells Cherry Pink' (2)
C = *Gaura* 'Perky Pink'
D = *Heuchera* 'Green Spice' (2)

Container Characteristics

The upright and moderately trailing plants are just right for this shallow bowl with a twelve-inch diameter. I love using stone planters like this one because—as you can see in the front center of the picture—they age beautifully over time, adding to their character. This bowl is part of a collection from Braun Horticulture that is more lightweight than many stone planters.

Care Clues

This is a low-maintenance design that requires no special care. The *Heuchera* is the slowest growing plant, so make sure that none of the others tries to outgrow it. If that happens, trim the faster-growing plants back. *Gaura* and *Heuchera* are both perennials hardy to USDA Zone 5. At the end of the season, you can take the plants apart carefully and plant the perennials in the garden. USDA Zones 8 and warmer can also plant the *Nemesia* and *Calibrachoa* in the garden.

Plant Personalities

This window box is very rich in texture due to the heavy use of foliage. Actually, only one-fifth of the plants used were selected for their flowers. But since there are only a few flowering plants, I selected those that make a great impact with their blooms. The vibrant red flowers here belong to *Calibrachoa* 'Cherry Pink'. Its hundreds of small, reddish pink flowers really jump from the canvas of foliage.

The dominant foliage elements contain two ornamental grasses, dwarf purple fountain grass and leatherleaf sedge. Dwarf purple fountain grass is a perfect selection for container gardens, as it stays much more compact than the regular form of purple fountain grass. Leatherleaf sedge is definitely the weaker accent, but it balances the right side of the container. It has thin leaves that grow upright and curl at the top. Both grasses bring height to the plant composition without overpowering because their fine texture is open and airy.

The purple of the fountain grass is echoed in two other foliage elements, 'Tricolor' sage and the *Heuchera*. By placing these two purple elements at the farthest corners of the window box, they visually hold the container together.

The remainder of the plants provides a few subtler and neutral elements with silver and gray-green variegated foliage. The green and white variegation of 'White-Edged' sage is echoed in the trailing English ivy, and the silver lavender cotton provides a cool, neutral effect.

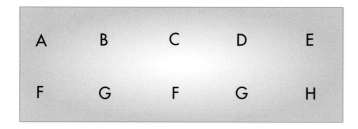

A = *Salvia* 'Tricolor' (sage)
B = *Pennisetum setaceum* 'Red Riding Hood'
C = *Salvia* 'White-Edged' (sage)
D = *Carex buchananii* (leatherleaf sedge)
E = *Santolina* (lavender cotton)
F = *Hedera* 'Glacier' (English ivy) (2)
G = *Calibrachoa* 'Million Bells Cherry Pink' (2)
H = *Heuchera* 'Amethyst Myst'

Container Characteristics

This container garden was planted in a seven-by-twenty-two-inch plastic window box, but a redwood version would also look stunning. If you place it in a spot where you only see the front, you can use the plastic version because the trailing plants hide most of it. But if you will be viewing it from all sides, spending a little more for a redwood window box would be well worth it.

Care Clues

None of the varieties used here require pruning, but you can use the flowers of the fountain grass in fresh or dried flower arrangements. If you live in USDA Hardiness Zone 5 or warmer, you can take the plants apart carefully at the end of the season and plant the sedge, English ivy, sage, lavender cotton, and *Heuchera* in the ground. Plant them early enough so that they have time to establish before winter. Areas with little or no frost can also plant the *Calibrachoa* and fountain grass in the garden.

Plant Personalities

This monochromatic combination in orange uses different daisy-shaped flowers accented by foliage. At first sight, you might only notice *Osteospermum* 'Orange Symphony', which clearly is the dominant plant in this design. It's a compact *Osteospermum* that will eventually cascade slightly over the edges. Where many other varieties might get too tall, the 'Symphony' series stays low, making it a good candidate for hanging baskets and shallow bowls such as this. 'Orange Symphony' has vibrant orange flowers and dark centers.

The second flowering plant in this design is *Arctotis* 'Sunspot'. This South African native has large, daisy-shaped flowers that remind me of *Gerbera*. It keeps its flowers well above the compact foliage. Depending on the age of the flowers, they range from dark orange streaked with red when they first open to yellow-orange once they're mature. Although you can't see very many *Arctotis* blooms in this picture, it is a very floriferous plant—it just hadn't reached its peak bloom when the picture was taken.

For texture, I added *Carex flagellifera* 'Toffee Twist', an ornamental grass with thin, bronze leaves and a weeping habit. Because this bowl is relatively shallow, we don't need a lot of height, so 'Toffee Twist' is just the right selection. In other combinations in taller pots you might see this cascading ever the edges. The bronze of 'Toffee Twist' echoes some of the colors in the flowering plants, especially as the sun reflects on it. 'Toffee Twist'

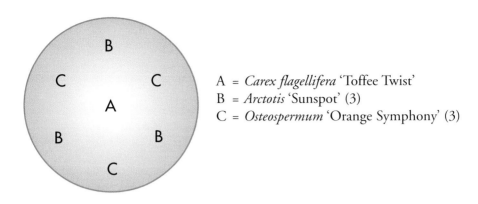

A = *Carex flagellifera* 'Toffee Twist'
B = *Arctotis* 'Sunspot' (3)
C = *Osteospermum* 'Orange Symphony' (3)

grows slower than *Osteospermum* and *Arctotis,* so look for a well-developed plant. Better yet, use the *Carex* in a six-inch pot and the rest of the plants in four-inch pots.

Container Characteristics

This blue bowl is an excellent complement to the orange flowers. Purple would also look outstanding. This glazed container reduces the water loss compared to more porous, non-glazed containers, an advantage in hot weather. This bowl is fourteen inches in diameter.

Care Clues

Both *Osteospermum* and *Arctotis* close their flowers at night and under low-light conditions, so make sure to give them a sunny spot. Both also benefit from regular deadheading and will respond with more prolific blooms.

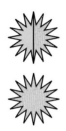

Plant Personalities

This is one of my favorite combinations for a partially shady location because it is so rich in texture. It's also a good example of color echoing.

The tallest plant in the center is *Carex buchananii*, also known as leatherleaf sedge. It adds texture and subtle height with its thin, bronze-colored leaves. The foliage looks and feels dry, even when the plant is in full growth. It's not a fast grower, so look for a well-developed plant and don't expect very much growth during one season. Another foliage plant is *Ipomoea* 'Blackie', an ornamental sweet potato with dark purple, deeply lobed leaves. Its color and its texture are repeated in the rex begonias. This variety of begonia from the 'Great American Cities' series has dark purple veins, which resemble the leaf shape of the sweet potato. Rex begonias are great for shady and partially shady locations. They need warm temperatures because temperatures below 45°F halt growth and temperatures below 40°F cause damage. In hot, dry climates, shade is important. Because they grow more slowly than the other varieties in the design, use begonias in five- or six-inch pots and the remainder of the plants in four-inch pots. If you can't find this particular variety, substitute with one of the many other varieties on the market.

I used two flowering plants to increase the color impact. *Torenia* 'Summer Wave Blue', also called wishbone flower, is a trailing variety with two-toned, purple-blue flowers. This *Torenia* echoes the color of the begonia, and a similar shade of purple can be found in *Heliotropium* 'Nagano',

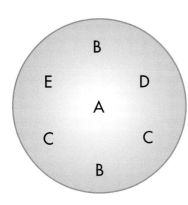

A = *Carex buchananii* (leatherleaf sedge)
B = *Begonia rex* 'Atlanta Jazz' (2)
C = *Torenia* 'Summer Wave Blue' (2)
D = *Ipomoea* 'Blackie' (sweet potato)
E = *Heliotropium* 'Nagano' (not visible)

which isn't visible in this picture. It's a fairly compact variety of heliotrope with a sweet scent reminiscent of vanilla. You can substitute another purple variety of heliotrope if you can't find 'Nagano', but look for a compact one.

Container Characteristics

This ornate gray container reflects one of the begonia colors, tying the plants and container together visually. It also looks great with the purple colors in the design. It's made of plastic, so it's lightweight and chip resistant. It's seventeen inches in diameter.

Care Clues

Begonias, heliotropes, and sweet potatoes like warm temperatures, so don't plant them too early in the season, but rather wait until the temperatures have warmed. Deadhead heliotrope regularly to keep the plant looking neat and flowering continuously. If the sweet potato gets too vigorous in the summer, trim it back. You can bring the begonias indoors for the winter and enjoy them as houseplants.

Plant Personalities

Here is another warm, spirited combination, this time in an oval planter for variety.

The backbone of the design is *Chasmanthium latifolium*, an ornamental grass also known as northern sea oats. Its golden, almost translucent foliage grows upright and gives the design the needed height. Although it's beautiful as it is in this picture, its foliage turns to bronze in the fall. In summer, it produces showy, droopy flowers that bring its total height to almost three feet. It's a truly stunning grass for container gardens.

Also toward the back are two plants with vibrant red flower clusters, *Pelargonium* 'Fireworks Scarlet'. This geranium type from a German breeder has beautiful, star-shaped flowers and appealing foliage with dark zones. Their intense red color is echoed in *Verbena* 'Tukana Scarlet', a trailing type with large flower clusters and broad leaves. By using the same color twice, the plants are connected visually.

Argyranthemum 'Courtyard Daisy Blanche' is planted in both corners. It has a low-growing habit, where many marguerite daisies would be too tall for this location. The white flowers with yellow centers sit atop silver-green foliage. The yellow centers are complementary to the bright red flowers and are echoed in the yellow foliage of the ornamental grass.

Although hard to see in this picture, there is another plant in the front that is more visible when the sun shines on the container from the front.

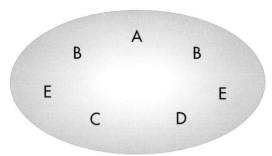

A = *Chasmanthium latifolium* (northern sea oats)
B = *Pelargonium* 'Fireworks Scarlet' (2)
C = *Verbena* 'Tukana Scarlet'
D = *Trifolium* 'Dark Dancer'
E = *Argyranthemum* 'Courtyard Daisy Blanche' (2)

It's *Trifolium* 'Dark Dancer', a low-growing plant with almost black foliage and light green margins. I used it here to add texture to the design.

Container Characteristics

I used an oval clay planter with approximate inside dimensions of nine by twenty inches. It's simple but elegant, with a subtle rim design. A matching planter might be hard to find, but you could use a rectangular planter instead.

Care Clues

Deadhead the *Pelargonium* regularly to promote continuous flower production. The marguerite daisy and verbena also benefit from occasional deadheading. Use a well-developed *Chasmanthium* plant when planting, because it grows more slowly than most of the other plants in the design. In this example, I started with a five-inch pot, whereas the others were four-inch pots. *Trifolium* is also a slower grower. You can either trim the other plants regularly so that they don't outgrow it, or let nature take its course: Enjoy the *Trifolium* in the beginning and accept that it might "disappear" over time.

Plant Personalities

This is a beautiful combination in different shades of pink and purple. It combines upright and trailing elements for a harmonic composition. By using only flowers that are fairly small and similar in size, it creates a well-balanced arrangement. Although it's a window box, you can see here that it beautifies almost any setting.

Bracteantha 'Sundaze Pink', a strawflower, dominates the back of the container. It's an upright-growing variety but stays more compact than many other varieties. Its flowers can be used in fresh or dried arrangements. The texture in the back center stems from China love grass. It has beautiful, pinkish-red flowers with an airy appearance. It adds texture and movement to this combination planter.

Blue and purple tones are represented through *Petunia* 'Supertunia Mini Blue Veined' and *Torenia* 'Summer Wave Blue'. While the 'Supertunia' is mostly white, it has a blue eye, which echoes the color of the *Torenia*. Both plant types are trailing and create a waterfall of color that cascades over the edges of the container.

Finally, the color composition is rounded out with *Nemesia* 'Candy Girl' and *Verbena* 'Babylon Light Blue', which is actually more a shade of lavender than blue. Again, the pinkish lavender color is echoed in both plants.

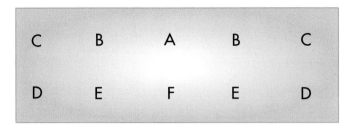

A = *Eragrostis* (China love grass)
B = *Bracteantha* 'Sundaze Pink' (2)
C = *Nemesia* 'Candy Girl' (2)
D = *Verbena* 'Babylon Light Blue' (2)
E = *Petunia* 'Supertunia Mini Blue Veined' (2)
F = *Torenia* 'Summer Wave Blue'

Container Characteristics

The container here is a redwood window box, although you can see only a very small sliver of it on the right. Redwood is always a classic and rustic choice for window boxes. Since the plants here cover the window box completely, you might be tempted to choose a lower-priced plastic version instead, but keep in mind that you can still see the container in the back and partially along the sides. So in the end redwood is a great choice. The particular size is an eight-by-twenty-six-inch window box. If you use a smaller or large container, adjust the number of plants accordingly.

Care Clues

To assure continuous bloom, deadhead the strawflowers and *Nemesia* regularly. The verbena also benefits from deadheading, but it's not required. This container garden uses a lot of plants that need a good supply of fertilizer, so it's especially important that you keep up your fertilizer regimen. If you tend to forget, apply some slow-release fertilizer to compensate.

Plant Personalities

This hanging basket combines the classic complementary colors purple and yellow. The combination of flowers and foliage create a high-impact basket rich in texture.

The dominant flowering plant in the front is 'Supertunia Mini Blue', a trailing petunia with an abundance of small flowers. Although it's called blue, its color is actually more purple, as you can see in the picture. Once this plant is older than the one in the picture, it's covered with small, bluish purple flowers. The second plant that was used for its flowers rather than its foliage is *Osteospermum* 'Lemon Symphony'. Compared to other *Osteospermum* varieties, the 'Symphony' series has a mounding, semi-trailing habit, which makes it a good candidate for hanging baskets, where many other varieties could get too tall. Its cheery yellow blooms build a nice contrast to the purple petunia flowers, and the purple centers of the *Osteospermum* blooms echo the color of the petunias.

Lamium 'Golden Anniversary' is one of the two foliage plants in this basket, although its purple flowers are also very attractive and complement the color theme. But its true asset is its golden-yellow and green variegated foliage that stays nice and full all year. It has a compact, mounding habit and fills bare spots in the basket quickly. Although hard to see, a second foliage plant is *Thymus* 'Golden King', a golden variegated thyme with a fresh lemon scent. It has a low-growing, creeping habit and an unobtrusive

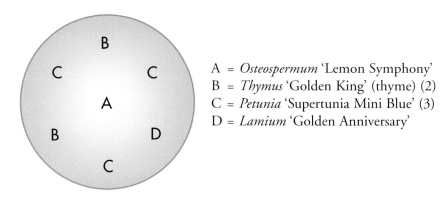

A = *Osteospermum* 'Lemon Symphony'
B = *Thymus* 'Golden King' (thyme) (2)
C = *Petunia* 'Supertunia Mini Blue' (3)
D = *Lamium* 'Golden Anniversary'

character. When it produces flowers, they round out the color theme with their soft purple tone. You can use this thyme variety in the kitchen as a culinary herb.

Container Characteristics

Part of the character of this design comes from the moss basket. Its natural look adds a rustic character and texture to the design. Plant performance is excellent in moss baskets because the natural fibers allow for good air circulation. Their only downside is that they dry out fairly quickly, which can be a problem in hot weather and once the plants are big. Some moss baskets come with a water reservoir in the bottom, which slows the water loss. In this design, I used a fourteen-inch basket.

Care Clues

This is a low-maintenance design that needs little special care. At the end of the season, you can plant the *Lamium* in the garden, where it is perennial to USDA Zone 5. Thyme is also a perennial and can be used in the kitchen garden.

Plant Personalities

A simple design with only three different plants can make a very attractive combination, as this planter in complementary colors shows.

To build height, I used *Angelonia* 'Angelface Violet' in the center. This summer snapdragon has tall spikes of purple flowers accented by lighter-colored centers. It blooms well throughout the summer, even as the temperatures rise. Because I used only one plant of *Angelonia* in relation to three each of the other varieties, I used a larger plant. Look for one in a five-inch or six-inch pot if all of the other plants are in four-inch pots.

The vibrant purple of *Angelonia* is complemented by the yellow flowers of the other two varieties. These two colors are on opposite ends of the color wheel and really make each other stand out if used together in a design. One of the yellowish flowers is *Osteospermum* 'Peach Symphony'. It has a semi-trailing habit that works well along the edges of planters. The soft peach-to-yellow flowers have dark purple centers that echo the color of the *Angelonia*. A bright yellow flowering *Osteospermum* with purple centers would also look great. The third variety is *Calibrachoa* 'Million Bells Terra Cotta'. With its miniature petunia-like flowers, it creates a charming trailing element. The flowers are multitoned, ranging from almost pure yellow to reddish tinges. In summer, when the temperatures are warm, the flowers are primarily yellow. Their earthy, warm tone looks particularly attractive in this rustic planter.

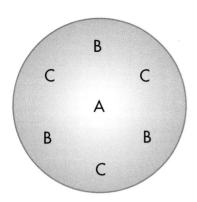

A = *Angelonia* 'Angelface Violet'
B = *Osteospermum* 'Peach Symphony' (3)
C = *Calibrachoa* 'Million Bells Terra Cotta' (3)

Container Characteristics

This dark brown terra cotta planter has an intricate design and a short, stocky shape with "feet." You are unlikely to find an identical one, but this design will look good in any terra cotta planter, especially one that's dark and ornately decorated. Because the plants are only moderately trailing, this relatively short planter is perfect for this design. Its diameter is sixteen inches.

Care Clues

Deadhead the *Osteospermum* regularly to ensure abundant and continuous bloom production. The other plants don't need any special attention.

Plant Personalities

The theme is clearly purple in this planter brimming with many different plants. The reddest nuance of purple is represented in *Verbena* 'Superbena Burgundy' in the back right corner. It's a vigorous verbena with a mainly upright growth habit and large flower clusters. If you can't find this particular variety, look for a similar color and similar habit. In the back left corner is *Nemesia* 'Safari Plum', a variety with deep purple-blue flowers and a yellow center. With its compact, mounding habit, *Nemesia* 'Safari Plum' is just the right plant for this spot, where you wouldn't want something that grows very tall.

In the front row are three more flowering plants, all in shades of purple. *Calibrachoa* 'Superbells Blue' has miniature petunia-like flowers and a trailing growth habit that cascades over the left and front rim. Its flowers are dark purple-blue and accented by dark veins and yellowish centers. It represents the darkest shade of purple in this design. In the front right corner is *Scaevola* 'Spring Rhapsody', also known as fan flower due to its fan-shaped blooms. *Scaevola* is a true heat lover and likes to cascade out of hanging baskets and over the edges of planters. If you can't find this fairly new variety, look for another blue flowering one, such as 'New Wonder'. In the middle is *Ageratum* 'Artist Blue', a compact ageratum with purple-blue flower clusters and an upright growth habit. With its compact, upright habit, it presents a nice transition from the taller upright plants in the back and the trailing plants in the front.

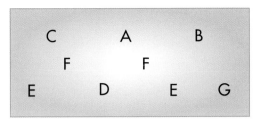

A = *Strobilanthes* (Persian shield)
B = *Verbena* 'Superbena Burgundy'
C = *Nemesia* 'Safari Plum'
D = *Hedera* 'Glacier' (English ivy)
E = *Calibrachoa* 'Superbells Blue' (2)
F = *Ageratum* 'Artist Blue' (2)
G = *Scaevola* 'Spring Rhapsody'

As foliage accents I chose Persian shield and *Hedera* 'Glacier', also known as English ivy. The *Strobilanthes* in the back is an excellent plant for container gardens. With its dark purple leaves accented with silver, it adds texture and structure to mixed plantings. In the garden in warm weather, it can grow three feet tall or more, but it stays more compact in containers and in moderate climates. The variegated English ivy echoes the color of the planter in its gray foliage with white margins. It's a popular trailing texture plant for mixed containers. There is an abundance of variegated ivies available today, so if you can't find this particular variety, you should easily find one similar in color.

Container Characteristics

A stone trough like this is a welcome change from the often round, predominantly clay containers. What I like about these kinds of planters in particular is their porosity, which not only provides the air circulation needed for good plant performance, but it also makes them age over time as water seeps through them, adding to their character. This trough's dimensions are ten by sixteen inches.

Care Clues

Deadhead the verbena regularly to encourage profuse bloom production. If any of the plants get too big, trim them back as desired. This might be the case with the *Strobilanthes* if you live in a hot climate.

Plant Personalities

The warm, spirited colors of this container garden combine foliage and flowering plants in yellow, orange, and red tones.

Carex flagellifera 'Toffee Twist' provides height and texture. Its thin, bronze leaves are very subtle. Although sedge is botanically speaking not a grass, it's commonly handled as one. This particular variety has a graceful, slightly weeping habit. The second foliage plant that was used for texture is golden sage, *Salvia* 'Icterina'. It also picks up the color theme with its green and golden yellow variegated leaves. With its mounding habit, it fits perfectly into this front center spot. The leaves are very aromatic and may be used as culinary herb.

Petunia 'Supertunia Red' is one of the few trailing, truly red petunias. It has large red flowers and a vigorous, cascading habit. 'Supertunia'—like most trailing petunias—can grow very fast and may trail up to three feet or more. *Arctotis* 'Sunspot' is the tallest growing flowering plant in this design. Its daisy-shaped, orange flowers are held high above the compact, silver-green foliage. Another orange flowering plant is *Osteospermum* 'Orange Symphony'. Compared to many other *Osteospermum* varieties, it has a very compact, semi-trailing habit that is best used along the edges of containers. It's also a very heat-tolerant selection and flowers throughout the summer. The yellow color spectrum is present in *Bidens* 'Peter's Gold Carpet'. This vigorous, trailing selection has five-petaled, bright yellow flowers with a sweet honey fragrance.

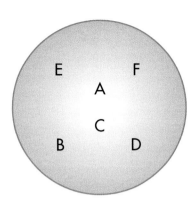

A = *Carex flagellifera* 'Toffee Twist'
B = *Petunia* 'Supertunia Red'
C = *Salvia* 'Icterina' (sage)
D = *Osteospermum* 'Orange Symphony'
E = *Arctotis* 'Sunspot'
F = *Bidens* 'Peter's Gold Carpet'

Container Characteristics

The warm color theme is carried through to the container with this classic terra cotta pot. Because I used a lot of trailing plants, you can't see much of it. This pot doesn't have the tapered shape of many simple pots, but it's wider and more bellied, which leaves room for more potting mix, which in turn allows for better moisture retention. If you can't find a pot in this shape, you can use any terra cotta planter. This pot is twelve inches in diameter.

Care Clues

Deadhead the *Arctotis* and *Osteospermum* regularly to keep the plants looking neat and blooming abundantly. If any of the trailing plants get too big for your taste, cut them back. The sage leaves can be used as a culinary herb. Both the sage and *Carex* are perennial, the sage to USDA Zone 5 and *Carex* to Zone 7. They can be planted in a perennial bed at the end of the season.

Plant Personalities

For a partially shady location, this combination of flowers and foliage plants creates a colorful, low-maintenance design.

The center plant is *Artemisia* 'Oriental Limelight'. Its yellow and green variegated foliage grows compact at first, but then develops tall, upright branches. Its colors are used a second time, this time in the most trailing element, *Sutera* 'Gold 'n' Pearls'. This is an unusual selection of a popular favorite. Where most *Sutera*—more commonly known as bacopa—have green leaves, 'Gold 'n' Pearls' has golden yellow and green variegated foliage. It doesn't flower quite as heavily, but the beautiful foliage more than makes up for that. The third foliage plant in this design is a rex begonia. Rex begonias are great for shady and partially shady locations. They need warm temperatures because temperatures below 45°F halt growth and temperatures below 40°F cause damage. In hot, dry climates, shade is important. Because they grow more slowly than the other varieties in the design, use begonias in five- or six-inch pots and the remainder of the plants in four-inch pots. If you can't find this particular variety, substitute with one of the many other varieties on the market, but look for a similar color.

Heliotropium 'Nagano' with its purple flowers echoes the color in the center of the begonia leaves. 'Nagano' is a fairly compact variety with a slight vanilla scent. If you can't find 'Nagano', make sure to look for a

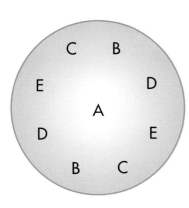

A = *Artemisia* 'Oriental Limelight'
B = *Begonia rex* 'Houston Fiesta' (2)
C = *Heliotropium* 'Nagano' (2)
D = *Diascia* 'Strawberry Sundae' (2)
E = *Sutera* 'Gold 'n' Pearls' (bacopa) (2)

compact variety as a substitute. Another flowering plant is *Diascia* 'Strawberry Sundae'. Its medium-pink flowers sit atop compact, mounding foliage with delicate leaves. As it grows bigger, it droops slightly over the edges of the planter.

Container Characteristics

This ornate container is made of plastic, which makes it lightweight and chip resistant. It's eighteen inches in diameter, but a slightly smaller one, such as sixteen inches, would be big enough for the number and sizes of plants used. Because there are few trailing plants in this design, you could also use a shorter one.

Care Clues

Deadhead the heliotrope regularly to keep the flowers coming more abundantly and to keep the plants looking tidy. Other than that, this is a low-maintenance design. Make sure to wait until the temperatures have warmed before you plant because rex begonias and heliotrope like warm weather. In the fall, you can bring the begonias indoors and use them as houseplants during winter.

Plant Personalities

This purple-themed planter dominated by verbena is planted into a topiary frame that's filled with moss and planted with English ivy. In other words, it's a "living planter."

I used *Phormium,* also known as New Zealand flax, to add height. It's one of my favorites to use in container gardens because it adds height without being overpowering. Availability is still limited in some areas, but *Phormium* comes in many colors, so use whatever color you can find. It grows a lot more slowly than the other plants in the planter, so make sure that you use a good-sized plant. Ideally, buy a six-inch or gallon *Phormium* and the other plants in four-inch pots.

Nemesia 'Blue Bird' and *Verbena* 'Temari Patio Rose' make up the second tier. Both are compact, upright plants of medium height in shades of purple. Unlike the other verbenas in this planter, the 'Temari Patio' series is upright growing, which is important for this particular pot. I also added a variegated thyme for its texture, 'Golden King'. It's quite inconspicuous compared to the abundant colors of the verbenas.

A broad variety of trailing verbena from the 'Babylon' series accounts for the trailing elements. I chose pink, white, and blue—which is actually a bluish purple—to continue the color theme. If you can't find these particular varieties, look for similar colors, but make sure that they are trailing.

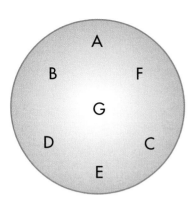

A = *Phormium* (New Zealand flax)
B = *Nemesia* 'Blue Bird'
C = *Verbena* 'Babylon Pink'
D = *Verbena* 'Babylon White'
E = *Verbena* 'Babylon Blue'
F = *Verbena* 'Temari Patio Rose'
G = *Thymus* 'Golden King' (thyme)
Also needed: *Hedera* (English ivy)

Container Characteristics

This container is actually a topiary frame from Green Piece Wire Art. It was completely filled with moss, but I took some of the moss out to create a sufficient planting cavity. The base of this urn-shaped planter is still solidly filled with moss and so are its sides. After filling the planter with potting mix and planting the plants on top, I planted English ivy along the edges and pinned its branches with bobby pins very tightly to the moss walls. Repeat this process as the ivy continues to grow until the planter is covered.

Care Clues

If you deadhead the verbenas regularly, you will get a greater and more continuous show of color. If you have a large number of spent flowers at once, you can give them a hard trim. If you plant English ivy along the moss, as in this example, make sure that you moisten the moss well before planting. For the first few weeks, you'll need to water the sides of the planter where the ivy is growing, because it won't yet have sufficient roots to retrieve water from the core. Once the ivy is well established, watering only from top should be sufficient, but check periodically to be sure, especially during hot weather. As the English ivy continues to grow, pin the branches down with bobby pins or cut them off after the topiary is completely covered.

Plant Personalities

This simple but effective design utilizes two plant types: verbena and petunia. Its main theme is purple, with white flowers used to brighten the design.

The center plant is *Verbena* 'Babylon Lilac' with its rich, purple flower clusters. Instead of using an upright plant and following the classic planting diagram, I decided to use a trailing variety instead. But since the plant is on top in the center and can't trail down, it spreads horizontally and covers most of the top of the basket. It gives it just a few inches of height in the center, which is especially good for baskets that are hanging at or above eye level.

The second plant is also a verbena from the 'Babylon' series, this time 'Babylon Light Blue'. It has the same ferny foliage and large flower clusters as the 'Lilac' variety, but this time in a softer, lavender shade. This shade complements the darker variety very well to create a purple theme in different intensities.

To brighten the design, I added white flower accents with *Petunia* 'Supertunia Mini White'. Compared to other 'Supertunia', the 'Mini' series is not as extremely trailing, which looks better with the moderately trailing verbena varieties. What I like particularly about this white variety are its snow-white flowers because white petunia blooms sometimes have a greenish or brownish eye.

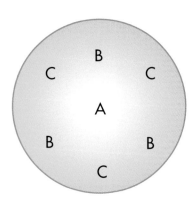

A = *Verbena* 'Babylon Lilac'
B = *Verbena* 'Babylon Light Blue' (3)
C = *Petunia* 'Supertunia Mini White' (3)

Container Characteristics

Once again I used my favorite—a moss basket—with a fourteen-inch diameter. But since these plants are so trailing, they quickly cover the basket, which allows you to use a lower-priced alternative. But if you want a great look from the get-go, a natural looking basket such as one made of moss or cedar is more than worth it. Since verbenas and petunias grow fast, baskets made of natural fiber can dry out quickly once the plants are big. If this is a concern, look for baskets with built-in water reservoirs.

Care Clues

The varieties in this design flower fairly early in the spring, so you can give this mixed basket an early start. It's a very low-maintenance design that doesn't require any special care other than regular fertilization, which is important to maintain good plant performance and flower power. Deadheading the verbenas regularly keeps the flowers coming in abundance.

Plant Personalities

The picture doesn't quite show the characteristics of this planter, but it's actually taller in the back than in the front. This demands special attention to careful plant selection. To add substantial height, I planted *Phormium* in the back. Also known as New Zealand flax, this is an excellent plant for container gardens. Nurseries also see its value and, as a result, *Phormium* has become much more readily available over the last years. For this color theme, I chose a red variety, but a brownish tone would also work.

The plants in the middle tier are of moderate height to create a transition to the trailing plants in front. *Cuphea* 'Firefly' is a fun plant with pinwheel-shaped, slightly ruffled flowers in deep magenta. It has a wiry growth habit, which makes it a prime candidate for mixed containers, where it can grow in between other plants. *Verbena* 'Temari Patio Rose' is an upright variety with a full growth habit. Its flowers are also a deep magenta color, echoing the color of *Cuphea*. If you can't find this particular variety, match the color, but also try to match the growth habit so you have an upright or mounding component in the center and not a trailing one. *Diascia* 'Little Charmer' is the shortest of the middle plants. It has compact, upright flower stems with pink blooms. When given the chance, it drapes over the edges of containers.

The front is made up of strictly trailing elements. *Petunia* 'Supertunia Royal Velvet' is a compact trailer with rich, deep purple flowers that look and feel like velvet. *Lotus* 'Amazon Sunset' is also known as lotus vine. A

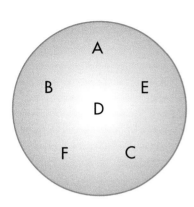

A = *Phormium* (New Zealand flax)
B = *Cuphea* 'Firefly'
C = *Lotus* 'Amazon Sunset'
D = *Verbena* 'Temari Patio Rose'
E = *Diascia* 'Little Charmer'
F = *Petunia* 'Supertunia Royal Velvet'

lot of designers use it primarily for its foliage, which is what I did here, and you might not even know that it flowers. But lotus actually creates beautiful, flaming orange blooms. It needs cool temperatures to start blooming, but 'Amazon Sunset' continues blooming longer than traditional varieties. Don't worry if you can't get yours to bloom—the needle-thin, silver foliage easily makes up for any lack of flowers.

Container Characteristics

This container is certain to make your neighbors do a double take! Put it on your front lawn and it'll look as if it's partially buried in the ground. Its Roman-inspired, antique styling looks superb wherever you put it. It's best showcased in a prominent spot.

It's taller in the back than in the front, which makes it a little trickier to plant. The actual planting surface is about fourteen inches in diameter. Fill it with potting mix to the lower rim and accept that there will be room in the back that you won't be able to fill. By placing tall plants in the back, you will fill that void. A planter of this size gets quite heavy once planted. It's best to plant it in its final spot, or have several pairs of strong hands available to move it.

Care Clues

Deadheading the verbena regularly keeps new flowers coming in abundance. If the petunia and lotus start to hide more of the planter than you want them to, cut them back as desired.

Plant Personalities

This petite bowl is great as a centerpiece for your summer party or as a summer-long decoration on your patio table.

The plant in the center is *Diascia* 'Summer Celebration Coral Belle'. It has a compact, low-growing habit and coral flowers. You'll want to have a compact variety such as this in this small bowl. While *Diascia* never used to be one of the best choices for hot summer temperatures, breeders have greatly improved upon those traits, and today's varieties hold up well through most summer climates, provided they are watered regularly.

The *Diascia* is surrounded by purple flowers, one of which is *Ageratum* 'Artist Purple'. 'Artist Purple' is a compact *Ageratum* that is grown from cuttings, whereas most ageratums are grown from seed. 'Artist Purple' has a long blooming period over which it produces an abundance of purple flowers with a reddish tinge. The second purple flower surrounding the *Diascia* is *Calibrachoa* 'Superbells Blue'. *Calibrachoa* has small, miniature petunia-like flowers and a trailing growth habit. 'Superbells Blue' has deep purple-blue flowers accented by dark veins and a yellowish center. It provides a welcome trailing element in this design.

To fit into this small bowl, I used a four-inch *Diascia* and three-inch ageratums and *Calibrachoa*. If you can't locate plants in three-inch pots, look for small plants in four-inch pots and gently remove some of the potting mix before planting. Or look for a larger bowl or planter, but if all

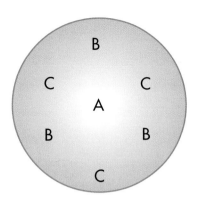

A = *Diascia* 'Summer Celebration Coral Belle'
B = *Ageratum* 'Artist Purple' (3)
C = *Calibrachoa* 'Superbells Blue' (3)

plants are in four-inch pots, the purple colors will be more dominant than the dominant coral in this design.

Container Characteristics

This small container has a nine-inch diameter and is fairly shallow, which makes it a good candidate as centerpiece for a patio table. Because it's glazed, it's less porous and looses less water than a non-glazed clay container would, which is especially good during hot summer weather.

Care Clues

This is a very low-maintenance design. If the *Calibrachoa* trails too much and hides more of the bowl than you wish, simply trim it back as desired.

Plant Personalities

This design in predominantly purple colors combines foliage and flowering plants.

The tallest plant is *Angelonia* 'Angelface Violet'. This summer snapdragon is heat resistant and will flower all summer long, even in hot climates. The tall flower spikes add height and color at the same time. As a medium-height plant in the same color theme, I used *Nemesia* 'Blue Bird'. With its soft purple-blue color and lighter centers, it softens the dark purple of two of the other flowering plants. The third purple flower is *Verbena* 'Babylon Blue' in the front of the design. Its growth habit is very low and trailing, which works perfectly in this particular location. Its color echoes the *Angelonia* flowers, which connects the design visually. If you need to substitute, look for a similar color and growth habit to keep the impact of the overall design.

Diascia 'Summer's Dance' adds a second color to the design with its soft peach-colored blooms. Their light shade reflects the light centers of *Angelonia* and *Nemesia*, although the colors are not identical. This guides the eye from one plant to the next.

To add more texture, I used two foliage plants. Although *Carex*, commonly called sedge, is botanically speaking not categorized as a grass, it is handled and known as an ornamental grass. This selection, also called weeping brown New Zealand sedge, adds movement and texture with its needle-thin leaves. Since this sedge grows more slowly than the other

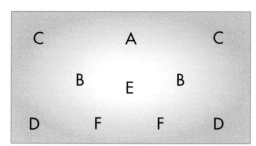

A = *Angelonia* 'Angelface Violet'
B = *Carex flagellifera* 'Toffee Twist' (2)
C = *Nemesia* 'Blue Bird' (2)
D = *Muehlenbeckia* (creeping wirevine) (2)
E = *Diascia* 'Summer's Dance'
F = *Verbena* 'Babylon Blue' (2)

plants in the container, you will want to look for nice, full, well-developed plant so that the other plants don't overpower it. The second texture plant is *Muehlenbeckia,* also called creeping wirevine. With its small, emerald green, glossy leaves and wiry growth, it's perfect for mixed plantings where it can weave through the other plants. It also adds a welcome trailing element along the edges of this planter.

Container Characteristics

I chose a stunning iron container that is full of character. Its elegant, formal look is softened over time, as it ages beautifully to an antique look. Its neutral gray color keeps the focus on the plants. The dimensions of this particular planter are twenty-two by twelve inches. When you find one like it, make sure that it has drainage holes, or drill some before planting.

Care Clues

Deadheading the verbena regularly results in more abundant and continuous bloom production. Besides that, this is a low-maintenance design. *Muehlenbeckia* and *Carex* are frost hardy to USDA Zone 5, so if you live in those or warmer climates, you can take the planter apart at the end of the season and plant them in the garden. USDA Zones 8 and warmer can also use *Nemesia* and verbena as perennials.

Plant Personalities

A container garden as rich in color and texture as this one is guaranteed to capture the eye. Dark foliage builds a dramatic backdrop for vibrant flowers. It has a good balance of flowers and foliage and a beautiful planter to set it off.

Leatherleaf sedge provides airy, unobtrusive height. Although not considered a grass botanically speaking, it is handled and used as an ornamental grass. Because it grows more slowly than the rest of the plants, look for a well-developed plant. Buy one pot size larger than the others if necessary. Its bronze-colored, needle-thin leaves grow straight up, with curlicue tips. Its dark foliage is echoed in *Persicaria* 'Red Dragon', a perennial with dark purple, almost black, foliage with silver accents. Although it produces small, creamy white flowers, they definitely play second fiddle to the stunning foliage. The trailing foliage element is *Muehlenbeckia*, creeping wirevine. It's a wonderful container plant because of its wiry growth. Its small, emerald green foliage weaves between the other plants and trails at the same time.

The vibrant flowers stand out against the dark foliage backdrop. The bright orange blooms belong to *Bracteantha* 'Sundaze Bronze Orange', an upright growing strawflower with a fairly compact habit and a floriferous, free-blooming nature. Its orange color is echoed in *Calibrachoa* 'Terra Cotta', which is mostly hidden in the picture but guaranteed to

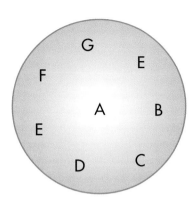

A = *Carex buchananii* (leatherleaf sedge)
B = *Bracteantha* 'Sundaze Bronze Orange'
C = *Muehlenbeckia* (creeping wirevine)
D = *Heliotropium* 'Nagano'
E = *Persicaria* 'Red Dragon' (2)
F = *Calibrachoa* 'Million Bells Terra Cotta'
G = *Cuphea* 'Tiny Mice'

get attention on your patio with its multitone flowers in warm, Mediterranean hues.

The heliotrope adds color and fragrance at the same time. Its dark purple flowers have a sweet vanilla scent. Its color is subtly repeated in the calyx of *Cuphea* 'Tiny Mice'. 'Tiny Mice' is a really fun plant with flowers that look like the face of a mouse—another attention-getter in this design!

Container Characteristics

I chose to use plants that show more of the container rather than covering it with trailing elements, simply because it's so beautiful. Its Mediterranean flair looks great in many settings. Its mouth is sixteen inches wide, but the entire pot is quite a bit larger, as it flares out in the middle.

Care Clues

Deadhead the strawflower and heliotrope regularly to assure continuous blooms. None of the other plants require special care. *Persicaria* and *Muehlenbeckia* may be cut back if they get too big. At the end of the season, take the plants apart carefully and plant the *Carex, Persicaria,* and *Muehlenbeckia* in the ground. They are frost hardy to USDA Hardiness Zones 6 (*Carex* and *Muehlenbeckia*) and 5 (*Persicaria*).

Plant Personalities

When I see this mixed basket, I automatically think of spring because of its soft, pastel colors. But it's a great design for any time of the year.

In the center is *Osteospermum* 'Cream Symphony', with soft yellow flowers. The 'Symphony' series is a good choice for the center of hanging baskets because of its compact, mounding growth. Where other *Osteospermum* varieties might get too tall, this series is especially low-growing and spreading. It has also excellent heat tolerance, which is what you'll want so that you have a continuous show of flowers throughout the summer and not just green foliage in the center.

The cheerful pink flowers belong to *Diascia* 'Strawberry Sundae'. Its growth habit is both mounding and semi-trailing, which makes it a good middle-row plant for hanging baskets. *Diascia,* also called twinspur, has intriguingly shaped flowers. The varieties available today are much more heat tolerant than those that first came to the market in the early 1990s, so you usually have good luck with them year-round.

The most trailing element in this design is *Petunia* 'Supertunia Mini Blue Veined'. Its flowers first open up with a soft blush of lavender before turning white once they're fully open. The dark blue veins maintain their color throughout each flower's life. While some 'Supertunia' can get three feet long or more, the 'Mini' series consists of more moderate trailers, which contributes to a round basket rather than an oblong one.

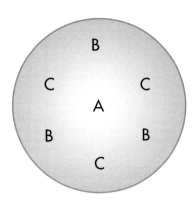

A = *Osteospermum* 'Cream Symphony'
B = *Diascia* 'Strawberry Sundae' (3)
C = *Petunia* 'Supertunia Mini Blue Veined' (3)

Container Characteristics

If you have plants that are very trailing, such as the 'Supertunia', you won't see the basket itself for very long, which would allow you to use a low-priced version. But I like using those made of natural fiber, especially moss. In this design, I used a fourteen-inch moss basket because until the plants are fully grown you can see part of the basket, and moss adds to the natural look. Besides, plant performance in moss baskets is very good.

Care Clues

All of the varieties in this design start flowering fairly early in spring, so you can start this mixed basket early. With proper fertilization and care, it'll last all summer. The *Osteospermum* benefits from regular deadheading, but none of the other varieties requires special maintenance.

Plant Personalities

This container in warm colors uses different shades of red and yellow. The intense red tones are represented by *Pelargonium* 'Fireworks Scarlet', a beautifully ornamental form with star-shaped flowers and foliage shaped like maple leafs. The 'Fireworks' series came to the U.S. from Germany and is new to the market here. The flowers of 'Fireworks Scarlet' come in large clusters of the most vibrant red. Their intense red color is echoed in *Verbena* 'Tukana Scarlet', a vigorous form with large flower clusters and a compact but trailing habit. These two plants set the tone for this warm, spirited combination.

While the two red shades are almost identical, the yellow tones are represented in a wider range of intensities. The darkest yellow is almost orange with *Arctotis* 'Sunspot', a daisy-shaped flower that might remind you of *Gerbera*. This dark-eyed beauty's petals intensify in color toward their tips, which makes for an intriguing color display. The second yellow flowering plant, *Osteospermum* 'Cream Symphony', is of the palest yellow. It's a mounding and semi-trailing type that fits perfectly into this spot, where many other *Osteospermum* varieties would get too tall.

To add more texture, I included an ornamental grass, *Hakonechloa macra* 'Aureola', a beautifully cascading grass with gold and green variegation that echoes the color of the *Osteospermum* flowers in its palest parts. To give it room to spill over the edges of the container, angle the verbena and *Osteospermum* so that they face outward—then the grass has room to

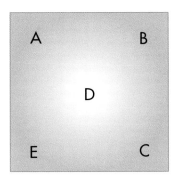

A = *Arctotis* 'Sunspot'
B = *Pelargonium* 'Fireworks Scarlet'
C = *Osteospermum* 'Cream Symphony'
D = *Hakonechloa macra* 'Aureola'
E = *Verbena* 'Tukana Scarlet'

cascade. Since ornamental grasses often grow more slowly than the other plants in this planter, look for a well-developed plant or buy it one or two pot sizes larger than the others.

Container Characteristics

This beautiful, brown glazed planter complements the warm color theme of the plants, but it's also subtle enough to keep the focus on the plants. This particular container is approximately nine inches square. If you use a larger or smaller container, adjust the number or size of the plants accordingly.

Care Clues

Deadhead the flowering plants regularly to encourage continuous flower production. If any of the plants tries to overtake the ornamental grass, trim it back. Watch for aphids on the *Arctotis*.

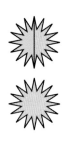

Plant Personalities

If you need a container garden for a partially shady location, try this combination of texture-rich plants.

In the center is *Acorus gramineus* 'Variegatus', a variegated sweet flag. It has creamy white and green striped leaves and a compact, clumping habit. This ornamental grass is popular for container garden because of its non-invasive growth. It doesn't grow very fast, so make sure to start with a well-developed plant. Its colors can once again be found in *Hedera* 'Yellow Ripple', a variegated English ivy. English ivy is a classic container garden plant and is excellent in shady spots where plant selection is often limited. There are countless English ivy varieties on the market today, so feel free to substitute a similar color if you can't locate 'Yellow Ripple'.

The remaining two plants represent purple tones. *Torenia* 'Summer Wave Blue', also called wishbone flower, is a trailing variety with two-toned, purple-blue flowers. It thrives in warm temperatures and likes partial shade, where its foliage remains lush green, whereas it turns slightly bronze and may even burn in full sun. Both its lighter and darker shades of purple are echoed in *Begonia* 'Albuquerque Midnight Sky', a rex begonia from the 'Great American Cities' series. This effect connects the plants visually by leading the eye from one plant to the other. Rex begonias are great for shady and partially shady locations. They need warm temperatures because temperatures below 45°F halt growth and temperatures below 40°F cause damage. In hot, dry climates, shade is important. Because they grow more slowly than the other varieties in the design, use begonias in five- or six-inch pots and the remainder of the plants in four-inch pots. If you can't find this particular variety, substitute one of the many other varieties on the market, but look for a similar color.

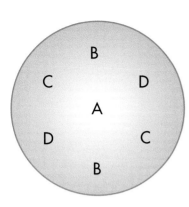

A = *Acorus gramineus* 'Variegatus'
B = *Begonia rex* 'Albuquerque Midnight Sky' (2)
C = *Torenia* 'Summer Wave Blue' (2)
D = *Hedera* 'Yellow Ripple' (English ivy) (2)

Container Characteristics

This bowl is very shallow, so it's OK to use a very simple, inexpensive one because not much of it remains visible. After the plants get larger, most of the bowl will be hidden. This bowl is sixteen inches in diameter.

Care Clues

This is a very low-maintenance design. None of the plants requires special care. In the fall, you can take the planter apart carefully and bring the begonias indoors to use them as houseplants during winter.

Plant Personalities

Here is a cheerful combination in a purple color theme that's sure to please you.

In the back are two different types of daisies, *Osteospermum* 'Dandenong Daisy Purple Blush' and *Felicia* 'Cape Town Blue'. The *Osteospermum* has large, white flowers with a soft purple blush and a purple ring around yellow centers. Although it closes its flowers at night and under low light conditions, the undersides of the petals are silver with a purple tinge. *Felicia* 'Cape Town Blue' is a bright blue daisy with a yellow center. Like the *Osteospermum*, it holds its flowers on long stems over compact foliage, which really shines the spotlight on the flowers.

Along the edges is *Sutera* 'Glacier Blue', also commonly called bacopa. Where many bacopas are white, this variety has large blue flowers and a cloudlike growth. If you can't find this particular variety, try to find one with lavender or blue flowers to achieve the same color effect.

The two flowering plants in the front carry on the purple-themed design. *Scaevola* 'Pink Fanfare', also known as fan flower due to its fan-shaped blooms, has lavender-pink, multi-toned flowers. It loves the heat and will start to cascade over the edges once it gets bigger. *Ageratum* 'Artist Blue' has purple-blue flowers and a compact, upright habit that builds a transition between the taller growing plants and the trailing ones.

Finally, for texture I added *Hedera* 'Glacier', a variegated English ivy with gray and white leaves that echo in part the color of the planter.

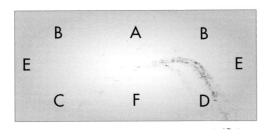

A = *Osteospermum* 'Dandenong Daisy Purple Blush'
B = *Felicia* 'Cape Town Blue' (2)
C = *Scaevola* 'Pink Fanfare'
D = *Hedera* 'Glacier' (English ivy)
E = *Sutera* 'Glacier Blue' (bacopa) (2)
F = *Ageratum* 'Artist Blue'

Container Characteristics

A stone trough like this is a welcome change from the often round, predominantly clay containers. What I like about these kinds of planters in particular is their porosity, which not only provides the air circulation needed for good plant performance, but it also makes them age over time as water seeps through them, adding to their character. This trough's dimensions are ten by sixteen inches.

Care Clues

You can deadhead the daisies occasionally to encourage profuse bloom production, but none of the other plants has any special care requirements.

Plant Personalities

A large planter chockfull with plants creates a stunning centerpiece on any patio or in the garden. This design focuses on different shades of purple.

Phormium, also called New Zealand flax, gives this design texture and height. There are many different varieties of *Phormium* available. I chose one with olive-green, purple-tinged leaves, but you can substitute a different variety. *Phormium* is an excellent container garden plant, and it's one of my favorites. Unfortunately, it's often hard to come by, but recently more and more nurseries have started offering it, so hopefully it'll be easier to find in the future. *Phormium* grows much more slowly than the other varieties, so start with a well-developed plant.

The purple theme is most prominent in the flowering plants. As mounding elements, I added *Osteospermum* 'Dandenong Daisy Purple Blush' and *Verbena* 'Temari Patio Rose'. Although the *Osteospermum* looks almost white in the picture, it actually has a very soft, purple blush along the tips of the petals. Its compact, mounding foliage sits well below the flowers, holding the blooms into the spotlight on long stems. The second mounding plant, *Verbena* 'Temari Patio Rose', adds the biggest color splash with its magenta-purple flower clusters. If you can't find this particular variety, make sure to look for one with a mounding or upright growth habit to best fill this spot.

The more trailing, purple flowering elements are *Brachyscome* 'Toucan Tango' and *Torenia* 'Summer Wave Blue'. *Brachyscome* is great for the edges

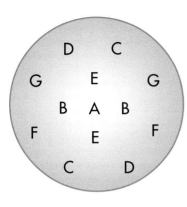

A = *Phormium* (New Zealand flax)
B = *Osteospermum* 'Dandenong Daisy
      Purple Blush' (2)
C = *Brachyscome* 'Toucan Tango' (2)
D = *Glechoma* 'Variegata' (2)
E = *Verbena* 'Temari Patio Rose' (2)
F = *Mentha* 'Nigra' (mint) (2)
G = *Torenia* 'Summer Wave Blue' (not visible) (2)

of containers, where it can cascade. The *Torenia* is not visible in this picture, but it has lovely, bluish purple flowers and a trailing growth habit.

To add more texture, I incorporated two foliage plants. *Glechoma* 'Variegata' has white and silver-green variegated foliage and a low-growing, cascading habit. Its white margins echo the color of the *Osteospermum* flowers and add brightness to the design. Black mint, *Mentha* 'Nigra', has dark, purple-green leaves that are very aromatic and can be used in the kitchen.

Container Characteristics

I love stone planters like this—they are full of character. Because they are porous and let moisture through, they age over time. Although hard to see in the picture, this one has already started to age, giving it a rustic look. This particular planter is a round pot with a twenty-inch diameter.

Care Clues

Deadhead the *Osteospermum* and verbena regularly to encourage profuse blooms. None of the other plants needs any special care. If some start to be more aggressive than others, trim them back to give the slower growers room.

Plant Personalities

A classic example of color echoing, this design frequently repeats yellow and pink tones in a combination of foliage and flowering plants. It's one of my favorite container gardens, not only because of its colors but also because of its asymmetrical design.

The ornamental grass in the center right is *Pennisetum* 'Red Riding Hood', also sold as 'Dwarf Rubrum' and 'Eaton Canyon'. While the regular version of this purple fountain grass would get too tall, 'Red Riding Hood' is just right, with its thirty-inch mature height. Its burgundy flower plumes mature to soft beige. You can find more burgundy foliage in *Coleus* 'Super Sun Plum Parfait' to the left. Plant breeders and collectors have brought fantastic varieties of coleus to the market over the last few years. They offer a wide range of colors, shapes, and heights to meet your design needs. You can use them in full-sun combinations such as this because they are more sun-tolerant than older varieties.

The lighter colored centers of the coleus foliage lead into one of the other main colors, pink. Its most vibrant hues are repeated in *Calibrachoa* 'Million Bells Cherry Pink' in the front right, a semi-trailing plant with small flowers resembling a miniature petunia. The flowers of *Bracteantha* 'Sundaze Pink' also repeat the vibrant pink shades on the edges of its star-shaped, paper-like strawflowers, but fade to a softer tint toward the center. The 'Sundaze' series of strawflowers has a compact habit, which makes them well suited as medium-height plants in container gardens. The soft

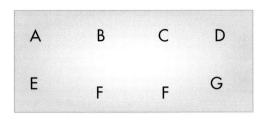

A = *Coleus* 'Super Sun Plum Parfait'

B = *Bracteantha* 'Sundaze Pink'

C = *Pennisetum setaceum* 'Red Riding Hood'

D = *Coleus* 'Amora'

E = *Calibrachoa* 'Million Bells Yellow'

F = *Vinca* vine (2)

G = *Calibrachoa* 'Million Bells Cherry Pink'

pink sections of its petals are echoed in the undersides of *Coleus* 'Amora', a beautiful, multicolored variety.

Another color that can be found repeatedly is yellow. Not only is it represented in the cheery yellow centers of the strawflowers, but also in *Calibrachoa* 'Million Bells Yellow', a plant similar in habit to the earlier described 'Cherry Pink', but with soft yellow flowers. Very soft tints of yellow can be found in the foliage of *Coleus* 'Amora', and, in its palest form, in the margins of vinca vine in the front.

Container Characteristics

Although hard to see, this design uses a rectangular stone planter with dimensions of ten by sixteen inches. These types of planters are rich in texture and character, as they age beautifully and take on a darker color when they are wet.

Care Clues

This is a low-maintenance design that requires little deadheading or pruning. You can trim spent flowers of the purple fountain grass if you don't care for their soft beige color. Deadhead the strawflower regularly to keep it looking tidy and blooming in abundance.

Container Garden Ideas

ere are a few more ideas for fabulous container gardens. Use them for inspiration or copy them. Most of all, enjoy!

WHAT DO YOU do with a tall, majestic planter like this? You certainly don't want to hide it because not only is it beautiful, but planters like this come with a hefty price tag. The right plant selection helps showcase your masterpiece, and it'll be worth every penny.

The challenge in this situation was that the diameter of the opening on top is small, but a tall planter asks for tall plants, which often come in large pots. By using *Phormium* (New Zealand flax), which grows tall, you can get the height you need with only one plant. *Muehlenbeckia* and *Hedera* (English ivy) provide trailing elements in colors that look good with the respective *Phormium* variety. Use small plants of the trailing varieties because you're likely to have little space left after placing the *Phormium*. Or buy larger plants that you can separate into smaller, individual plantlets.

PLANNING A TEA party in your garden? Here is a unique decorating idea. This container garden is planted in a topiary frame shaped like a

teapot, from Green Piece Wire Art. When I received this topiary, it was completely filled with moss. To plant it, take most of the moss out, leaving it only in the handle and bottom. Leave enough moss to thickly line the bottom and sides of the frame. The sides should be covered to about one third or one half of its height. Fill the moss-lined portion with potting mix and start planting with small, nonaggressive plants. Thread some branches through the wire frame and some along the handle. The particular plants used here are vinca vine, *Sutera* (bacopa), *Acorus* (sweet flag), *Brachyscome*, *Heuchera*, and *Armeria*.

ARE YOU looking for an unusual gift idea that can be assembled in minutes? This miniature wooden house was planted with one four-inch pot each of red cyclamen, *Ficus pumila,* and a fern, but you could easily substitute different plants. This planter can be placed in a shady spot outside or

in a bright window in the house. Once the plants are past their prime, you can replant it with fresh plants or use it in a whole new way, as a bird feeder, for example, or you can decorate it with dried flowers.

THIS ROOSTER won't wake you in the morning! I used a topiary frame from Green Piece Wire Art that's entirely filled with moss. Before planting, make sure to moisten the moss thoroughly. You can do this best by letting it soak in a tub of water for a few hours. If you water it with a hose, you most likely won't get it wet all the way to the core.

Some of the plants used are succulents. Succulents are great for topiaries because they need little water and they root easily. Select different succulents and snip off small cuttings, which you then insert into the moss. Besides the succulents, I used *Ophiopogon* (black mondo grass) on the head and neck, *Trifolium* 'Dark Dancer' on the back, *Ajuga* 'Chocolate Chip' on the chest, and variegated *Glechoma* on the wings. For the tail "feathers," I chose two ornamental grasses—*Scirpus cernuus* (fiber-optic grass) and *Acorus* 'Ogon' (variegated sweet flag)—as well as *Vinca* 'Illumination' to trail down. Because these plants were already rooted, I had to use very small plants, otherwise I couldn't have gotten them into the wire frame. I divided the plants I had into individual plantlets so that they would fit.

The biggest challenge for a topiary frame like this is to keep it watered. By choosing plants that can tolerate shade, the water need is slightly reduced, but you might still have to water daily. A good way to keep the moss moist is to put the frame's "feet" in a tub of water.

Next to the rooster are two topiary slippers, also planted with succulents.

THIS WREATH, seen at Molbak's in Woodinville, Washington, is a wonderful way to greet your visitors at your front door. It is planted with

bromeliads, impatiens, ferns, and lobelia. The pink-striped bromeliads echo the color of the impatiens. The result is a beautiful, eye-catching design.

Before planting, moisten the moss well by letting the wreath soak in water. Use small plants and a knife to insert the plants into the moss. Make sure to water thoroughly and often. By using plants that tolerate shade, you reduce the arrangement's water needs, making its care and maintenance a lot easier.

YOU COULD SAY that this pot takes container gardening to the next level, because it gives you a display of flowers on two tiers.

This lantana standard is underplanted with an abundance of colorful flowers, including fuchsia, *Sutera* (bacopa), zonal geraniums, lobelia, *Scaevola*, and *Brachyscome*. A lantana standard like this is several years old and can be overwintered in a relatively bright, frost-free basement or garage or on an enclosed porch. Some nurseries even accept customers' plants as "houseguests" over winter and care for them for a fee. The plants in the bottom are best replaced every year, unless you live in a frost-free climate, where you can enjoy the entire design year-round.

CONTAINER GARDENS don't have to have flowers at all. This example is planted with a wide variety of the many beautiful lettuces that are available today. Containerized lettuce like this is especially practical for condominium gardeners who don't have access to a vegetable garden. But even if you have a big garden, you might still want to have this  planter on your patio for the times when you need only a few leaves and don't want to make the trip to the vegetable garden.

One of the things that I like especially about this planter is the type of container used: A harvest basket like this looks great when planted with vegetables.

NOT EVERYTHING you create needs to look like it came out of the pages of *Fine Gardening* magazine. If you're into whimsy, this container garden might be for you. Clay planters like this are available in many different animal shapes. This one is planted with petunias, verbenas, marigolds, lobelias, and dianthus, but you could choose any annu-  al or perennial that you like, provided it stays small. Don't expect this container garden to last from April until October, but it sure makes a great gift item that your friends will treasure for many weeks or even months. After that, it can be replanted.

A CONTAINER garden doesn't need to be brimming with plants. This tasteful design resembles a miniature rock garden. It's planted with succulents and other typical rock garden plants and embellished with tree roots

and rocks. Because rock garden plants don't need much water and fertilizer, this arrangement is quite easy to care for. Use a shallow container, such as this terra cotta bowl, and a sandy, well-drained potting mix. This miniature rock garden looks great where it can get the attention it deserves, such as in a prominent spot on your patio or next to a water feature.

MANY HOUSEPLANTS BENEFIT from spending the summer outdoors. But instead of just moving them into a corner of your patio, why

not turn them into an attention-grabbing container garden? This ficus tree was placed in a large terra cotta planter and underplanted with shade-loving plants such as ferns, begonia, and impatiens in soft colors to complement the variegated foliage of the ficus. Your houseplant gets the fresh air treatment it needs, and you get an almost-instant container garden.

If you move your houseplants outdoors, make sure to protect them from frost and acclimate them to outdoors conditions gradually. Remember that light intensities outdoors are usually a lot higher than indoors, even if you had your plant at a bright window. In the fall, discard the annuals and bring your houseplant back indoors.

If you live in a mild, frost-free climate, you can enjoy a container garden like this year-round.

GROUPINGS OF container gardens that share a similar color scheme are especially effective. Just the way you might plant an entire flowerbed in one color scheme, a grouping of similar container gardens results in a higher color impact.

The planter in the back right corner is the same as featured on page 174. The lotus vine from that design is used again in the planter in the back left corner, and the *Bergenia* is used again in the planter in the front. I also used the *Phormium* (New Zealand flax) twice. You can't help but let your eyes travel from one planter to the next. Besides using identical plants twice, I also used similar ones repeatedly. For example, the color of *Helichrysum* 'Icicles' in the back left is similar to that of lotus vine. I also used two varieties of *Diascia*: 'Coral Belle' is in the back left, while 'Little Charmer' is in the planter in the front. The two texture plants in the front planter are *Muehlenbeckia* (creeping wirevine) and *Carex flagellifera* 'Toffee Twist', a sedge.

I also used similar, but not identical, planters. While the two designs in the back use stone planters, the one in front is a galvanized metal bucket. The two types of containers bring enough similarities to make the grouping look harmonious, but they also have enough individuality to keep the interest and eye-appeal high. If you use a galvanized metal planter like this, make sure that it has drainage holes before you plant, or drill some if it doesn't.

USDA
Frost Hardiness
Zone Map

Agricultural Research Service, USDA, Beltsville, Maryland.

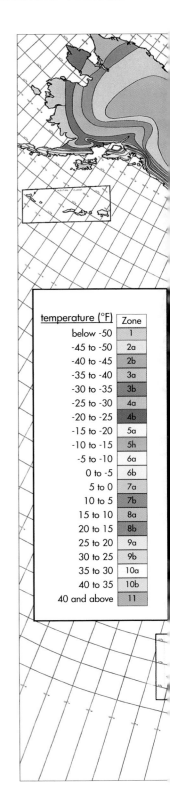

temperature (°F)	Zone
below -50	1
-45 to -50	2a
-40 to -45	2b
-35 to -40	3a
-30 to -35	3b
-25 to -30	4a
-20 to -25	4b
-15 to -20	5a
-10 to -15	5h
-5 to -10	6a
0 to -5	6b
5 to 0	7a
10 to 5	7b
15 to 10	8a
20 to 15	8b
25 to 20	9a
30 to 25	9b
35 to 30	10a
40 to 35	10b
40 and above	11

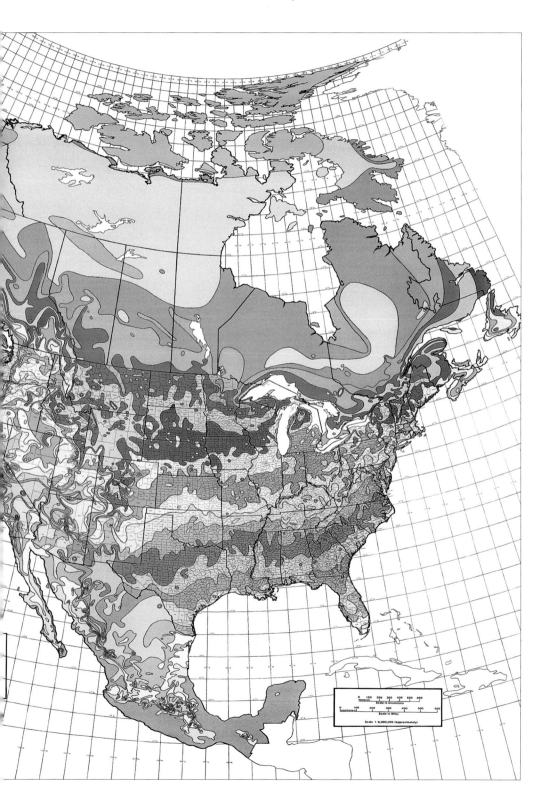

Glossary of Terms

Some of the terms used in this book might be new to you. The following is a glossary of terms to shed some light on the sometimes confusing language of horticulture and designing with color.

Analogous colors. These are colors that are next to each other on the color wheel. They are related and similar, such as blue, blue-purple, and purple. Also called harmonious colors, they are pleasing to the eye and unobtrusive. By expanding an analogous design to include another neighboring color—such as red-purple in our example—the design becomes less harmonious but increases its impact.

Calyx. The sepals of a flower as a group; the outermost parts of a flower.

Color echoing. The technique of using a color more than once in a container garden. This effect connects the design visually by guiding the eye from one plant to the next, wherever the color is repeated. The simplest form of color echoing is to use a certain flower color twice or more. A more refined and advanced way is to repeat a color in different areas, for example, to repeat a yellow flower color in yellow and green variegated foliage, or to repeat red veins from a flower in red stems of a foliage plant. Designs become especially intriguing if you use one color more than twice and if you echo more than just one color.

Color wheel. A simple tool that displays colors in a circle around a wheel. It's especially helpful in determining complementary colors and analogous colors. Color wheels are fairly inexpensive and available at artists' supply and crafts stores.

Complementary colors. Colors displayed on opposite ends of the color wheel. As the name implies, they complete each other or enhance each other. Each color appears more vibrant if used with its complementary color. A popular combination of complementary colors in plants is purple and yellow.

Corolla. The petals of a flower as a group.

Day length. The duration of daylight that's available any given time of the year. Some plants flower only after being exposed to a certain amount of daylight. Those plants are called "day length sensitive." Among day length sensitive plants are those that need short days to initiate blooms, and those that need long days to initiate blooms. Plants that flower regardless of the duration of daylight are called "day length neutral" or "day length insensitive."

Deadheading. The process of removing spent flowers. Deadheading keeps plants from producing seeds and encourages continuous bloom production.

Habit. The characteristic form in which a plant grows. Also referred to as "growth habit," frequently distinguished habits are trailing, spreading, cascading, prostrate, mounding, and upright.

Hue. Synonymously used for "color."

Monochromatic. A monochromatic design is made up of only one color, but in different saturations; for example, light blue, medium blue, and dark blue. A monochromatic design is always harmonious and pleasing to the eye, but might lack impact for some tastes. Paired with the right pottery, a monochromatic plant design can be very elegant and impressive.

Sepal. An individual leaf or part of the calyx.

Stamen. The pollen-carrying part of a flower.

Umbel. A cluster of small flowers that arise on a single stem, forming an umbrella-like shape.

USDA Frost Hardiness Zone. Based on the map published by the United States Department of Agriculture (USDA), which divides the United States into eleven zones based on the average annual minimum temperatures in each zone, with Zone 1 being the coldest and Zone 11 being the warmest. Generally, a plant listed as "hardy to Zone 5" means that it will survive temperatures in Zone 5 and higher. The data provided in this book is based on the map published in 1990. By the time this book went to print, a revised version was in the works but hadn't been published yet. Besides minimum temperatures, other factors such as plant cultivation practices and stress factors also influence the winter hardiness of plants. USDA zoning data provided in this book is intended as a guideline only.

Vegetatively propagated. A term used for plants derived from asexual propagation. The term "vegetatively propagated" is common in horticulture for plants grown from cuttings, but it also applies to plants propagated by division, runners, or other means of asexual propagation. The opposite of vegetatively propagated plants are those grown from seed, or "seed propagated."

Index to Plants in Recipes